CENTRAL AMERICAN WRITING IN THE UNITED STATES

# The Wandering
## song

EDITED BY

*Leticia Hernández Linares*

*Rubén Martínez*

*Héctor Tobar*

TIA CHUCHA PRESS

ISBN: 978-1-882688-53-1

Book Design: Jane Brunette

Cover art: Mural image from "Enrique's Journey" on Balmy Alley, San Francisco's Mission District, by Josué Rojas. Used with permission.

English translation of "El canto errante" copyright 2008 by Gabriel Gudding. All rights reserved. Used with permission.

Published by:
Tía Chucha Press
A Project of Tía Chucha's Centro Cultural, Inc.
PO Box 328
San Fernando, CA 91341
www.tiachucha.org

Distributed by:
Northwestern University Pres
Chicago Distribution Center
11030 South Langley Avenue
Chicago IL 60628

Tía Chucha's Centro Cultural & Bookstore is a 501 (c) (3) nonprofit corporation funded in part over the years by the National Endowment for the Arts, California Arts Council, Los Angeles County Arts Commission, Los Angeles Department of Cultural Affairs, The California Community Foundation, the Annenberg Foundation, the Weingart Foundation, the Lia Fund, National Association of Latino Arts and Culture, Ford Foundation, MetLife, Southwest Airlines, the Andy Warhol Foundation for the Visual Arts, the Thrill Hill Foundation, the Middleton Foundation, Center for Cultural Innovation, John Irvine Foundation, Not Just Us Foundation, the Attias Family Foundation, and the Guacamole Fund, among others. Donations have also come from Bruce Springsteen, John Densmore of The Doors, Jackson Browne, Lou Adler, Richard Foos, Gary Stewart, Charles Wright, Adrienne Rich, Tom Hayden, Dave Marsh, Jack Kornfield, Jesus Trevino, David Sandoval, Gary Soto, Denise Chávez and John Randall of the Border Book Festival, Luis & Trini Rodriguez and others.

# 2
*En Voz Alta*

# 3
*La Poesía de Todos*

*To the work of*

ROQUE DALTON
*cuyo canto errante nos abrió el camino*

VILMA RUTH MARTÍNEZ DE ANGULO
*madre, poeta, sicóloga, inspiración*

PRUDENCIA AYALA
*writer from Santa Ana, El Salvador;*
*first woman to run for president in the Ámericas.*
*She demanded a seat at the table.*

TOM HAYDEN
*worked tirelessly with organizations like Homies Unidos*
*and helped to establish Central American Studies*

# Stories from Our Unincorporated Territories

HOME WAS BEHIND US, always somewhere else. Born into 1970s Los Angeles, a few months after my parents arrived in the United States, I experienced El Salvador as a distant place we referred to as "back home." Civil war disappeared the possibility of return, and yet, my parents' country transplanted itself within the walls of this other home, colored our beans, determined our verb conjugations and our difference. "Back home" shadowed our lives here; my parents baptized me *en la Parroquía Sagrada Familia,* the church in my father's neighborhood, *la Colonia Centroamérica,* and thanks to his uncensored storytelling, I am aware that my conception occurred at *la Playa San Diego, La Libertad.* Most of my family remained in El Salvador and we called them on rotary phones, often communicating through static-filled calls with delays that underscored the vast space between us.

I developed a deep bond with "back home," despite the distance and thanks to the thick thread of my father's stories. Donning the folkloric dresses my grandmother would send north, I would put on shows for family and friends, making up the steps no one taught me. My father, bass player for *Los Lovers,* a bilingual Salvadoran band, and my mother who crocheted and did ceramics taught me who I was through memory, lyrics, and handmade things. As I came of age, textured stories wrapped me tight in a web of nostalgia and wandering, all despite my privileged place of birth.

Home was behind us, always somewhere else. The only other place my family and I traveled, other than back home, was the Mission District of San Francisco, the Central American heart of the Bay Area; the trip, the soundtrack—the very road itself—were equally important parts of the experience. As a twenty-something, I returned to the Mission. I came following in the footsteps of an uncle who taught me how to heal and how to own the indigenous and the migrant in my blood. I came here in pilgrimage to be part of a thriving community of artists and writers, and have lived on the same block since 1995. Ironically, during the last year, my poet-husband Tomás, our two sons, and I have been fighting an eviction from our home. We have lived under an expiration date on how long we can stay in this community of neighbors, murals, action, and *convivencia*—at least that's what it was once. Only the latest victims in a terrible epidemic of displacement by eviction or by fire, we live with a sense of impending exile from this, my longest, and our sons' only home.

Writers of the Central American diaspora have occupied shaky literary and historical ground —until now. For so many years the voices in this book have, largely unbeknownst to one another, hummed the melody of a wandering song. My co-editors, Rubén Martínez, Héctor Tobar, and I present a chorus of writers, artists, and performers who unequivocally answer a critical question: yes, there really is a Central American Literature and it includes a complex, bilingual, and multinational space. This book offers a literary soundtrack where there was mostly silence, and assembles a spine that can withstand the telling of who we are in this country.

In his study, *La Lengua Salvadoreña,* Pedro Geoffrey Rivas reflects on the importance of tracing the geography of language, and how *"el mundo es el lugar donde uno vive lo que se ha dicho y queda escrito... adónde uno habla. Donde está la voz o su ausencia. La voz es el mundo."* ("The world is the place where one lives what has been said and remains written... where one speaks. Where the voice is, or its absence. The voice is the world.")

Rivas writes of how inscription makes and unmakes place, and claims that his study, a tribute to homeland, will only capture the Salvadoran voice of a certain time because language is ever-changing with place. The earth is not the only part of our landscape that moves. We compile and present all these words here, in this time and place, without proposing to define or limit what Central American Literature is or will be. Rather, we offer a significant piece of a much larger picture.

The various stages of Central American immigration to the United States have largely emerged from situations of extreme violence and poverty. While movement and presence can be traced to the 1950s and 1960s, war and its long devastating aftermath in Guatemala, El Salvador, and Nicaragua was the principal impetus for immigration patterns in the 1970s and 1980s. Frequent earthquakes, hurricanes, the importation of gang violence from the U.S., and ongoing economic instability continue to push our gente to make the journey. During the last few years, "surges" of unaccompanied children arriving in the

U.S. provoked renewed attention. Now more than four million Central Americans reside in the United States, and no less than two of our home countries in the so-called Northern Triangle of Central America are considered the most dangerous in the world. We are immigrant and refugee, first, second, and even third generation.

This book enables us to retrace our steps and chart the unincorporated territory of our stories.

We hope that you, *Chapín* in Los Angeles, *Guanaca* in D.C., *Nicoya* in San Francisco, *Panameño* in New York will feel at home in these pages and invite friends to take the journey with you. In the first section, *El Camino Largo,* we travel back and forth in time and between here and there, rendering different aspects of the journey that forms the foundation of our community and this anthology. In *En Voz Alta,* poets and performers string together voices and pieces of language to craft terms to define themselves. While spoken word and performance writers appear throughout the book, this section privileges the act of storytelling and community engagement as a substantive part of our literary craft. In *La Poesía de Todos*, we feature work that bridges a multiplicity of themes and genres, leaving the path ahead, beyond this book, open.

Ultimately, *The Wandering Song: Central American Writing in the United States* embodies our *canto popular.* This Tía Chucha Press anthology demonstrates how we continue to shift the map, what no amount of anti-immigrant sentiment and xenophobic backlash will erase. As Rubén Darío implied in the poem this book is named after, we offer salve through our singing, and we hope you will sing along—loudly, *y con ganas.*

—*Leticia Hernández-Linares*
La Misión, San Francisco
November 28, 2016

# El
# canto
# errante

El cantor va por todo el mundo
sonriente o meditabundo.

El cantor va sobre la tierra
en blanca paz o en roja guerra.

Sobre el lomo del elefante
por la enorme India alucinante.

En palanquín y en seda fina
por el corazón de la China;

en automóvil en Lutecia;
en negra góndola en Venecia;

sobre las pampas y los llanos
en los potros americanos;

por el río va en la canoa,
o se le ve sobre la proa

de un steamer sobre el vasto mar,
o en un vagón de sleeping-car.

El dromedario del desierto,
barco vivo, le lleva a un puerto.

Sobre el raudo trineo trepa
en la blancura de la estepa.

O en el silencio de cristal
que ama la aurora boreal.

El cantor va a pie por los prados,
entre las siembras y ganados.

Y entra en su Londres en el tren,
y en asno a su Jerusalén.

Con estafetas y con malas,
va el cantor por la humanidad.

En canto vuela, con sus alas:
Armonía y Eternidad.

—RUBÉN DARÍO

# The
# Wandering
# Song

A singer goes all over the world
impassioned or bored

In a little train or a white train
by the gulls or through the grain

A singer walks into wars and peaces
into civil wars, trench wars, trade wars

through discord or concord
a singer goes to all these places

A poet moves in the world

On the ridge spine of the elephant
into the narrows of the Hellespont

On a palanquin, in gemmy silks
she crosses glaciers in the Alps

On a cloud backed and glinting jet
into Buddhist and bright Tibet

In a car into St. Lucia
On a dark train through Galicia

Over the pampas and the flats
on American colts

She goes by river in a canoe
or props herself in the banging prow

of a pelagic freighter
or she simply rides an escalator

She brings her nose to archipelagoes
And carts her ears into Tangiers

On a dromedary across the sands
by jiggling boats, she visits lands

She goes to the tundra's edge
on an expeditious sledge

And far from the equator's flora
she thrills to the boreal aurora

The singer strolls through hissing crops
across the rows and by the cows

She enters her London on a bus
her Jerusalem on an ass

She goes with mailbags
    and pouches of the State
to open doors to eternal things

To salve the sores of human beings
is why she sings.

—Rubén Darío

# 1

*El Camino Largo*

MARÍA ISABEL ALVAREZ

# War

I TRAVEL THROUGH NORTH AMERICA at the expense of strangers. In Massachusetts, I sleep on the twin bed of a little girl who never reached the age of ten. Her mother receives me in her arms and leads me to the tiny second floor bedroom, wood-plank stairs creaking beneath her pale bare feet. The room appears dusty yet tidy. The silhouettes of floating ballerinas border the blush pink walls, delicate lace the color of bone drapes the single bedroom window, and a floral comforter lays stiffly over the mattress as if handwashed in starch. The mother points toward the bathroom and offers a set of towels, a spare key dangling from a lanyard, and a gentle reminder that she'd prefer if I return each night no later than eleven. I ask this question of every one of my hosts and each time I receive a vastly different response: What compels you to open your home to strangers? The mother's answer echoes how I feel about the home I've left in Guatemala, that through the continual exchange of strangers she has learned to overcome the residual madness of grief.

In Texas, I toss and turn from the humidity, my neck and thighs seeping in sweat. In New Jersey, I fall dormant to the angry screams and then savage lovemaking of an Italian couple. Then in Louisiana, I never sleep. I lay immobile among the cotton sheets, my forehead pressed flat against the cool plaster as I attempt to decipher the language in which my host is weeping. And though I never discover what heartaches ail her, or what tragedy visits her dreams, once dawn casts its nuanced indigo light, I conclude that her sorrowful crying sounds as haunting and harried as mine once had.

I learn to sleep on sofas and loveseats, some clean, some covered in dog hair; down comforters spread in layers across the floor, leaky water beds and children's bunk beds—sometimes vacant, sometimes not; day beds and trundle beds and outgrown racecar beds, canopies slung heavily in curtains, rubber air mattresses, a single army camper cot, the rear seat of a Cadillac sedan, and an eco-chic, Japanese-inspired platform bed made entirely of faux bamboo.

My favorite remains the hammock strung between two California palms, the crosshatch twines pressing against my arms and legs as the repetition of waves rippling like black silk hypnotize me into a sleep so deep and continuous that I wake the next morning as though I am finally well-rested.

When I arrive in Minnesota it is spring, and I am unprepared for the sleet that pelts the pavement. My host's name is Reta, an Ojibwe woman of the White Earth nation of Northern Minnesota, and she is as simple and quiet as the house in which she lives. The interior is coated in a deep shade of crimson and unlike many of the other homes suffocating in family portraits and opulent pieces of art, her walls are void of any distractions. The house possesses a kind of uncontaminated spirit, as if those who lived within its corridors summoned every known indigenous ritual and cleansed it of impurities.

Reta speaks curtly and selectively, in a low and smoky voice, and relies heavily on hand gestures to relay emphasis on certain key phrases. The kitchen is there. The bathroom is upstairs. There is no telephone. I am intrigued by her economic way of speaking and feel it imprudent if I don't employ the same courtesy, so I simply nod in understanding and thank her for her hospitality, never asking what motivated her to open her door to a nomadic, Latina woman with nowhere to sleep.

She shows me to the bedroom parallel to hers. The room contains only three pieces of furniture: a twin bed swathed in a vibrant indigenous blanket, a cherry wood bureau affixed with brass hardware, and an old wicker rocking chair that seems to mysteriously sway.

I unpack my duffel bag, extracting toothbrush and travel shampoo, washcloth and hand soap before submerging myself into the well of a clawfoot tub. I rub the bar of soap under my breasts, lather the crevices between my thighs, scoop water into the cavities of my collarbone, rinse the oil from my roots with baby shampoo, my brown skin pruning like dehydrated fruit as the minutes turn into hours and the hours turn into sleep.

I dream about my family, remembering how we bathed with buckets of cold water drawn from a well. My mother had washed all six of us in a large yellow tub outside our tin house, taking a kitchen cloth to our baby skin and scrubbing the dirt between our toes, the sweat from under our chins.

"My children are clean children," she'd say in our native Spanish. "Because my children are God's children."

During the summer, she'd boil a stockpot of water and wait for it to cool before draining it over our mosquito-bitten backs. Then she'd leave us to play and we would splash each other and poke each other and huddle against one another after the leaf-laden water had lost its appeal, oblivious to the fact that half of us were girls and the other half were boys and we were all naked.

And then our bodies became less like taper candles and more like kerosene lamps, shapely and heated from within. Us girls were forced to plead with our neighbors about bathing in their private showers, offering to sweep the dust from their floors, feed rice to their many wailing children or stir their simmering pots of homemade recado. And sometimes they'd oblige, immediately propping their colicky babies into our arms, but other times, because these were war times, we were left to wander outside the city and into the lush countryside for fresh river water, only to discover that the rivers had become bloodied with bodiless limbs.

After the war, after the Ixil and the K'iche and the Q'anjob'al had been wiped from their communities, after their homes had been set ablaze and their children trampled like stalks of weeds and their wives and daughters raped as repeatedly as shells are shot from a submachine gun, we found that the rivers could no longer sustain the sins of our country, could no longer dilute the transgressions of war, so we stopped bathing altogether.

My brothers were the first to succumb to the bloodshed, one after the other they were slaughtered like pigs with corroded machetes, dropping to their knees into the wet earth, their carcasses devoured by ravenous white maggots.

My mother and sisters—they weren't nearly as lucky.

Our neighbors, church fellows and distant relations, they fled to the mountains, believing the myth that the highlands would save them, that the closer they were to God, the better they could evade death.

Death found them faster than sound travels.

I dream these things each night. Each night the dead haunt me for having survived; each night their cries strangle me in my sleep.

CAROLINA RIVERA ESCAMILLA

# Night Memory:
# The Mansion in the Middle of a Gully

IN 1980, I am a theater student at the only arts high school in the country. Every evening I come home from school, eat and then climb a ladder to sit on the cement edge of the unfinished mansion's terrace letting my legs dangle in the air.

Slowly, gradually, I disconnect myself from the problems of our household and the hillside *colonia* where we live. I feel a bit nervous, as though one little bat flits in the pit of my stomach. Fears like thin baby worms cling to my feet, as I look down onto the parched patio. I stare straight off into the faraway city, volcano on my left and hills on my right. I become a large orange kite, a crazy wild thing kids play with. I turn into a bird, a red *guacamaya* with indigo and yellow aspect, feathers flying toward my nest atop the high terrace of the mansion.

On the terrace, this is when and where I really live. Reality these days is a huge armored war vehicle, and I am like that vehicle of traction, like the one that Papá used to start building this half-finished mansion five years ago. I am both conflict and conflicted. Our mansion has become a mausoleum, an ancient Roman ruin jutting out of the earth. It has windows, a lot of them square, and heavy pillars to hold up three stories, strong with heavy walls, and three thick cement ceilings and floors. To look up at me where I sit from down the hill below the house, this must seem like a tall apartment building. But from the street level immediately behind me in the Colonia Rubio, *pelo de elote*, one sees only a one-level house.

When I get off the bus at the bus stop at the edge of the *colonia*, I hear their comments. "She lives in the house that looks like the cathedral." They are neighbors referring to the cathedral of San Salvador, which is also only half-finished. "I see her sitting on the edge of the building. Maybe she goes up there to pray." Gossip, gossip. I am sure it is the woman who sells tortillas who tells others about the mansion and me. Everyone seems to know about everyone in this neighborhood, this field of ruins. I am learning to detach from ordinary people, since I started art school and began reading art books and history. I read hiding under the bed, eventually paying as much attention to my shadow as to anything else. My shadow is changing from within and has begun to change its outer shape into a young woman.

"It has to be of an Italianate construction to survive earthquakes and hurricanes," Papá says opening a drawing my older brother designed, as a first-year architecture student at the National University. Papá does not really follow the exact design; he has his own plan, square and boxy, but well built. He makes excuses, "What else can one do to turn this gully into a home?"

"You're not following our son's design." Mamá criticizes.

The mansion smells of soft new rain and old humidity, as it waits in silence to be whole and complete. Our mansion is not the only unfinished construction site; the whole country looks like ancient Rome, or more like its ruins. At least Rome had its splendor, its glory, and its achievements. Here we have none of these; all is started and left unfinished, unless you are rich.

A 1975 winter of a few years past calls itself forth. Under a September Saturday's yolk-colored sun, the Bee Gees are "blaming it all" on the "Nights on Broadway" from the shiny marine blue stereo console Papá bought the previous Christmas. He stands at the edge of the newly dug horizontal trench with a rusted shovel in his raised right hand, his left resting on the hammer tucked into the brown belt of his corduroy pants. He calls us, his children, to carry pieces from the rock pile to drop into places he indicates along the long trench. As we watch, he mixes sand, gravel, water, and cement. In turn, he gives us each a shovelful of mixed concrete.

I manage to avoid spilling my shovelful, even though it seems heavier than any rock I've ever carried. He helps each of the littler brothers with a spadeful of concrete. He quickly scoops in the rest of the concrete, and then tells us all to jump into the trench full of wet concrete to stamp on it. He says the wet concrete will kill our foot fungus, although we do not know what foot fungus is, and we are fairly sure we do not have any. A few days later, layers of dead skin peel from our feet. We compete after lunch and after school to see who is faster at peeling off all the dead skin.

"Sweep away all the dead skin," Mamá says. "Do not leave it on the floor, because the animals will come inside the house to eat it. You do not want the hens to taste like your feet, do you?" We laugh. Mamá gives us her look; she is not joking.

"We build this mansion in fulfillment of your mother's dream that will be yours, too." Papá says placing a nail between his lips.

"Hurry up then," Mamá says sarcastically, meaning for him to finish the mansion or at least the task immediately, so they can go buy food. She is dressed to go out, lips colored orange-red. "I am ready to go to the Central Market."

But it is his dream, not ours, or maybe we just don't understand. We know Papá never had a home. He ran away from his grandmother's house after his mother and his father died. He was not even seven. (But my paternal grandparents and great grandparents… that is another story). He does not dare call what he is building just a house; he does not even allow us to call it a house, but a mansion, because mansions are what he has built all these years for the rich in their *colonias* farther up in the hills. One day, I suppose it crossed his mind: "Why not build a mansion for myself?"

The Bee Gees' energetic rhythm, the yellow sun, the motion of people passing by the house greeting us from the street, all of it encapsulates for me the confetti- showering, laughing happiness of that Saturday morning, as we imagined a future mansion, that included that day's gentle puffy clouds moving through our blue sky. As Papá spoke and Mamá interrupted him, I swear I could see a bedroom of my own with curtains, lamps, bookshelves, closets, and a table where I sit reading something intelligent.

In 1980, it turns out to be Albert Camus who tries to speak to me from a book on a Thursday evening in September overcast by dark clouds in a rainy month. But 1975 hums within me still—"Hurry up, let's cover the cement or it will all be washed away"—as Papá hurries to finish the beginnings of a first foundation, under Mamá's slightly impatient gaze. This night memory flashes and is gone. My bedroom might never be finished. Bee Gees' music still sometimes plays on a neighbors' radio, but now its melodic rhythms embitter both past and present. The Mansion is still unfinished. It serves as an emergency barracks for the family, a refuge where we go individually to think up tactics for survival. Mamá takes the immense concrete stairway to the second floor midmornings to dream up strategies to keep us alive through this hell of economic starvation.

The city is gray this evening, like ashes fallen from the sky. This afternoon I was at Parque Libertad waiting for the bus home. There I saw children with their little hands holding Gerber baby food jars to their mouths, inhaling shoe glue. It reminded me the way my little brothers would eat their baby food, spooning it in as fast as they could eat. The label on these baby jars shows a healthy white baby. Is this jar of shoe-glue food for these children, who are usually hidden away in a corner of the park, each child with a baby jar of glue? Their own two hands push it to their mouths.

Each child sucks and breathes in the poison, dreaming of a bottle of milk they might never have.

In another corner of the park, a young prostitute sells her body to a petty thief. The prostitute is the daughter of the man with the painted face who performs the fire show in *el parque* Libertad every day after five o'clock. The audience drops miserable coins into the hands of the clown's assistant, his daughter. Poor students like me go there for the free entertainment. I like to see the show: the father of the young prostitute takes a bottle of alcohol or gasoline, puts it in his mouth, then, in a single gesture he spits, torches it with a lit match, and spews a cloud of fire, its yellow, orange, purples the same colors as the afternoon horizon of *celajes*. If not for the line of trees at the bottom of the house that has grown up with me, I could see the whole city from the terrace. I wonder where the fire-eating father, his daughter-the-prostitute, and the children are sleeping in the park.

I hear steps, definite and slow, come up to the terrace on the old wooden ladder. It is Papá; we are the ones who hold consistent vigil here. That is not entirely true, as I sometimes meet here with my older sister to talk about boys, music, and places around the world to which we would like to escape. "Russia, Costa Rica, Hungary, Czechoslovakia, but Russia for sure!" Then we lie down on the cool humid cement of the terrace to count stars until Mamá reminds us to go to bed no later than ten o'clock.

I look down at the line of white trunks of avocado, coconut, and eucalyptus trees on the patio below. Papá whitewashed the bottom half-meter of the tree trunks. I don't know why. Among the trees' fallen decaying brown leaves and branches are two big rust-colored ceramic frogs that someone scavenged for Papá from one of the rich houses he builds. When dead leaves rustle on the ground, I could swear a frog just moved.

Everything grows wild here. We've got nothing fancy growing, like the roses or camellias in the gardens of rich people's houses. Here green wild vines climb from the ravines below, where soapy water runs down into the earth to twist tree roots. The trickle of white water flows from my Tía Yita's morning laundering.

I bend my head like a duck to gauge the distance from the top of the terrace to the patio. I grab the terrace's edge with my four fingers like a parrot on its perch. I will not slip accidentally. What would happen if I were to dive from the terrace to the patio? Would I survive the fall as Papá did two years ago? Perhaps not. Papá was very drunk, but I'm not drunk like him. I'm worse than drunk. I am delusional to think I am an artist, an actress without even owning Stanislavsky's actor's manual. I have no money to buy it, and even if I had the money, the book does not even exist in the bookstores in this flea-sized country. Why would I kill myself anyway? Why not just go to *El Cerro de Guazapa* that the *guerrilleros* have taken. I could have gone with el *Cadejo Negro*, as I call my new friend from the Art School, to fight against the armed forces. At least my death would be worth something then. I sigh as I pull myself back from the edge. I try again to measure the distance, but I've never been good at measuring. A ray of moonlight has filtered through the trees, revealing changes in this clod of dirt I have known as home since elementary school.

When my father first brought us to see this piece of land, it was just a littered gully back then. Now the large, solid, unfinished cement house stands in the middle of the shady space, surrounded by maturing fruit trees that were as small as me back then. The mangos, *sunzas*, avocados, and a few leftover coffee trees were already there, before Papá transplanted the others. Now instead of a gully, there is a yard where chickens and ducks sleep. The trees grow, fertilized by memories of recent years and the *ca-ca* of domesticated birds. The coyotes sometimes scavenge for something to eat in the *barranca*. Tía Yita sets up a small space each evening to sleep close to the trees in case the coyotes attack the hens. Tía Yita knows how to get rid of them. She chants like an owl, or pigeon, or even like a wolf or another coyote. Let them try to eat Tía Yita, I laugh to myself. Those coyotes would be sorry, because she keeps a long eucalyptus stick with a sharp hook like a nail on the end. No animal could escape her strike. The coyotes make me feel the place is haunted with live animals and dead ones, too. I fear the coyotes will carry me away to other ravines where La Siguanaba lives, that wandering madwoman who appears beautiful to men, but once they go with her, she kills them monstrously. That's one story I heard about her.

Where we live is called *colonia* Rubio. The whole neighborhood's land still bears the name of its original owner, old man *Rubio*, whose name means blond like corn silk. He sold Mamá and Papá this gully as though it were a real piece of land, but it was only a *barranca,* a gully or ravine with coyotes, owls, snakes, some fruit and coffee trees. Whenever it rained, the whole gully filled like a lake. My father hauled tons of earth and put three heavy stone walls and another foundational wall to create some real land. He was sure to divide it from another *barranca* next to us that was also full of coffee and orange trees. That gully still belongs to the *colonia* owner Rubio.

The first year we came to the *colonia*, a hurricane hit the whole country. It was one o'clock in the morning when our beds were floating in different directions. Mamá carried my two little brothers, a three-month-old baby and a one-year-old. Papá was not there. He was building a mansion somewhere else in another part of the country. The Formica table, a big rusty frying pan, the water barrels and ourselves were all we rescued from that disaster.

"As long as we are alive, we can always start over," Mamá said while making a fire when the rain lightened on the only flat piece of land up close to the so-called Main Street. Four strong wood poles, mango tree branches and a corrugated metal roof were what my older brothers managed to put back up during the hurricane. The neighbors closest to our *barranca* brought us coffee and bread. The whole *colonia* was wrecked, but we did not have a house. Even the house we had before the hurricane was improvised, anyway.

When Papá came home the next night, it was still raining the last of the hurricane. He brought with him two of his old coworker friends, el Chato Nicolás, and el Chele Pavián. Tío Polo, Tía Yita's husband, showed up, too, without letting us know ahead of time, as if there were a way to let us know they were coming. The hurricane summoned Papá and Tío Polo back to our house. Tío Polo worked at another construction site that Papá also managed. The bigger fallen mango tree branches served as a good roof structure during the last of the rains. Papá directed us to hang sheets of plastic over the branches and leaves to form an enormous umbrella. Three days after father's return, by the third morning we had a new solidly improvised house, as Papá, el Chato, el Chele Pavián, Tío Polo, and my older brothers worked even at night.

This temporary house was stronger and bigger, so my Tía Yita and my two cousins could be with us to help in the next catastrophe. It is not that Tía Yita was far away from us when the hurricane happened. Her settlement was close to our *barranca*. We heard her screaming for help with her two children on top of her back as water and mud pulled at her, as she held on to a mango tree. Papá and Mamá decided to leave everything buried, as the mud was too thick and deep to find the rest of our belongings.

FROM THE MANSION TERRACE I look down at the dirt patio and wonder how long it will take to finish this mansion. It is 1980, and Papá has lost his construction employment. A war has broken out throughout the country. We are living on the savings Mamá had hidden away. They sold the land they owned to make a farm outside the city to keep us all alive. Papá is here with me on the terrace. We sit together quietly. The silence between us inspires us to excavate memory. "Do you remember when we first came to this *colonia*?" Papá asks me, gazing at the moon over the hills of Guazapa. "Yes," I say. I ask him, "Do you remember when you said, 'We'll be fine?' that's what you said before the hurricane hit us." "Hija, war scars the soul worse than any natural catastrophe. Men are killing each other." I follow his gaze.

Do we build up the future like we built up this *barranca*? How does one do that? I wonder whether Papá knows which hammer and nail to take…

and I wonder how to take the right path to the center of this labyrinthine universe where children are homeless, where the unprotected sell their bodies, where women cry for their disappeared, and elders suffer strokes and heart attacks because of ceaseless worry for food and for their children. Sons and daughters are leaving to save their own lives from disaster here. They flee violence, look for better lives and a just society. Mamá calls Papá and me. It is time to sleep.

1975 speaks to me still, and I swear I can no longer see the bedroom with curtains, lamps, bookshelves, closets, and a table. Instead, I read something intelligent as I sit on the terrace of my brothers', sisters', and my unfinished mansion.

CAROLINA RIVERA ESCAMILLA

# In a Corner of Your Country

In a corner of your country
a shadow has stopped,
or perhaps it is a soul.
Sunday is ringing church bells absent of echo.
The empty streets… where are the people?
This is not the church who offered me shelter
when the world was upside down.

I am caged in a corner of faded yellow, red, orange,
colors of the Californian grapefruit sun.
I am dreaming of a world,
my world,
a world without a pillow,
a world embroiled and scowling
in sour lemon, roiling inside my veins.

A baggy eye world,
Hypochondriac.
It drifts like a leaf that I wanted to catch
from the river when I was seven years old.
Oh distant world!
The tree at my house yields yellow flowers,
like tropical summer jewels.

It is not my fault you do not want to enter my world.
How stupid to think that my universe is important.
It is assumed from before my departure,
that it was me who had to mend your world onto my skin.

You know,
I detest Sundays.
How wretched you are, who still believe in that day.

You argue that something must have happened to me on a Sunday,
that there is no reason why I should hate it.

Sundays have always seemed to me an idle luxury for fools.
Many die of thirst, from wars,
as the world opens its secret sorrows on blind walls.
On Sundays I am consecrated to curse
the dictators of my adolescence.

On Sundays sometimes I have company.
A voice restless and heartbroken accompanies me on Sundays.
She who, like me, has the same fate relegated.
She fills herself with song,
"Thanks to Life" "*Gracias a la vida*"
Violeta Parra.

On Sundays in exile,
I meet her in a dark house,
a confused hour of late afternoon,
a cloudy Sunday—tousled—
a house inhabited by women of different territorial directions,
wanting to change the world.

Their girls play and sing in English,
"Row, row your boat..."
They fight in English,
"I hate you..."
Mothers do not understand
that the world is already wounded.
You did not do it.

She (The Banished) like me carries a memory,
and memories in a plastic jar,
or as a fabric of woven *arpilleras*,
Violeta Parra style,
like a dream, these plastic jars
where women of our territories used to store water
that is collected from the river a little foamy from washing,
and they drink it together with their children.

She sings a song of Silvio Rodriguez
and you like to hear the song.
It is as close to your experience
as the year of the Redmoon Revolution.

Then she goes... "There are echoes in our memories.
I write words with wings that do not take off.
And like this we spend the unsavory Sundays in exile."

In my world there is a lot of water.
The water has an owner.
Water is cared for similarly
to my care for memory
in this corner without umbilical cord.

Children killed, rivers poisoned
by great masters of the universe,
despots of the world.

Them I curse double on Sundays
and every day of the week.
They owe me; they owe us much.
There is no echo in this town.
There is no echo in this town…
Its freeways majestic,
rulers of the city,
gods of Los Angeles' destiny
and I am on one of them.

I think:

Women rooted in the graves of their sons and daughters.
Cicadas recite the seasons.
And so mine… yours… years pass in this corner of whose country?

The magpies embittered
soak the winter season.
The mountain sings.

Last night I dreamed of a black girl in my arms.
Last night was Sunday.
What an arrogant night it was.
Night put a black girl in my arms,
while stairs to my nest were overthrown.

So many haltering steps in my soul.
And the girl shattered into the marble,
gilded lamps tied in the mountains,
no one cried for her. Another one.
Is there no echo in the corner of your country?

She was born in a country that still paints her history
with children, women and men coming out of landfills,
a country filled with clowns.
Children and men hang around
like statues with drawings on their bodies.
Their memories are a language encrypted.

People avoid them. After a revolution!
The lords of the universe conquer one more time,
while women and girls are raped.
Here in a corner of this country
I invent rosaries filled with curses
against invading boldly and loudly,
now one million dead,
more than one hundred thousand in my country.
And still they laugh in the face of the world. Mine... yours...
Mine, yours. Is there no echo in this town?

They have you believe in freedom.
You buy a television.
Memory has a bad smell.
The tomb comes to you.
They owe me; they owe us so much, I say...
Sunday, I am metamorphosis in this corner of this country.
How much can I endure... in exile?
The moon reminds me of that dogs howl,

and fear invades me
while night covers me.

Night comes like a bullet of silence.
The memory of soldiers,
their rifles tips nip into a corner of my body,
there remains anchored inside me…
how do I—how do you cleanse them?

Sundays—I will curse them:
The devastators of peace!
Why does no one stay angry?
They… you watch the screen.
I hear an echo. Bla bla bla… CNN
Teeth chatter over Hollywood moonlight.
In a corner of your country.

# To the Reader

I WILL BEGIN with my name. It should have been Leonel like my father, the way they planned while in love, before I was born, but they fought so the story changed. I learned of this three years after his death; I learned of this before embarking on my journey to the United States. My aunt Alba told me; she looked after us because my mother would leave early in the morning and return late at night. In the Chinandega market, she sold discounted products to provide for her five children. I was the youngest. My aunt would tell us stories, from when she and my mother were young girls. She punished us when we misbehaved, fed and sheltered us. To me she was more than my aunt, she was a second mother. Though later I would find out the truth, I had thought that my name was in honor of the city of León. It didn't seem such a farfetched idea because León was my home: the narrow streets where I learned to play baseball with a rolled up sock, the colonial style adobe houses, and the parks where I felt my first kisses. Besides, it wouldn't take long for any foreigner to imagine that León was the city of Ruben Dario, who at one time said, "León is today for me like Rome or Paris." That verse was enough to justify his image on public signs, murals, statues, and even in jokes. León is not the city where Dario was born, but it is where he grew up and began as a poet and where he died an alcoholic.

My father also died an alcoholic, during the war, on February 10, 1985. He was about to turn 45. I saw him vomit chunks of blood. The puddle splattered the walls with black stains. He looked pale, but stayed calm and composed himself as he dressed to go to the hospital. My mother wasn't at home; she had gone to Honduras to see my brother Sergio, who was in exile. I was the only one who had stayed with my father. My sisters had gone to my Aunt's house. I waited for him at the front doorway; I wanted him to tell me something. He embraced me like he always embraced me and said to me, "I'll be back soon." He looked melancholic when he climbed into the taxi, surrounded by his friends. He passed away the next day in surgery at 2:10 pm, while they operated on his liver. They say he was very intelligent with numbers; he was a renowned mathematician in the city. I remember him as a charismatic man with an agreeable smile. He never hit or mistreated me. I know that he had children by other women; the neighbors made sure to let me know, pointing, "that girl walking over there is your half-sister." My father also enjoyed poetry. He taught me the first poem I learned from memory: "The Bullet" by Salomon de la Selva. I wish I had known him better, but he came to stay with my mother almost at the end of his life. My Aunt Alba didn't think too highly of him. She said that she did not want me to be named Leonel because she feared that I would end up like him, an alcoholic and a womanizer. The fight before I was born made my mother, as a gesture of revenge, erase the last two letters in Leonel. The accented syllable in my name should have absorbed the blow: León. That accent was supposed to carry out the revenge; my mother, in complicity with my aunt, registered me under that name in public records, and that way they made sure that my father would not leave his copy in me. They achieved it. I was never like Leonel, though for many years I attempted to be.

Names are always an imposition, but sometimes accidents happen that save us. I used to think that my origin had been distorted. I came to feel as some kind of impostor, and many times I even introduced myself to people as Leonel. Another event intensified the farce. So the authorities would grant me a permit to leave Nicaragua, my mother paid a lawyer to draft a false birth certificate that would make me six months younger. Young men were required to register for military service at the age of 16. I was 15 and a half.

The falseness appeared on another level; my education falsified. It was difficult for me to read; to read a paragraph was to enter a hostile and elusive territory. I was one of the worst students in elementary, but my bad conduct allowed me to hide my poor performance in school. Many years later, when I arrived at the University of California, Berkeley, I heard talk of a type of learning disability. A friend told me of the symptoms, and right away I diagnosed myself with that problem. I had dealt with it, battled it on my own, always questioning my capacity and mental sanity. Now it took on for me an unfamiliar name: DYSLEXIA. I remember an incident from when I was 12, months after my father had passed away. I sat in a corner, waiting for some friends, who like me, would not enter class. A cloth banner hung among the electric wires of a light post; it had a white stripe with blue letters. I wanted to read what it said. I don't know if I read "Dario Dario" or "Radio Radio." I have forgotten that detail because at times I remember things backwards, turned upside down. Even dreams randomly become part of my collection of anecdotes. In any case, I thought that the banner made no sense. I reread it, perceived the same message. I understood that the anomaly was in me because I had experienced it before, letters altering themselves not unlike the way today electronic marquees shift their announcements. I concentrated, lifted my gaze so that I could read the sign again. This time I knew that the banner read, "*Radio Dari*o." Letters altered their order, slipped in front of my eyes to form their double. It could be that the distorted reading of "Dario" made me more conscious of my visual slippage; at the same time and without knowing it, I was slipping away—from my country, from my family, and from my two mothers—to the north.

The feeling of impostor intensified when I entered as an undocumented immigrant into the United States. I felt like an intruder. I walked across the Rio Grande because it was dry and rocky. Later, after passing bushes, I climbed out of the river bank onto the parking lot of a supermarket—I believe it was called Ralphs—and that's how I discovered America in the city of Brownsville, Texas. This anecdote has been poetized by Javier O. Huerta in his immigrant epic poem, "American Copia." Years later I realized that that border crossing constituted a federal crime. At the time, I didn't even know what the word "federal" meant. When I didn't have documents or had to rely on false documents, I tried to assume an American citizenship at times. Quickly, the accent, the culture, the gestures would betray me. I had to be happily one more Mexican.

I became obsessed with learning to read another language so I became a good student. After 11 years I was able to normalize my legal status. I applied to the university and was accepted. I had to propose a dissertation project after passing my doctoral exams. One day I was reading a poem by Carlos Martinez Rivas and came upon the idea I was after: "Because it is true that we commit fraud," the verse said. That is my word, I thought. I met with my professors. They laughed when I told them that I wanted to read Dario through the lens of fraud. Realizing I was serious, they asked, "Why fraud?" "Because it is true that we commit fraud," I responded. "Because even at the expense of fraud and of word games, we continue to perpetuate the threat, to invent necessity, to uphold the danger." Attentively they listened to my theoretical justifications about the connection of those verses with Dario's aesthetic. One said that he was interested in the project because it pointed to a different reading of Dario; the other two, though not opposed, maintained their reservations. As I finish the second chapter of my dissertation I think disconcertedly: it might be certain that certain acts are repeated, first as tragedy and continued as farce. But in which crossing does the plot, the slippery effect of fraud, begin; to what skies do its swings aspire and in what clash does the question originate.

LEÓN SALVATIERRA

# To the North

(SEPTEMBER 24, 1988, SOMETIME AROUND 3 PM)

HE TOLD US we couldn't stop running, *Caballo Blanco*, a quiet man with rough features—I didn't know why they had given him that nickname. We had to run several miles down a rocky path when we crossed the border from Guatemala to Mexico. In Mexican territory, we ran even though no one was chasing us. But we were running in a big pack of 40 people (women, men, and even children), the majority from Central America, one, two, or three from further down South. It was under these circumstances that what happened happened, with frightened souls not knowing whom we were running from. They said that it was from the Mexican Border patrol, but I never really saw them chasing after us. The landscape seemed peaceful, sunny, and green, but it was a dry heat. The Tecun Uman River had left us exhausted. It was even worse for those of us who said we knew how to swim, and on top of that smoked, because those who could not swim across the river crossed it on tire tubes guided by locals. I almost drowned because of exhaustion and had to let the current carry me like 200 yards down the river. But that isn't what I want to narrate. I want to tell what happened to Don Eduardo. I believe that was his name, and if it wasn't, that will be his name in this story. No one knew of Don Eduardo's sickness. He probably hid it because he was afraid that *el Caballo Blanco* would refuse to take him. In one of several conversations, while staying at the motel Monte Carlo in Guatemala City, which was frequented by criminals, transvestites, and prostitutes, he confided in me that his two daughters were waiting for him over there in the United States, that they had married gringos and that he already had American grandchildren. He proudly showed me the photos. He said that they had finally bettered the race. I laughed, imagining with a certain joy how beautiful it would be to have kids with a blue-eyed blonde woman, a face like Brooke Shields when she starred in The Blue Lagoon. I was running and taking long strides; running next to me was *el Venado*, a young man from the Atlantic coast of Nicaragua, excellent dancer, good with the jokes and the drinks. He got his nickname during our stay in Guatemala.

While we waited for *Caballo Blanco*'s "cargo" to fill up, he passed the time drinking that cheap rum, *el Venado*; it was for him the best thing he had ever drank because it had a strong kick, he said. I hung out with him at my almost sixteen years. I liked to talk with him because he made me feel like an older person. I thought that we would continue to be friends once we got to the United States. I never saw them again, not *el Venado* and not Don Eduardo. But in the case of Don Eduardo, it was different because he was never able to step on American soil—his dream, his promised land, only a few family photos. He had seen it by way of the faces of his progeny, who were much whiter than the nephews and relatives that he had left behind. We had run a long stretch when Don Eduardo collapsed. He was of medium stature, thin, and recently had turned 55. *Caballo Blanco* had sent him ahead, and shortly afterwards we found him fallen on the path, spewing white foam from his mouth and convulsing like his soul was possessed. His words unintelligible, his eyes turned inward, and his head was slamming against the ground. Only *el Venado* and I stopped—the two drunks of the group. Nobody there knew what was wrong with Don Eduardo. *El Venado* grabbed him by the legs because he was stronger and Don Eduardo kicked uncontrollably. I tried to calm his head, which was bleeding from pounding against several rocks on the ground. We held him like that for a long time. Everything came to a still, even the convulsion that made his chest jump. It was a strange sensation. I had never seen anyone die, much less had anyone die in my hands. In that moment I would have liked to trade places with *el Venado*, holding Don Eduardo's legs. Perhaps I would not have felt his death as much. But it was on me to hold his graying head, his cranium, his eyebrows, his nose, his mouth, his twisted tongue, his jaw, his neck. All of it was extinguished in an instant. The white foam continued to spew from his mouth like inertia, but Don Eduardo's soul had already crossed the border. I had seen something similar many years before in my hometown, a young woman that sold cheese on the sidewalk at the market. The cheese tray had turned over because she had collapsed on top of it, and the cheese began to roll on the ground. Several people helped her. I was a child then and was frightened by the white spit that gushed from her mouth. All I could think of doing was running back home. But I didn't. I wanted to see what would happen to her, and that's when I saw that some of the same people that were helping her were stealing her cheese.

ALEXANDRA LYTTON REGALADO

# La Masacuata

MÁMA CARMEN SAID Ada came to burden her life because she was born blue-eyed. Not that milky grey that most new mothers boast about. Later, you see those same babies propped on their mothers' aproned hips: sunbrown and skinny, eyes dark as *azabache* stone with a stick-straight shock of black hair. Same as every other man, woman, and child from Canton Chancala.

This was not the case for Ada. The *partera* swabbed a cloth across her brow, handed her over to her mother still bleeding on her cot, and she gasped when Ada opened her eyes, blue as mints. "*Dios guarde,*" said the *partera,* and took a step back, making the sign of the cross. Like no color found in nature, Máma Carmen thought. Like the slap-dash coat of turquoise paint intended to give cheer to cemetery headstones. People stood whispering under the eaves of their ranchos all day long.

Her husband came staggering home two days later, stinking of *guaro,* took one look at Ada's blue eyes and called Máma Carmen a *puta.* She convinced him Ada had his lips, the unmistakable stamp of the Gonzalez, a fish pout their older children shared. "I've called her Adalia, after you, Adán," she offered. "Adalia Eduvigis with her saint's name." Adán fiddled with his hat brim, his face deeply tanned and creased from years of cutting cane. Máma Carmen intoned, "*Amorcito,* can't you see she is a gift from God after all those babies we lost?" For a couple of months, he stuck around, just long enough to see downy blond curls sprout from Ada's otherwise *coco-liso* head. Then he spat on the floor, turned without saying a word, and disappeared for good.

Máma Carmen says Abuela Consuelo was also blonde and blue-eyed. She who died in the Chalatenango mountains at the onset of the civil war. A snapshot tacked to a bedpost, the only photo ever taken of Consuelo, showed a little girl standing on the roadside, carrying a flower-print umbrella and squinting under a backlit halo of blond hair. Abuela Consuelo's rancho was burned to the ground by guerrillas and Máma Carmen, just a teenager, was led crying and screaming across the river by her tia and tio. Ada's older brother and sister were both dark-haired and dark-eyed. And a decade later, the war over, Abuela's photo turned to ash. And so nothing to prove she really was Adán's child.

Ada was a colicky child and even though she wore the red wool cap and red socks, the red bead talisman around her wrist to keep away the *mal de ojo*, Máma Carmen was certain a jealous visitor had given her child the evil eye. After Ada's birth, Máma Carmen had more sewing business than usual. Neighbors brought dresses to tailor, pants to mend, and though Ada wailed in the back room Máma Carmen insisted the baby was asleep. Always, these visits ended with clients cooing to Ada in their cradled arms.

Unlike her older children who had only mewled once or twice before falling asleep, Ada was willful, having mastered a stabbing cry that culminated in blue-lipped breath-holding, arms and legs stiff as a corpse. The only thing that soothed her was being nursed. Bare-breasted, Máma Carmen spent hour after hour crouched over some woman's shirt, embroidering birds and flowers while in her lap, her daughter drowsed on a cracked and bloody nipple.

Then, as suddenly as the colic started, it ended, though the cure proved more disturbing than all those nights filled with Ada's cries. It was the peak of *zafra* and more than half the cane fields had been harvested. Their house stood at the dead end of a dirt road. A rusted chicken wire and *izote* fence enclosed a small patch of backyard. Then the pitted gully of a stream, and beyond that, vast, waving cane fields.

To cut the cane, they first had to set fire to the field so the razor-edged leaves wouldn't slash to ribbons the harvesters' arms. Cane fires always sounded like the spit of rain on dry leaves. Then, the suck of oxygen, flames towering like a roaring ocean. The night lit up in a blaze of sunset oranges and the fleeing animals ducked into safe burrows, scrabbled up trees, or through the cracks of neighboring houses. The next day, everything dusted with ash, the only green was the lush canopy of a centennial ficus tree standing at the corner of the razed field.

Máma Carmen imagined the snake out feeding when the fire was lit. Imagined it sliding over the smooth stones of the creek bed, through the rivulet of water, across their backyard, and through the eave to the rafters of their clay-tiled house. For two weeks, Ada had slept through the night, and although she looked pale and a little thin, Máma Carmen didn't afford it much importance. "Such a good baby," she cooed.

It wasn't until two weeks later, when Josué, her eight-year-old son, awoke with a middle-of-the-night fever, that Máma Carmen discovered what had happened. Josué parted the curtain separating her bedroom from the main room and screamed, dropping the flashlight when he saw the snake.

In the candlelight, Máma Carmen slept sitting up on her cot, her breasts bare and dripping milk onto her lap where Ada was cradled. Josué backed into the corner and cried out, "Mamá, Mamá! *La masacuata! La masacuata!*" and pointed to the rafters. Máma Carmen held out her arms and Josué ran crying to her bedside. She looked down at Ada's face, her lips pouted in a perfect "O" and her tongue and cheeks moved as if suckling on something invisible. "The snake, Mami, it was drinking. It was drinking from your *chichita*," he sobbed. "Ada was— was sucking on its tail." Máma Carmen put her hand over her breast and felt the electric heat of her milk coming down. She had heard the stories about *la masacuata*, every woman in every pueblo had heard them. "Shh, *hijito*, you're burning with fever," she said and smoothed his hair. "It's a bad dream."

In the guttering light, she scanned the room, the darkness of the peaked roof. Snakes were attracted to milk, she knew that. She'd seen the limp body of the seven-foot *masacuata* they'd dragged out of Don Manolo's barn. Eusebio Sanchez had held up the bloody blade of his *corvo*, said he'd discovered the snake suckling from a cow, the newborn calf tight in its coils.

But that night in her rancho, Máma Carmen never closed her eyes. She slept with her fevered son and newborn tucked at her side; she thought of her oldest daughter sleeping alone next to the sputtering hearth but didn't dare get up until sunlight. She never saw a trace of the snake, not a wafer of shed skin, no pellets studded with hair or feathers. But she also never did see another mouse, spider, or beetle in her rancho. And though Máma Carmen took care to bind her breasts tightly each night, assuring no smell of milk would escape, Ada slept the whole night through, quietly in a hammock. Sleepless, Máma Carmen prayed rosary after rosary as she watched Ada suck, trance-like, at the air, the tip of her tongue peeking out from her pink, parted lips.


PEAK OF THE DRY SEASON, a hot gust swayed the canefield, silencing the cicadas' shrill alarm. Ada walked between the planted rows although Mamá had forbid her to enter the field. No matter that in September other nine-year olds, her own classmates, would be wielding machetes alongside their parents. Day in, day out, Ada traced a path through the canefield to her hideout. The knee-high leaves looked harmless, the green of lizards and sour candies, the mounds of newly tilled ground soft beneath her feet.

Knapsack slung over her shoulder, Ada reached down to grab a handful and pressed it together to form a tight ball. If she could toss it up and catch

it whole, she could break her promise. Mamá had sent her for firewood—
*and if you bring me thin green branches I'll use those to whip your shins, girl!*—
but there was something she had to do beforehand.

She caught the ball of dirt neatly and then crushed it in her fist. Once
more to be sure. Again, she launched it up and the ball landed intact in her
palm. But as she approached the end of the planted rows, she packed a third
ball and launched it forward. Perhaps because the field was more sand than
dirt it broke apart between her fingers. And that's when she ran towards the
giant ficus.

Near the rocky patch at the field's edge she stumbled to her knees,
though she didn't stop to examine her injuries until she reached the shade.
Bright blood crowned her kneecap. She clapped the dirt off her hands and
used the hem of her school uniform to wipe her wound. Though the scratchy
navy fabric didn't show the stain, she smelled the dried blood on her under-
pants. Not one word of it to her mother; Ada was sure it meant she'd been
bad, that her heart was honeycombed with lies. Not two days before, she
had dawdled on the way to fetch water and arrived after the town pipe had
run dry, found it leaking its last drops, enough to fill her *jarra* with three
sorry mouthfulls.

For nights she'd wanted to ask her mother to sing her to sleep. *Dormite
niñita, cabeza de ayote, si no te dormis te come el coyote.* But her mother would
not. Any child old enough to fetch water and gather firewood knew better
than to ask. "It's the end of the day," Mamá would say. "I've got nothing left
to give." Ada would not invite those words. To fall asleep, she stroked her
own head, gliding her fingertips over her lashes and brows, smoothing the
hair on the top of her head. *Si no te dormis,* Ada sang the lullaby but the
threat of the words snapped clear once they lost that sweet incantation of
her mother's voice. *Shhhsst* went the candle flame, snuffed.

The sun pressed a bright ring around the ficus' canopy, the fat trunk en-
graved with hearts and condemnations. She walked between the undulating
roots, traced the tree's scarred bark, the puffed letters of the older inscrip-
tions, the jagged cuts of the newer carvings. Some letters repeated, some let-
ters crossed out. Hanging vines created pillars and archways, secret caverns
and pockets, and to enter her hideout she had to turn sideways into the oval
slit where she then squatted and hugged her knees to her chest, the buds of
her breasts pressed to her thighs.

How was it that a man and woman fit together? At school she'd discov-
ered the Encyclopaedia Britannica's picture of a many-layered woman. She'd
turned the first page and peeled off the transparent skin, exposing the land-

scape of pink muscle, the birdcage of bone, until the woman was stripped to a puzzle of multi-colored organs. The mystery had to do with love and pain, like a thin hot wire across her entire body. Like how she squeezed pinpoints of blood from the scrape on her knee.

The pink sac between the woman's legs was not unlike the ficus' secret pockets. Not unlike this place she'd discovered, and where, over the years, she'd found a knife wrapped in a dirty handkerchief, a nest of empty eggs, a bundle of love letters, a lace-edged panty, the papery skin of a snake that crumbled between her fingers.

For the last two nights, a *masacuata* had visited her dreams, the snake's coils squeezed tight around her waist. In the morning she'd found a rust-colored stain on the sheets between her legs. The second night Ada pleaded with the snake, tried to pry open its jaws to see if it would talk. It spoke only with its eyes. If she wanted to stop bleeding she would have to give him her only doll. Though she was too old, it was the only toy she had ever owned. Anita with the flower diadem, blond curls, and click-clack blue eyes.

She slipped the pack off her shoulder and placed it to one side. In the farthest recess of the den, she dug a shallow grave. She wanted to open the bag's flap but seeing Anita's sleepy eyes would only make her cry. Instead, she slipped her hand inside the bag and placed her finger in the doll's curled palm. Then, she pushed the dirt back and sat atop the mound. The cicadas started their wailing and through the oval slit she looked out at the cane spears. It seemed it would never rain. She squeezed her cut kneecap again and pressed her lips to the jeweled blood

AT TWELVE, Ada protected her waist-long hair by braiding it in tight coils. When she was little, her mother had tried to shave it bald, saying, "It's not a punishment, it's the *piojos*," and pretended to crush a louse between her fingernails. Ada saw the speck of dirt and knew better, that her mother hated the draw of her blue eyes, hated how people always wanted to touch her hair. Mamá claimed she hated it too, but kept the white-blond baby ringlets and all the sun-streaked tips in a shoebox in her top drawer.

Each morning when Ada reached the paved road she let down her hair and spread it like a mantle across her shoulders. All her life, neighbors, old or young, teachers, classmates, street vendors, everyone treated her special. But each afternoon her mother, who spent her days sewing and eating *pan dulce*, would huff as far as she could up the street. She'd stand in a patch of shade, the wide stratas of her breasts, belly, and hips balanced over calves crosshatched with veins, and call out, "Get in here, Ada," and snap her wrist. "*Niña condenada.*"

Mamá stopped sending Ada on errands, gave her no money to buy sweets after school. And yet each day, Ada came home with a baggie of peeled green mangos or a square of sugar-dusted *semita*, the telltale purple of snowcone honey impossible to wipe from her lips. Her forearms were often covered with bruises, that tight grip of fingers and pinchmarks left by her mother.

But that Easter Sunday, her hair loose and her arms unmarred, she walked to church in her best dress. The one she'd worn for every special occasion, years in a row, now sizes too small, the pink satin stretched tight across her chest and so she'd left two buttons undone, and the straps off the shoulder. The dress dug into her arms as she hefted a Styrofoam cooler from one hip to the other. Mamá's earnings from sewing were not enough and so on weekends they sold tamales after mass at the soccer field. The 9:00 a.m. sun sparked the tin roofs of the neighboring houses. It seemed the first rains always fell on Good Friday but that year, though storm clouds threatened each afternoon, the ground was still tinder-dry.

Canton Chancala seemed hinged between two seasons, rain and drought, thrive and survive. Along the road the scrub-brush sizzled with insects, strewn trash, plastic bottles like alien eggs in nests of dried leaves. The countryside a patchwork of browns except for the flowering trees' pom poms of yellow and pink snagged in bare branches. *Wait*, they seemed to say. *Just wait, we can live beyond this.* The trees in the field, how they told it over and over.

Ada liked to hang back, her mother a silhouette through the flowered nylon of her umbrella, her hips and shoulders swaying as she walked. "A woman is like a *jarra*," her mother liked to say. "Like a clay jug, perfect and whole. But let that pot fall—no matter if you put together all the pieces— it will never hold water again." With each footstep, a small explosion of dust rose from the baked ground. Ada attempted to step inside those wide footprints and smile at boys pedaling their bicycles, without her mother noticing.

"Teach yourselves not to want the things of this world," was how the priest opened his sermon. Ada looked at the banners of cheap lace that arched over the congregation, the women hooded in makeshift kerchiefs of a folded hand towel and little girls itching at their spangled, stiff skirts. Fans stirred the hot air above the plastic chairs, as men stared blank-eyed into the empty bowl of their straw hats. In the back, their sons played catch with an oily rag or munched on fried plantains, sucked on copper-colored sodas from plastic bags. What was there to want in all of this? A skin Ada wished she could shed, like the splitting seams of her satin dress.

What had the things of this world taught her? That she was different. That people would treat her the way they do all things they misunderstand, a corner-of-the-eye sidestep, equal parts curiosity and dread. And lately, those girls at school all baring their teeth.

A few rows ahead, her classmates Rosalia and Yancy stood straight-waisted as boys, their empty bustiers sagging as they leaned over to kiss each other's cheek as a sign of peace. Rosalia must have felt Ada's eyes on her because when she turned, she lifted her eyebrow and mouthed, *Que?* Ada tried a smile, but Rosalia whispered into Yancy's ear. Ada took a deep breath, inched her dress down, her breasts bulging out over the top like the textbook pictures of Spanish queens as she kneeled along with the rest of the congregation. My body, she thought. What say did a snake have of its markings, a bird the color of its feathers? She was that kind of animal, showy and bold.

Beyond the single line of coconut palms that separated the church from Chancala's soccer field, came shouts from those already warming up for the Sunday match. She cracked open the cooler lid, the tamales still warm. Her mother swatted her hand; throughout all of Lent she had tried to use her most patient voice. The time of sacrifice, Ada thought, was coming to a close.

When everyone lined up for Holy Communion, Máma Carmen and Ada slipped out and made their way to the sidelines where they set up their stall beneath the patchy shade of a cocoplum tree. Ada plucked a ripe fruit from a low-hanging branch and popped it in her mouth, the flavor of spun sugar spreading across her tongue with each small bite.

On the sunny field, the boys yipped and whinnied as they sprinted up and back the entire length of grass. Those on the sidelines bounced soccer balls from knee to knee, sometimes to the crowns of their heads. Aside from the water vendor, her cheeks splotched with maroon birthmarks, Ada and her mother were the only women on the field. Men gathered on the sandy slope beneath the coconut trees drinking *guaro* from plastic flasks and cheering on their sons. In the far corner, a young man leaned on the hood of a faded Datsun with its flame appliques and a racing fin. When Ada met his eye, he started to walk over.

Over the years, legions of boys, as well as many older men, had tried to *cuentear* Ada, she with *eyes like jewels, hair of gold*. But this man just smiled and held her gaze, while Máma Carmen tended to customers. He approached Ada's side of the stall. A dusty blue cloud floated over the iris of his left eye. She made sure to select the fattest *tamal* and wrapped it in the brightest green leaves. When he smiled at her, she imagined herself as a kite floating in a sun-struck sky.

After the customers left and the man returned to his Datsun, Máma Carmen turned to Ada. "You think I don't know what you're doing?" she said, and when she gripped Ada's arm, Ada could feel the crescent moons of those fingernails piercing her skin. "Men like him will chew you up and spit you out. *Te comera viva!*" She stepped in front of her daughter, away from the bystanders that had turned and stared. Then she gripped the neckline of her daughter's dress and yanked it up. "You may look like a woman, but you're still a child."

The noon sun intensified, the heat winding around Ada's body and her mother leaned close and whispered, "What you have, *niña*, it is both a blessing and a curse." A thin moustache of sweat formed across her mother's lips. Ada closed her eyes and in the background she heard the slurred shouts and sniggers of the men, everything gone quiet in the lull of the soccer game.

Between the branches of the cocoplum the air was laced with dust. Mamá took a step forward, ran her hands across her daughter's hair and said, "Listen to what I tell you." Ada could tell her mother's intention was gentle, but when her fingers snagged in the tangles of Ada's hair, she whipped her head, stepped away and said, "What could you know? You who couldn't even keep your own husband!"

Máma Carmen's hand came down hard across Ada's lips and cheek, though she didn't cry until she'd made it all the way to the church courtyard. Obey, obey. Mamá had meant to knock her clear of her stubborn ilk. Instead, each word had served to reinforce Ada's will.

Ada walked along the road, kicking at stones and grinding insects into the asphalt. Near the turn off to her house, the Datsun with the flaming door panels pulled alongside. The man looked over, leaned across the seat and flung open the passenger door. She settled into the hot vinyl, and within seconds the wind was tugging at her hair, like a white flag, a sail, a ghost hand trailing from the open window.


ADA SEARCHED the smoke and alcohol of his tongue, wondering what he tasted in hers. They'd driven into the hills and parked beneath a tree between the chicken-wire fence of a pasture and a canefield. *Shush*, the cane waved its lavender plumes as he ran his hands across her body. She felt the heartbeats of animals crouched beneath the dry skirts of the underbrush. Maille-skinned *zumbadora*, vesper rat, savior beetle—one thing chases another, a never ending chain of open mouths.

Gray clouds gathered in the east, swallowing the hills of overgrown cane.

Of him she knew only this: every time she tried to ask his name, his age, anything about him, he leaned in with his rough beard, pushed her harder against the seat. He sucked on the curve of her neck, traced his lips along her clavicle. *No*, she wanted to say. *No*. But her words were like the bare scratch of a matchstick. He pulled down her dress and as he licked her skin, her heart guttered and waned, and she felt her whole body pulse in wicks of flames. "No," she said, finally, and inside her, that *no* flared. Her body lit up like cane fire, the heat climbing the stalks inch by inch, flames tight on the field's green hips.

As she tried to push him off, he whispered into her ear, "No, *niñita*, don't pretend. You know you're going to give it up." Followed by the rumble of thunder and in the corner of the window above her head, the first few drops of rain. On this switchback road, they hadn't passed a house for miles. Might this be like being buried alive? Ada closed her blue eyes, click-clack and the sound of rain in a steady *ssshhhhhh*.

He gripped her neck as he grunted above her. She was a stupid girl. In sheets of water the lacquered leaves nodded *yes*, *yes*, and *yes*. She was broken. In curtains, veils, everything slipped from her hands. She thought of her mother's words and she felt them whole and perfect. She would carry them all the way home, down the long stretch of road, all that guilt balanced on her head like a jug of rainwater.

When he went to unbuckle his pants she lunged for the door. He shoved her back, slapped her full across the face and as she clawed and bit and kicked, the tinny taste of blood filled her mouth. Her ears rang with her own screams; the rain warped to the sound of fire. She imagined it rising, sucking the air to cellophane, opening its throat of smoke to a roar, a water-fall of sound that even tomorrow the men would claim to hear as they angled their machetes, sent them singing into the stalks. Even the cane field would say—*Search the ashes, I am here, press my flesh until my veins run clear. Sweet is my strength, grip the burnt stalks, and throw me to the ground. I will never be yours.*

ALEXANDRA LYTTON REGALADO

# Ode to *La Matria*

"Tengo Patria y Matria"
—Claribel Alegría

From the starched white sky, the sun
    sparks the tin roofs on Easter Sunday,
slants a sheen on the banners of satin
    and laces the arch over the congregation.
Women hooded in makeshift kerchiefs—
    the folded square of a hand towel—bow their heads
as girls itch their spangled, stiff skirts.
    Fans stir the hot air above rows of plastic chairs,
as men stare into the empty bowls of their straw hats;
    their sons play catch, others munch on fried plantains
or suck on copper-colored sodas in plastic bags.
    *Teach yourselves not to want,* the priest says,
*the things of this world.* The sun glints into this.

\* \* \*

Salvadoran woman,
walking home from church,
the only thing
between you and the noon flash
is the flowered nylon
of your umbrella.

You admit
your back-lit silhouette,
the outline of your calves,
but I walk
alongside, invisible,
while your canvas flats
track prints in the dust.

Rays cut through cloud;
in this landscape are the two of us
no more significant than leaves
scraping across pavement?

\* \* \*

Each year the country witnesses two seasons
of thrive or survive; summer smothers
the idyll green, unmasks heaps of roadside trash,
    plastic bottles in nests of dried leaves.
The cicadas let loose their sirens, wailing
    and mating until it all goes up in flames.
But the bare trees insist; unafraid
    to stand naked, unable even to feign death—
*wait* they tell us, *just wait*—
    *we can live beyond this.*

\* \* \*

O Salvadoran woman, who is me
and yet not me; we travel
beneath a mantle of white.

Are we like the right hand
that pinches the left hand?
One stands by, giving its flesh
to be nipped, while the other
knowingly tweaks the skin?

I've had the privilege
of pretending, but
not without consequence.

Look into the light—
what does the sun know
about observer's guilt?

Petals cover the tinder-dry grass
with their light
pink skins.

* * *


Maquilishuat blossoms cling
        like puffs of spun sugar snagged
in bare branches—were it not for them
        the entire countryside would believe it is dying.
Who taught you, Salvadoran woman
        with your head bowed, veiled in lace,
to begin again with nothing more
than the promise of green?

# País

Amo un país lejano
Donde tiembla día a día
Un país verde
Luciérnaga pequeña
De lejanos inviernos

Recuerdo
Una viejo
Allá en el campo
Buscaba mangos
Y decía
—La lluvia les saca
Los gusanos
Del Corazon a los mangos
Ya no sirven—
Y temblando se fue
Empujando hojas con sus pies

Amo un país lejano
Que tiembla
Como tiemblo yo
Hoy me encontré
Con un sobre que llego de El Salvador
Hace treinta y cuatro años
La carta esta dirjida a mi
La enviaba mi padre

Hoy recorde al viejo
Aquel pais lejano

Hay dentro de mi un niño
Que se ha hecho hombre

Un niño que se hizo triste
Un niño que se hizo alegre
Un niño que se hizo hombre
Un niño que sigue siendo niño
Y busca en aquél pais lejano
Un Corazón que no le salgan gusanos
En invierno ni en verano

DORA OLIVIA MAGAÑA

# A la altura de la vida

AL POETA AMILCAR COLOCHO CAÍDO EN COMBATE EL 30 DE OCTUBRE 1990,
VOLCAN DE SAN SALVADOR, EL SALVADOR.

"NOSOTROS NO SOMOS NINGUNA GENERACIÓN ESPONTANEA ESTAMOS HECHOS
A LA ALTURA DE LA VIDA Y NUESTRO GOLPE A MANO DE FUTURO"
—AMILCAR COLOCHO

"A la altura de la vida"
tu poesía exige de la mía
el recuerdo de luciérnagas
en húmedas noches del tópico,
cuando el olor intenso del peligro
vibró en nuestro valor
y fuimos espadas al asalto.

"A la altura de la vida"
tu poesía exige de la mía
la verdad en la marcha
apostando, apuntando al hoy del futuro.

"A la altura de la vida"
tu poesía exige de la mía
la compañía
de la que vive lo que ama
y ama lo que vive
porque el sueño…
… sigue entero.

DORA OLIVIA MAGAÑA

# Era tiempo de guerra

Nicaragua 1980

Era tiempo de guerra
no me pude quedar,
me llevé en el cuerpo
tus montañas verdes.

Era tiempo de guerra
no me pude quedar,
me llevé en los ojos
tus atardeceres.

Era tiempo de guerra
no me pude quedar
estabas recién parida
te dabas a la tierra
en colmenas, cooperativas,
colectivos, comunidades,
comités de barrios,
solidaridad.

Era tiempo de guerra…
… El Salvador esperaba.

JOSÉ B. GONZÁLEZ

# Scene with Pancho, *The Cisco Kid (1950-1956)*

THE FIRST YEAR with my uncle my belly starts to flatten. He says it's because New York water is cleaner. He doesn't let me talk much about my grandmother and tells me that I need to bury my country.

I tried to bring up the times that she and I went to movies, but he usually stops me by the time I start to mention a scene. Bury it, he says.

He never had his own kids, but that's good. For me anyway. He leaves me alone in the apartment and doesn't worry about me crossing streets, the way my grandmother did.

I thought of asking him about my _____. What he was like growing up. I want to know if my _____met my _____ when they were in second grade. But my uncle keeps saying to bury it. So I stay quiet.

He has this small TV in the living room, where I sleep. He doesn't watch it much but he tells me that I need to watch as much as I can so that I can learn English. That's what he did, he says. That and burying, I bet.

There is only one Spanish channel, and that one is fuzzy most of the time. Playing with the antenna does nothing. So I have no choice but to watch TV in English anyway.

One channel plays the same show over and over. It's about two cowboys, Cisco and Pancho, who ride their horses across deserts and fight outlaws. They both have accents that don't sound like my uncle's.

Pancho's English sounds like it's for laughs, but there are no laugh tracks. He speaks in short lines and does what the Cisco Kid tells him. The time he gets kidnapped, Cisco scolds him, "Be quiet, Pancho."

I know those words from teachers at school. "Be quiet." By the end of the show, Cisco fistfights the outlaw while Pancho points a gun at a woman. The episode ends with the two of them riding free.

Each time I watch an episode, I wait for their families to show up. But they never do.

By the end of the year, I can understand most of the jokes that Pancho makes. And I can tell that they never mention their families. Not Cisco's. Not Pancho's. It's like they don't exist. Like they had to bury every part of them in order to ride into new sunsets.

ROSANNA PEREZ

# Back and Forward

San Salvador, *5 Junio 1983*

Margarita,

This morning, the fresh smell of coffee wakes me up. The sleepy body would like to continue embracing the blanket's warmth. But the million things to do are screaming for my mind's attention… The adjectives, the verbs, the first sentence to begin the journey of moving back and forward… Nearby the radio spits out the news in the neighborhood, which by no means is news at all, isn't it. Always the same thing? Everything and nothing at the same time, the confusion of ideas. And lately, the feeling of shame and guilt that is left for the survivor… It is ironic that to continue living one has to leave one's country or confront the consequences of staying where one is not wanted…

\* \* \*

Where do I begin to tell a story that is always in the making, the exposure of deep feelings that nobody wants to hear? Then, I guess, it is the body that becomes an instrument of memory, of the language that can provide us the axioms, the clauses, the syllogism, to create and re-create the story. A story told by this body that has been my companion, my witness, the temple where I take refuge when the overwhelming reality fails. But a body that you see but don't differentiate from any other body because I do not have it posted all over telling about my experiences. My body is tattooed with a history unknown for many and painful for the ones who know about it. Still I carry that story with me, like all of us do. All of us carry with us a family story, a country history, all that baggage that makes us who we are, we carry our customs, our habits, our ancestors, the ones who came before us… and the ones that came before them… I would like you to know that when we left El Salvador I would have liked to exchange these words with *abuela* but for whatever reasons at that moment I could not do it. But here they are: *Abuela*, we didn't exchange many words on the way to the airport. I have wanted to thank you for your support in these past months. It has been, the least to say, difficult for all of us. The escalation of the tension on the streets have imploded in our bodies and exploded at everybody's home and in the whole country. Seeing dead bodies on the streets, and seeing my Rodolfo… and friends disappeared or get killed—it has been deeply painful. There are things that do not need to be said. Departures are always painful besides—words cannot do justice to the feeling that eats my heart at this precise moment. The adjectives and verbs will keep the story going for years to come. My body still feels numb by the whole experience of being held without my will, and without knowing when I might be released. It feels like a bad dream you don't know if it is ending or beginning at once. I remember the first night after I was released, waking to the sounds of the avocado tree branches over the roof. I got scared and then realized I was at your home. It was still dark outside and a sense of confusion and emptiness enfolded me. I didn't know what to make of it, but I stayed there in silence listening to the early sounds of the morning. No, fear is the verb that better describes it. Not knowing what the future holds for us, and now this, abruptly leaving the country. I guess this dreary reality is taking over everyone's life, keeping us prisoners of fear and silence. Who knows for how long—what if it is forever? Seems like we are suffering a collective shock, confused, lost in our thoughts and worries. Nobody seems to know when things will be "normal" again. Perhaps it is a momentary *adios,* and we'll see each other soon. I just want to grasp this moment, and take with me your teary brown eyes, which are telling me everything at once. I will keep it in the most sacred part of my body. And I will look at it whenever I need comfort… Then we said bye…

\* \* \*

San Salvador, *Junio* 1992

Margarita,

I hope these lines will find you well. I heard the news this morning. They said that peace agreements were signed in January, and that was so long ago. Although, many of us thought that it would come sooner. Thirteen years waiting for the sun to come… and now that it is finally here a cloud of darkness has fallen over our heads. Once again uncertainty is taking over us… It has been almost ten years since the last time we departed without saying a word. I just remember giving you my baby daughter and looking into your eyes to keep calm under those horrible and uncertain circumstances. The men knocking at your door were armed to the teeth, without uniforms, and with clear orders to take me with them. I could not put up resistance; your son and mother were present then, and my baby daughter too. There was no reason to have all of us killed for no reason. There was no sense to run or hide. I guess fighting for utopias is not allowed in our country… outside your house a couple of cars waited for me. The night was cold. It was raining at that moment I wanted to gulp everything through my body, the darkness of the night, the falling rain, the smell of wet soil that is a vernacular part to our country. A country where the coffee plantations stand at the core of our economy, and ironically enough the land belongs to fourteen families, not even primeval to the country. I wanted to take everything with me, but suddenly, the darkness fell into my eyes, my body was tied up. The blows and punches began and a fall into an endless spiral. But the mind didn't want to let go of the rain, the night, the smell of wet soil to keep me alive. Being blindfolded and tied up is frightening under any circumstance; one loses control of one's body and becomes a passenger on someone else's trip. Many times the body loses its identity and does not feel like one's body anymore, numbed, tired, fragmented, in pain. Meanwhile, the mind drifts in the depths of the brain looking for help. Then the body will remember the good moments in life, and like a floater in the middle of the ocean, it sustains undergoing the adverse circumstances. There is always brightness in the darkness. A baby's smile, a hug from a loved one, singing with friends, the multitude of crickets singing by the creek after a good rain at night, the sound of the water going down the stream. Even running on the streets becomes an escape to that inferno. But one must remain SILENT. The interrogation begins and one cannot provide names, addresses, no faces to remember. It is forbidden! One must find the way to keep grounded to reality without letting them break one into pieces, which is their intention. In the meantime in isolation and blindfolded between four walls that one can only imagine because one is not allowed to see them. For the first time after all these years I am able to ask you, how are you doing? I have been trying to get in contact with you, but the distance since I moved out of the country and the fear that reigns in it have been obstacles to getting in touch with you or anyone else. I don't know where Rodolfo, my friends, my classmates, my professors are any more.

My companions are adjectives and verbs, which better describe what happened to us. I am sorry that things ended up this way. I imagine that is the only way it could happen. Who would think that something like my capture would happen in your neighborhood, which is a military town? However, I am glad that we can more or less talk about the event, at least to acknowledge that it was a horrifying experience for all. I am glad that we have survived the most difficult part of it and now we'll have to witness the future… Write when the time allows you…

\* \* \*

Los Angeles, *Agosto* 2006

Margarita,

The sky is blue this morning like the January sky in El Salvador. A veil of nostalgia covers my heart, and I feel my body is a pastiche of cultures: Nahua-Pipil, Northern African, and Spanish. I don't understand borders. What is a border anyway? The delineation of an imaginary line, that we are not supposed to cross. I wonder is this border outside or inside of us? The body has a memory of its own… remembers the land, the comfort food made by hands that took care of me as a child… besides the pains inflicted in it by the ones who wanted to control us… It is difficult to live in this country; more than once I have gotten lost in the city. It is the seagulls' fault. They make me think I am getting close to the ocean when we are only around MacArthur Park. This is the park where a lot of people from Central America get together. They sell food and gather their hopes and dreams under the palm trees every Sunday morning, precisely, the only place they can afford to take their kids to play. It is called inner-city, a green patch of land where the Christians congregated to proclaim the divine word offering the heaven that poor cannot have in life… The *paletero* sells sweets and comfort to the kids who cry to the heat of the afternoon. And a man with all kinds of inflated plastic toys brings happiness to the little ones by the sand box. Radios and rockolas scream at every corner in the park. There is a buzzing of noises accompanied by the snores of the lazy buses that sporadically run at this time of the day. This is a strange city—people want to put you in little boxes, accordingly, to your color, sex, way of speaking, the way one looks, etc. I was giving a presentation to build up solidarity for the community. Then, after the presentation I opened space for questions. A man in the audience called me "exotic." But I was not even standing on my hands or making any kind of tricks. Immediately, I thought about the Talapo, who goes to visit my *abuela* with his long tail and the little feathers at the end of it with a make up like Cleopatra. The Talapo that visited *mi abuela* for a long time, always looking for the food she'd put out for him... since my *abuela* left, he hasn't come around anymore...

*Hasta pronto...*

\* \* \*

Los Angeles, *Julio* 1983

Margarita,

This evening the smell of wet soil made me nostalgic and I thought about El Salvador... Suddenly, one's whole life is in a question mark. Was I right or wrong? I don't know, I was only doing what I thought was the right thing to do. Rodolfo and I were young and dreamers—we really believed in the rivers of honey and milk for all. But taking things into action has consequences. Often times, we might not be aware of the way it may affect us. There is a reaction to every action, perhaps that was the way everything started. Union laborers marching on the streets. The teacher's union, the nurse's union, the university students in solidarity, the campesinos wanting their land to plant coffee, sugar cane, and cotton with their eyes foreseeing a better future. Our actions like an avalanche rolling down a hill taking down everything in its path. After all, what lasts is the body and the memories that remains with it... besides the language that helps to deconstruct history in order to pick up the pieces to continue walking. Reading and writing can become a forbidden action if it is used to question the reality one faces. Being a woman who knows how to read has its implications in countries where women are expected to be quiet and submissive. There are countries where they think that education is not necessary for women. If women's main purpose in life is to procreate, they do not need an education. They just need to obey, and that subjugation can only occur in the vacuum created by the lack of education. I wonder, but as I walk and pick up the pieces of life that remain, I assure myself that I must continue my path and confront my fears and history... Arriving in Los Angeles is one of the great challenges I have faced in life... I am writing to you from this faraway place, it is a long way from home, three thousand miles of land separates us! Besides, a border that is more protected and guarded than anything one can imagine. At the line, I got scared of the men carrying their guns and the helicopters buzzing around. It did not bring good memories to me. I was thrown to the streets in San Salvador. We were marching, carrying the lifeless bodies of a couple of union workers who had been killed. We were on our way to the university to give tribute to these men. But on the way there, the police started to shoot at everybody. People ran everywhere… and then like now, I see faces and recognize that feeling of uncertainty and fear, which I am still acquainted with. Persecution and violence have many faces, which often times are unrecognizable. They fool us but sooner than later, take over, and there is not much one can do. However, I don't want to bother you with my stories, on the contrary, the reason of this letter is to tell you how thankful I am for the education that my parents allowed me to have. If not for this I would be in a worse situation. Living in exile is very difficult. The distance is like a second death. This city is a metropolis—the rhythm of life run everywhere. All places are at a distance. One has to give extra time to get to one's destination on time, because the buses are always running late. Or they are so full that they don't even bother to stop to pick up more passengers. It is very frustrating! People don't pay attention to others. No one makes contact with strangers. And new arrivers like me are swallowed into the guts of the beast without even being noticed. We become invisible like the shadows on the streets. The jobs that we get are the low pay jobs. You might think I studied at the university for nothing. Well, I would have to have my academic credentials to work a decent job. Since I don't have them, I've got to do whatever is available. In the United States, you need papers for everything. I guess that it would be even harder if I did not have the opportunity to cultivate my mind. It has been less difficult to develop the necessary skills to survive in Los Angeles. Culturally speaking, it is like day and night! This is a country with a different language, habits, customs, people, etc. I am trying my best to catch up, but this language is difficult. The pronunciation and the writing are different. There are sounds we don't even know in Spanish. But let's not talk about it. I guess everything in life can get somewhat difficult at times, but it is not always going to be this way. That's what I hope.

Please visit my parents when Cronos allows you.

Imagine if I'd gone to France…

DARREL ALEJANDRO HOLNES

# Bread Pudding Grandmamma

Crack open the coconut
and mix the fluids of *el coco* with cow's milk,
        like I mix words with grunts and moos
        when speaking with my childhood fable friends.
This is my grandmother's recipe for bread pudding
        when I come home heartbroken from high school.

We bake everyday pains into guilty pleasures,
mix in torn apart bread-loaf backs,
always in a ceramic bowl,
and watch them move like tectonic plates.
We play as God does in California,
        the geophysics of Caribbean cuisine
turn the earth at force with your spoon
        like turning through stages of teenage rebellion
        where nothing stands firm beneath your feet
        and your mind, like bread, is an uneven sponge.

Add in brown sugar *to taste* she says,
and eat some as you bake to feel better
        about being called a *brownie* today in class
a little glucose for her day of tasting tears that
        run down her cheeks as old age
        runs with my grandfather's mind.
Add white sugar, then vanilla, no almond extract,
        unless your monthly check has come on time.
If it hasn't, your palette will taste a richer sweetness
        the soulful truth of Caribbean cuisine:
almond absence brings the vanilla out more.

Our hands mush together our pains with
a few grains of salt,
        *for style* she says, with
a few slices of butter:
        *the secret to life,*
in each mixing bowl.

I'm the darling grandchild,
        her favorite, I believe.
At school there is trouble,
        and medication for her is expensive,
so we make bread, bake bread,
        the sweet kind to satisfy our appetite.

She digs from the bottom of a jar for
fruits soaked in wine,
        only the best ones.
We add this last.
        *This is what gives it that taste man,*
        *any liquor is all right.*
She talks, I smile.
        Eighty-six years old
I believe her old hands and weak eyes
        but strong legs and big smile.

We empty it into the pan,
        bake it, and trade our worries for the aroma,
pour in the ingredients
of hard work on a hot afternoon,
        forget that children can be mean,
and that with wisdom comes age,
        but with age comes ailment.
Bake for one and a half hours,
    and devour.

DARREL ALEJANDRO HOLNES

# Poder

FOR THE SURGE OF 70,000 CENTRAL AMERICAN MIGRANT KIDS


The difference between poetry and rhetoric
is being ready to kill
yourself
instead of your children
wrote Audre Lorde.
I say this now to the mothers who sent
their children north,
risking their babies' lives
for a better living
than chasing paper or running
from drug dealers
on the streets. The difference
between art and design
means being ready to die
for what you desire
others to achieve
through your work,
hours of your life gone forever
making a little, shiny, fragile thing.
I write to the mothers who send
their children north
never knowing if they'll make it
but hoping that even if they don't
their creations might mean more than just
the flesh and bone with which they're made
because they moved, because they desired.
So many are quick to dismiss
*desire* as too general a word
or this language as too simple
to power the constant thrust

toward betterment we call *life*,
but poetry is sometimes made of such things,
words used so often we take them for granted
and forget their power is in how they unite
existence through a common tongue. In Spanish the word
for *power* is the same as the word for *I can*.
*Poder*, one simple word banging the drum rhythm
made by children's soles thumping against the earth:
*po-der, po-der, po-der*; the power of doing
in each disyllabic step of metric feet
moving us further and further
away from the word being just rhetoric,
into the structure of its design
where we find the power to turn suicide
into sacrifice, the power to turn beasts
into man, and man into martyr or miracle.
This is what makes miracles: a desire path
stretching seventeen hundred miles
through an armed border wall,
through electric barbed-wire fences—
a surge surmounting
all odds to rise beyond the stratosphere;
knowing this too is poetry.

DARREL ALEJANDRO HOLNES

# Angelitos Negros

In the film *Angelitos Negros*, both parents are Mexicans who are as white as
    a *Gitano's bolero* sung by an *indigena* accompanied by the Moor's guitar
bleached    by this American continent's celluloid in 1948
    when in America the world's colors were polarized into    black & *blanco*.

In the film, Pedro Infante plays Jose Carlos    and sings
*Angelitos Negros* in a chapel, the film's title song,
    asking the painter of the church's art to paint a picture with black angels
who look like Jose Carlos's dark-skinned daughter, a child his wife refuses to accept.

    *¿Pintor, si pintas con amor, porque desprecias su color*
        *si sabes que en el cielo    también los quiere Dios?*

Tonight I sing the same song for my morenos absent from these cathedral walls:

O painter, painting with a foreign brush to the *rumba* of its old *bolero.*
    Listen to our angel's chorus of *inocentes morenos muertos.*

We *morenos* in the barrio create a *gumbo quilombo*, our little taste of heaven
    with matches and propane and coal stones under a pot of *cabra y culebras.*
We *morenos* are brown turned black,    burnt by fire fired from *guardia* guns
    making us *congos* for the    *chanchudos* of a *rabiblanco legislador.*

Listen to *los pelaos* in the favelas kicking
    around the soccer ball  *de pie a pie de pie a pie de pie a pie cabeza cabeza*
            *gol!*
forced out of their homes  by a world class stadium    they can never afford to
    get into,    forced into a life in the prison    of their streets.
They too deserve to be painted, *pintor*, in your *fresco Adoración.*

*¿Pintor, si pintas con amor, porque desprecias su color?*

Eartha Kitt sings *Pintame Angelitos Negros*,
the same Andrés Eloy Blanco poem *Infante*     set to song
on thrift store vinyl               playing in homemade YouTube clips.
     Kitt raises her voice high enough
to swallow morning     if it does not give her a sky
             with dark-skinned angels in its clouds tonight.


     Then dusk falls over the continent built on
shadows, shackles, and shame.


Broken-winged Blackbird    three shades of jade, just fly into dark matter in outer space.
     Perhaps up there is a better painter, better god for us all    to obey.

WILLIAM ARCHILA

# Bury This Pig

Behind the cornfield, we scaled the mountainside
    looking for a foothold among the crags,

rooting out weeds, trampling on trash,
    the trek as if it were a holy crusade:

bodies armored, mounted on horses,
    banners fluttering in the air.

Then one morning, we stumbled upon the thing,
    dead, cramped in a ditch, covered in ants,

trotters grimy, a purple snout of flies
    and not a dollop of blood,

but a thick piece of hide, cradling
    about fifty pounds of hog.

Someone said, "Kush! Kush!"
    as if to awaken the thing.

I thought about the carcass, blood-slick,
    staggering into the room,

grumbling and drowning as if deep in the mud,
    eyes buckled in fear,

bones breaking down to the ground, open
    to the chop and tear of human hands:

pork and lard, forefeet, fatback cut into slabs,
an organ fattened and butchered.

It continued for weeks, a few of us
    meeting in the afternoons

just to look at the steaming belly, maggots
    stealing the gray of the brain,

each time, one more barefoot boy
    probing the eye socket with a stick.

Some of us came back armed
    with picks and bars, shovels dusty in our hands,

until the ground groaned with war.
    The sky fell and cracked the earth.

How was I to know
    they would be hooked, hacked,

snouts smashed on the wall,
    their bodies corkscrews on the floor?

How was I to know
    I would bury this pig, rock after rock?

WILLIAM ARCHILA

# Guayaberas

In my boyhood, all the men

wore them, a light body shirt
with pleats running down the breast,
two top pockets for pens, notepads,

two bottom ones for keys or loose change,
each sewn with a button

in the middle of the pouch,
a complement tailored to the slit
at the side of the hip. If you look

at photographs in family albums,
men stand against palm trees,

their short-sleeved *guayaberas*
caught in sunlight, their Panama hats
tipped to the sky. There's a black and white

of my father, stumbling along fields
of cane, head full of rum,

mouth in an "o," probably
singing a *bolero* of Old San Juan.
On days like these, the sun burned

like an onion in oil. Women hung
*guayaberas* on windows to dry.

Shirtless, men picked up their barefoot babies
off the floor, held them against their bellies
as if talking to a god. Even my school uniform

was a blue *guayabera*, but nothing
like my father's favorite: white,
long-sleeved, above the left breast

a tiny pocket, perfectly slender for a cigar,
arabesque designs vertically stretched.

When the evening breeze lulled
from tree to tree, he serenaded

my mother, guitars and tongues of rum
below her balcony; the trio strumming,
plucking till one in the morning.

I don't know what came first,
war or years of exile,
but everyone—shakers of maracas, cutters

of cane, rollers of tobacco—stopped wearing them,
hung them back in the closet, waiting

for their children to grow,
an arc of parrots to fly across the sky
at five in the evening. In another country,

fathers in their silver hair sit
on their porches, their sons, now men,

hold babies in the air, *guayaberas* nicely pressed.

WILLIAM ARCHILA

# Dig

I can tell you this much because I
 always begin with picks & shovels,
pencils & spoons, because I always
 return as a worm, six feet below,
 breeding a thing of leather & bone,
because the skin breaks over the nose,
belly sinks into a ditch of gas.

I can tell you what rose to the surface
 because of the arrowheads washed
& catalogued, because of the mountains
crumpled like butcher paper, graver
 & vessel found in the strata, because
of the ravines broken off into chasms,
releasing fossils back into the waters.

And if there's more, it'll be my father,
 always trudging uphill, lugging
his two hundred pounds of flab,
 exhausted, nostalgic & melancholic,
 because come daybreak, he'll be at it again,
his shirt hanging on a branch, spade turning
the earth, exposing the loam to light.

And if there's truth in work, I learned it
 from him, among the junkyards
of auto parts, brake drums & pistons burned,
 in the preserves he delivered as a boy,
 exiled from childhood, from Munich
to Morazán, from the curl of a flugelhorn
to the spirals in a sundial or weathervane.

If there's more to say, it's because I loved
 in fathoms & groundwork, in hieroglyphics
that slip through a hole in the wire fence
 in trochees & dactyls, the volume
 of the ocean, the eye of a whale sounding,
daguerreotype of a leviathan
thrashing, the captain to the wheel strapped.

I can tell you this much because it's always
 my father who handles the claw hammer,
screwdriver speckled with rust, because
 it's my father, without tape or yardstick,
 without compass or pocket loop,
who tells me, lying under the house,
cutting a trench for the pipe, "Dig, son. Dig."

SHEILA MALDONADO

# Holy Heat (Semana Santa Spa)

At the table in the Queens Korean spa restaurant during Easter spring break
Ma was remembering *semana santa* in Honduras, how they couldn't
do anything from Wednesday to Friday because they were remembering
how Christ suffered in this time, how he was captured, how he was crucified.
They couldn't even pick up a broom to perform the cleaning penance
they enjoyed so well. They sat there in the heat with the memory of an old story.

From the table, she watched amazed, all these people, including herself now,
who didn't stop all they were doing during the days Christ suffered.
I asked her what about before Christ, what did they do then,
and she remembered the little bit of school she had where they told her about
*el puesto del sol*, the position of the sun and *un dios de maíz*, a god of corn.
I had never heard her remember a god that wasn't Christ.
The kitchen called our number and I picked up our order from the counter.

After we ate, we went to sweat in the rooms of gold and jade.
"All I think about is your father here," she said. Because he worked with stones
and gems I answered in my head, because we were the Maya and jade was our gold,
I imagined. "*Para los riñones*," she went on, these stones, this heat
might have helped the kidneys that failed him. But he wouldn't take care,
get air, leave the house, come to a place like this, give his body some relief.

She sat up in the domed sauna, eyes closed, belly unfolding beneath her,
and I saw that she looked like my brother, that he looked like her,
that I looked like them, that we are this tribe of bellies unfolding.
She sat up in the jade room, sweat dripping out memory,
vessel emptying on a straw mat, *petate,** *pop,*** in the matrix of time.
One position in the universe, ancients charting a figure on a mat
as a point on a grid, one point in a domed hut remembering, releasing.

* *Petate (Spanish/Nahuatl origin) means "mat" in English*
** *Pop (Maya word) means "mat" in English*

SARA CAMPOS

# Guatemala

*Madrecita, Guatemamá*
I played jacks on your cobblestones
hid inside the folds of your volcano skirts
scraped knees, drank Tio Landelino's jokes and ghost stories
like melon juice in Tia Chayo's kitchen.

*Guatebonita:*
Neruda rhapsodized your virtues
prometheus birds and kaleidescope *huipils* against
sea-hued skies
I snapped photos
touristed.

Remember me, *Guate-tontita*?
your prodigal *gringita*, bourgeois diaspora daughter
snug tight inside your rigid little boxes
you taught my walnut milky skin
brightens only with the gleam of gems upon my fingers.

*Guate-maliciosa*
You raced me, classed me, grabbed my ears,
held my aquiline profile before mirrors,
showed me rungs of the world,
lessons only you could teach.

*Porque, Vos?*
You stomped unshod feet
violenced your maize people bearing
the poetry of you?

*Nombre, Vos*, you pillaged the Ixil and Kanjobal
chewed Maya children between your teeth

because you craved the sensibilities of old world kings
feudal serfs for your plantations,
pedigreed sons sipping whiskies
making love inside compounds laced with shard.

*Guate-puta*
You sold your very flesh
peeled baby fingernails
daggered wombs
because Gringos opened fat purses
because of some cold, hot, tepid war
or the shame of your color wash?

And me?
I peek beneath the folds of your *traje*
unearth stories
longing to see your face
to write you
understand you
so I can love you again.

ADOLFO HERNÁNDEZ

# When You Think of Yoga

When you think of Yoga,
think of Jorge Ramirez Valenzuela.

They say as a boy,
He would hear voices that no one else could hear.
When He turned 18, the voices told Him, He was to go to India.

But He was a poor young man from Guatemala,
without a cent to His name.

The voices told Him to buy a lottery ticket,
so He did and He won.

When He got to India, He was greeted by
a bearded man familiar to Him only
in His dreams.

He trained in India as a mystic,
until He returned to Guatemala in the 50's.

He came to offer His knowledge
to the poor of Guatemala.

He taught them Yoga.
He taught them the Dharma.
He taught them how to ease their suffering—

and suffering, along with coffee beans,
was one of the few things
Guatemala had an abundance of.

My mother told me, that when she first met Him,
she was skeptical the way teenagers are,
and dared Him to prove His mystic powers.

That night an entity made of light woke my
mother and aunt up while they slept.

They screamed in fear, but
she never doubted Him again.

He once told His followers of the *Templo Yoga*
to protest the corruption of its country's leaders.

In Guatemala that's something you don't do.
The government took Him.

Some say, letter writing and Amnesty International
got Him out, but a political prisoner getting out of prison alive,
in Guatemala in the 60s, is nothing short of proof of a higher power at work.

And through Him
the ascended master teachers would speak

*Karishnanda*
*Krishanda*

They would speak the words
so desperately needed in this world,
but heard by so few,

practiced by even fewer.

And when He died
the temple moved to a smaller
location.

His followers dispersed.

And the practice of Yoga
in Guatemala went into decline.

When He died,
there was a little more suffering in the world.

They say at night,
there is light that still emanates from His grave.

When you think of Yoga, think of
Jorge Ramirez Valenzuela.

FELIX AGUILAR

# The People vs. Us

"JUECES SOMBRÍOS HABLAN DE PUREZA CON PALABRAS QUE HAN
ADQUIRIDO EL BRILLO DE UN ARMA BLANCA."
—LA CASA DE LA JUSTICIA ROBERTO SOSA


Jesús Cruz,
the translator is not here.
You are accused of violating
the law.
Do you waive your right
to a speedy trial?

*La ley es la ley.*
The law is the law.

People are shuffling papers
in court
as easily as flying kites,
detached.
White people
dispensing justice to
dark people.
People smile on the other
side of the wooden fence,
where there are no pews.
It is just another day at work.
The public defender
speaks fast-learned words.
Terror is dispensed over
papers and coffee cups,
and under fluorescent lights.
One side of the little wooden fence
is us, brown, foreign;
on the other side words are spoken
that cut like dull knives and
have the whiteness of bread.

People vs. Jesús Cruz
Do you plead No Contest?
—*No entiendo* (I do not understand)—
Do you understand the charges?
—*No hablo inglés* (I don't speak English)—
Do you waive your rights?
—*No sé* (I don't know)—
Jesús is confused with
the strange language of the law.
The judge sneers.
The defender orders Jesús
in accented Spanish,
*¡Diga sí!* (Say yes!).

GINA MARIA BALIBRERA

# Age of Indigo

EXCERPT FROM THE NOVEL THE VOLCANO-DAUGHTERS

IN THE DREAM we return to the room where we died, to watch our great-grandmothers crouch over buckets. Three enormous vats fill the room: one of dark water, a pile of stones beside it, another of water that floats with large muddy flakes, and the last vat brimming with our great-grandmothers' piss and the piss of the forty other women working beside them. Some beat the waters of the second vat with a splintery oar, the liquid changing color before our eyes: from a rancid gold, to a green, to an impossible aquamarine, to a still-stranger lavender, which deepens into a deep blue-violet that shimmers like a beetle's back. We are as dazzled by the properties of these poisonous waters as we are by Graciela's famous face.

Our great-grandmothers were the last of the age of indigo. An ugly job, with pretty ways of being described. They reeked of piss no matter how much they washed, how long they lived past the age of indigo. Coffee came in during their youth, but their brains and wombs were already poisoned. Later, when we were children, the wooden beams of this room held our great-grandmothers' scent, along with rotten red coffee berries softening from their stones in piles heaped high enough to warp a body.

In the dream, some women reach into the vats and pound the pulp with stones, their arms thrashing beneath the surface of the waters. Some women fish for garbage in the vat, pulling up ceiba leaves, pebbles, a clot of menstrual blood, human hair. Some women crouch on the floor, using their machetes to cut muddy bricks of iridescent blue into squares the size of a baby's palm. The best pieces of indigo are named after the throat of a dove because of the way these pieces catch the light. These pieces are harder and lighter than the other indigo.

Our great-grandmothers' hands, up to the elbows, are a deep violet-blue. Stiff, thick fingers, burned bloody to the quicks, ochre shadows where the nails should be. We hold their hands as long as their work lets us. In the dream, each of our great-grandmothers carries the same golden glow in their faces. This radiance is jaundice, the poison beginning its work on their beautiful bodies from the inside.

Another chapter of the dream: we stand in the fields where the coffee grows now, and watch our great-grandmothers plant the seeds during the dry season in rows, dusty pale dirt mounds like infant graves. The plants come up a yellow color that develops into a sickly green after a few weeks. We see our great-grandmothers packing tobacco into the sides of their mouths, and spitting it into the fields. We watch the ceiba birds roost in their ancient tree, leaving and returning like clockwork.

Our great-grandmothers' words dried up before we were born, but the building where they made indigo, where our mothers sorted berries, where Graciela last confided in us, and where we all died, still stands today. We figure the slatted wood should have rotted through, crumbled to the ground, or have at least been burned in the years of violence. The building belonged to one of the Fourteen Families, though we are not quite sure which one. From the dream, we have learned that history can be told by its monuments: what was constructed and what was torn down over time. For a while after the long dream of our great-grandmothers, we dream only of buildings. All kinds of buildings.

Some dreams give us ruins. In one, a woman's face is carved into a stone wall. We move through the shapes of concrete, steel, wood, and glass. Over-alled men climb the iron tower in France, hauling shining metal. The Eiffel Tower in Paris, 1899, constructed in preparation for the World's Fair.

When the dream returns to us we stand in a field, watching the harvest. Our young great-grandmothers pull weeds, plow the dry ground, and, when the stalks match their heights, chop down the plants with machetes hanging from their tiny waists. Our great-grandmothers wrap the stalks in twine and throw the bundles on their backs. When the bundles of indigo hunch their backs, our great-grandmothers head up the path to the room at the top of the hill, past the ceiba tree, which is as miraculously full then, of birds and branches, as it is now. Inside the sorting room the women allow their bundles of stiff branches to fall to the ground, and they kick the bundles into a pile beside the first vat. They throw the bundles into the water and count to 100 together, their voices a soft chant. Fat flies thicken the hot air with their dark deathly bodies, hovering over the vats, scattering outside after a few hours, when the plant oxidizes in the beaten water and changes form, and turns the waters too foul for even the attending insects of rot.

Somehow, our great-grandmothers live. The other women in the room have five years, tops, left in their lifelines. Their wombs die empty, polyps colonizing their lungs and their brains.

At night, some of the women fall asleep coughing blood into their mats. They complain of headaches and drop into dead faints, blaming the heat.

Their men find them dead: one girl sprawled lifeless on the floor, on one of the sacred mornings Izalco deigns to erupt, pulmonary blood darkening the ground, one girl collapses dead at the festival of the Black Virgin in Juayúa; one girl, pura india, goes missing for a week and is found broken, at the bottom of a well. Hers is one of the sadder cases. They say she suffered visions, hallucinations, momentary paralysis, and days of blindness. But our great-grandmothers live.

Our great-grandmothers give birth to our grandmothers, to our mothers, to Graciela's mother, the poison radiating from their indigo-dyed wombs into their infants' bones, and then they return to the *finca* to make indigo. Our mothers work hauling berries after indigo disappears. And after Graciela disappears, we work inside the same splintered walls. If not for these walls, and for Graciela, all of us would go without leaving a stain on the earth. And all the years we remember, the purple-fingered *viejas* sit silent, calling to us only after we have disappeared as well.

KELLY DUARTE

# Burning at the Lake

WHEN I WAS YOUNGER, I used to think Lake Isabel was the ocean, the turquoise waters seemed to have no limit. If I squinted, I could maybe see the sliver of *Sapodillas* that lined the shores of the lake on a clear day. It was only during our holiday from school in December that the sun was the highest in the sky and we would spend every day in the water. We would run down the hill, our sandals slamming into the dirt, nearly face-planting with every step, as if our legs weren't sure where to go next. My mother would shout at me to watch my sisters and then mutter prayers until she was out of sight. I would dive headfirst into the lake, I preferred to let the water hit me all at once while my sisters, Elena and Sofia, would move a couple inches at a time. Sometimes it would be an hour before they were fully submerged. We would swim, get out only to eat the lunch of bread and chicken our mother would provide for us and then go back to the water. My favorite thing to do was to sit in the sand once it had cooled and listen to the small waves. The sound reminded me of a dog lapping up water.

But today was different. My mother left for work early for the cannery. She had to work more hours now that she was the only one bringing in money. I knew she was in a rush because her blue glass rosary beads and her coffee mug were still on the kitchen table. She hadn't packed a lunch for us. We inched slowly toward the kitchen as if *la llorona* was waiting there, stirring a pot of beans. We could still smell the mix of sweet plantains and cream and our stomachs rumbled. It was so close but we didn't dare put a foot on the red tiles that separated us from the food. We weren't allowed in the kitchen, my mother was worried that if she let us go in there she would return home to find one of us injured or dead. I could imagine the wooden spoon on our backs if we even dared try to get anywhere near the stove. So we set off without lunch to the lake.

We played in the sun and never got out, we didn't need to since there was no food waiting for us on the shore. My skin got a deeper and deeper shade of brown. Elena's too. But we didn't notice that Sofia was burning. Her skin turned pink and then red. We laughed when we noticed and we called her a little *cangrejo*, which caused her to protest and splash water at us until we stopped laughing. She said her skin felt hot so we told her to just get deeper into the water. I looked at her, her peach skin now the color of an over-ripe mango. Maybe we should get out of the water, I thought. But I didn't want to. It was the only time I was able to be a child. I didn't have to worry about my sisters every second of the day. No chores, no nagging, no caretaking. The lake was the only place where I didn't have to act like an adult.

After hours of playing, we pulled ourselves out of the water. Elena and I were the color of coffee while Sofia was a chile pepper. She was too tired to walk and I carried her, and when her skin touched mine, it burned. Every time I shifted my weight, she would slightly gasp and clutch me harder, her tiny claws trying to pinch the skin off my back. I carried her to the house and set her down on the first step of our porch. My skin was still warm as if she was still clutching me.

My mother screamed at us as soon as she saw Sofia and ordered me to get aloe vera from the backyard. When I did, she ordered me to bite it. I bit hard and heard it crack and tried to spit out the bitter juice and flesh but my mother ordered me to swallow. That is nothing compared to what your sister is feeling, she said. She took the plant from me. She cut it open and started rubbing the clear goo onto Sofia's already peeling skin. Strips of red were coming off her back to reveal pink underneath.

Sofia screamed the whole night as my mother kept rubbing in the aloe vera deeper and deeper into her skin. I couldn't sleep, rolling around and pulling off my cotton sheet that was suffocating. Watch your sisters, my mother only asked that of me.

YOLANY MARTÍNEZ

# Pájaros de sombra

Pájaros de sombra salen
de un abismo incierto. Tu boca
esa
que es una noche de alas cerradas
fosa común para el transeúnte
lugar de abandono para el renegado
ciudad errante en tu cuerpo.

Pozo sin muros es tu voz
que viaja confundida entre sombras
y que se extiende en ondas sordas
simulando vida.

Tu lenguaje es un sarcófago vacío
que remeda el destino de hospedar la caída
y la carne muerta de la justicia.

Hay un temblor en las piernas
cuando los pájaros de sombra visten figuras humanas
y todo parece percibirse a través de sus espectros:
una ciudad aparente
con estaciones de llegada
partidos de fútbol
y taxis colectivos.
Pero en el fondo
hay sudor en la frente
y un espejo turbio detrás de las pestañas.

Hay niños descalzos
y un horizonte que termina detrás de montañas de basura.

Sin embargo, ellos son los únicos
que no han sido engañados por los pájaros de sombra.
Ellos son los únicos que han promulgado una herejía al miedo
a las explosiones de armas de fuego
al impuesto de guerra
a los cadáveres en los bordes de las calles que les provocan pesadillas.

Ellos han promulgado una herejía al miedo
para huir de la asfixia que les grita el cuerpo
y vivir disfrazados de humanos
con una piel y una espera que no les pertenece.

Pájaros de sombra salen de un abismo incierto
mientras la noche devora
los sentidos con su tinta críptica,
todo está saturado en esta cámara de dudas
donde el parpadear es un acto de rebeldía
y una protesta por los miles de ojos
que han quedado fijos
sobre este espacio tildado de cielo
cliché
casi un conjuro.

YOLANY MARTÍNEZ

# Birds of Shadow

TRANSLATED BY ARTHUR DIXON AND YOLANY MARTÍNEZ

Birds of shadow fly out
of an uncertain abyss. Your mouth
that one
that's a night of unopened wings
mass grave for the passer-by
forsaken place for the renegade
wandering city in your body.

Your voice is a well without walls
that travels confused between the shadows
and spreads out in muted waves
simulating life.

Your speech is an empty sarcophagus
that mimes the mission of hosting the fallen
and the dead flesh of blind justice.

Legs begin to shake
when the birds of shadow dress in human forms
and everything seems to be seen through their spectres:
a deceitful city
with its arrival stations
*fútbol* matches
and shared taxis.
But inside
there is sweat on foreheads
and a turbid mirror behind eyelashes.

There are barefoot children
and a horizon ending behind mountains of trash.

Nonetheless, they are the only ones
still undeceived by the birds of shadow.
They alone have spread a heresy against the fear
against the gunshot flashes
against the street gangs' tax of war
against the bodies by the side of the road that give them nightmares.

They have spread a heresy against the fear
to flee the suffocation screamed by their bodies
and live disguised as humans
with skin and hope that do not belong to them.

Birds of shadow fly out of an uncertain abyss
as the night consumes
the senses with its cryptic ink,
everything is saturated in this camera of doubt
where blinking is an act of rebellion
and a protest by the thousands of eyes
that have become fixed
on this branded space in the sky
cliché
almost magic.

HENRY MILLS

# The Indigo Field

Galileo sits with me on the porch,
his tail is still, matching my quiet.

No stars to study, only the field
of indigo above my hometown.

I stare at it and wait for a vision
and what comes is my own pulse.

I can feel it behind the clouds,
feet stomping macerated leaves

'til they darken the blue dye
Europe doesn't want anymore.

But the indigo keeps churning
as if dead indios still marched

across the hills of Cuzcatlán
to the iron gate of an *hacienda*.

HENRY MILLS

# Earthenware

Despite chemo-blunted taste buds, my *tia*
maintains each tortilla on the *comal*'s surface
puffs with its predecessors' essence.
I'm not one to believe a titan's hands
sculpted from muck the first people
but marvel at how earthen *comales* survive
metallurgy, the skillet, what'd otherwise be
machine-made, molten poured, blasted clean.
This is from before the first bomb,
before the old languages turned to shrapnel—
a well-crafted tortilla right off the *comal—taste it,*
she says, *something endures.*

# Ghost Bullet

We're sitting in the conference room of a church.
It's January, the sidewalks of DC are glazed with ice

but the *pupusas* have kept hot in their cartons.
*The captive soldier thought* guerrilleros *ate children,*

Francisco says, mouth full of pork and cheese,
the *pupusa* steaming where he bit in.

Pausing to chew, he's no monster, breath stinking
of roasted toddler, nor does he morph from *masa*

into the action hero I dreamt as I child.
He pats his belly, no longer the man from the photo

in my parent's living room, weighing little more
than his M16. *This is where the bullet got me,*

(left ass cheek) *it bounced into my gut but the exit
was here,* he motions with the knife of his hand,

and in remembering, the bullet splits the decades
(to the right of his nutsack) and makes him wince.

# Juvenal

WHENEVER MY SISTER CALLS it's to tell me someone I know has died. So, when my phone rang and I saw her name on the screen and that picture of her when she was little, angry at having to wear an outfit she didn't choose herself, I sighed into the warm air of my empty apartment and answered.

"Guess who died," she said. In the background I heard running water and the clinking of plates.

"Who?" I stopped trying to guess a long time ago. There was something morbid about mentally rifling through all the people I knew to figure out who could have died and under what circumstances. She never let me guess anyway.

"Juvenal."

"Who?"

"Juvenal! The kid you guys used to harass in school."

Juvenal. I knew this Juvenal. I remembered freckles.

"How did he die?"

"He was shot six times. Apparently it was a mugging. Poor kid."

Proximity to death impacts one's sense of time. I was quiet, trying to recall all that I could about Juvenal.

I remember when he moved into our town. I was six or seven. My friends and I were busy with a game of marbles, trying to establish the rules for that particular match. I don't remember which version of the game it was. Maybe it was the one where we lined up marbles and tried to hit them from a distance. Those marbles we hit we could keep. He was small, smaller than me. I never hurt him physically, but I know from the time Juvenal came to our school to the time he left, I'd been complicit in inflicting deep emotional scars. Before Juvenal arrived I was the target for the older kids, who constantly taunted me with comments about my height and my torn clothes. Words like "midget," "little turd," and "little beggar" sat on my shoulders every day, like parrots, whimpering their names right into my ears. When Juvenal arrived the focus of those insults shifted on Juvenal who was shorter than me and, from the look of his clothes, poorer than me too. Some days he wore clothes too big for him, and other days he wore clothes too small for him. That first time we saw him it was his grey slacks that were too big. He kept them up with a black string tied like a bow, like he was a small, delicate gift. That first day the other kids surrounded him. He didn't know what was coming. His eyes, eyes that had not experienced shame and ridicule, still flashed tiny specks of hope for friendship and, I assume, acceptance. I could see it in him. He was happy to see other kids. But, someone untied the bow and someone else pulled his pants down. That was the first time he cried, the first time any of us heard the catch in his throat. His small brown hands begged for the string while everyone around him laughed and pointed at his naked bottom. Then, Miguel, who, at nine, was the oldest kid in the group, punched him in the face and told him to "shut up." Juvenal cried louder, until Miguel silenced him with a kick to the stomach.

"Let's go back to the game," Miguel said. Juvenal stayed on the ground, bent over, crying in between gasps, his hands on his stomach.

Eventually I'd take part in the emotional abuse, though I never hit him. From time to time, I joined the other kids in the usual taunting and actually authored a song that followed Juvenal for the rest of his years at our school: a *Cumbia* which I titled "Juvenala." The music I stole from a *Cumbia* that was popular at the time. It played on every radio in every house and every jukebox in every whorehouse. I made up the lyrics to say something about Juvenal, something about how he liked boys and how he was a little girl. A line about how Juvenal was a female prostitute pretending to be a boy was my pride and joy. He hated the song. I wonder if he knew I came up with it. Whenever we ran into him on the street or at school he would stand still, aware of what was coming, his arms limp at his side. We'd sing and dance around him while he waited patiently for us to grow tired. We'd grab his small hands, like a puppet, making him dance with one of us as we shouted, "See? He likes to dance with boys!" He tried to run away once. Miguel chased him. The rest of us waited. When Miguel came back he told us how Juvenal had tripped on one of the railroad tracks and landed on his face on the rocky dirt. When I saw Juvenal the next day he had a black eye and bloody scrapes on one side of his face.

I liked watching him. Sometimes he moved as if he was in a hurry to get somewhere, dragging a cloud of dust behind him, moving to a place as far away from us as possible. His greasy straight hair hung lazily to the sides of his face. He liked to sit under the almond tree, his little hands played with the ripe fruit that lay littered underneath the tree. Occasionally he must have imagined he heard his *Cumbia* and he would jump up and his arms would go limp on his side, waiting for an imaginary attack that never came. When he realized that no one was coming for him he went back to playing with the almonds or digging a hole on the ground. Other times he'd walk slowly, lost in thought. He'd talk to himself, too, long conversations, though he was never close enough for me to hear what he said. Once, I was watching him hurl some rocks to the ground, angry at something or other, when I noticed him taking something out of the front pocket of his pants and put it in his mouth. He did that a couple more times. It couldn't have been fruit. He was wearing blue slacks that were tight on him. Fruit would have been obvious in his pockets. He must have felt the weight of my eyes on him; he turned and looked at me. His face was stuck on a frown.

One rainy day my friends decided it was better to go to the beach to look at the engorged waves than to go to school. Skipping class, for me, would guarantee a beating. All the other kids knew about beatings. They didn't mock anyone's fear of them. I was alone at school that day. Juvenal sat in his usual spot digging holes on the ground, sheltered from the rain by the almond tree. I was still curious about what he'd been putting in his mouth. I'm not sure why, really. It's one of those things children are curious about, like how magnets work, or why those squiggly floaters in the eyes move the moment one tries to look at them. For whatever reason, I felt it was a good opportunity to go and talk to him. I walked toward him, my hands out of my pockets so he knew I wasn't carrying any rocks.

"What do you want," he said, looking up at me. He'd dug a couple of holes around him.

"What do you carry in your pockets that you can put in your mouth?"

"It's none of your business," he said.

"Why do you like to dig holes? What do you do with them?"

He didn't answer. I knew how to make him answer. I pushed him hard. He fell to the ground, bounced back and pushed me down to the floor where he began to punch me in the stomach. I couldn't breathe. I kept trying to tell him to stop but I couldn't make a sound and I doubt he would have heard me. A teacher came by and pried him off me. I cried, loudly. He was crying too. I'd never seen that type of anger before in anyone. This kid hated me. We were both hit with rulers on the palm of our hands. The principal gave us notes to take to our parents. When my father came home my step-mom gave him the note. He was angry. He yelled at me for behaving like an animal. He said, "This is not what you've been taught at home." He threw the note at my face and slapped me. He grabbed my arm and jerked me into the bedroom. There he made me strip. I was already crying as I pulled my pants down. He removed his belt in one swift motion and began to strike my back and the back of my legs. It was difficult to stay still but it was the best way to avoid getting hit in other places. Like always I pleaded with him to stop. I promised I wouldn't fight again. I told him, in between sobs, that I was sorry. I never got used to the beatings. At the end of each one I always felt like I couldn't breathe, like I was collapsing into myself. At the end of each one I would watch my father throw up into the bushes.

The next day my father told me I had to go to Juvenal's house and apologize to him and to his mother.

"I already apologized," I said to my father, angry at the thought of being seen at Juvenal's house.

"You'll do it again," he said, moving closer to me, keeping his eyes on mine until I had to look away.

Juvenal's house was smaller than my house. It was made entirely out of metal sheets. There was no door. In its place was a blue shower curtain decorated with cartoon ducks. I knocked on one of the walls and Juvenal's mother came out.

"Come in," she said.

His house was one big rectangular space with beds on one corner, a small place with wood for cooking and a little dining table with four chairs around it. When he saw me, Juvenal jumped up from where he sat playing with half an action figure and came toward me. I moved back a little.

"You don't want to be here. I don't want you to be here," he said, looking straight into my eyes. I'd never been that close to him before. I'd never noticed the tiny brown freckles on his nose, like they'd been carefully drawn with a pencil.

"I'm sorry I pushed you," I told him, trying to sound as unfriendly as possible. I turned toward his mother and said, "*Lo siento mucho.*" She smiled at me, ruffled my hair.

"Why don't you take him to the corn field," his mother said. "He can help you plant the new crop."

"No!" he said, moving toward his mother with quick little steps. "I will not take him back there. That's *my* corn!"

"Juvenal! You will take him back there because that's what I'm telling you to do. Do it!"

He didn't respond. He looked down at his bare feet and walked out of the house. The shower curtain rustled as it came back to its place.

We made our way to the back of the house where half of the field was filled with dry corn plants while the other half was bare. He picked up a metal container with corn seeds and walked to the empty field. I followed, not sure what to do. When we reached the empty field he grabbed a bunch of seeds and put them in the pocket of his pants. He grabbed one from the metal container and threw it in his mouth.

"Can I have one?" I asked him. He offered me the container and I pulled out a single corn seed and threw it in my mouth. The middle part of the seed was easy to eat; it was sweet. The rest was too crunchy for my taste but when he offered another one I took it.

I watched him work. I watched as he bent down and dug a hole into the soft soil and then another and another. When he was done he dropped corn seeds inside each of the holes. Then, he used his foot to drag dirt on top of the corn. He did that on his own for some time before he turned around and asked if I wanted to help. For four hours I walked side-by-side Juvenal, planting corn seeds, watching him smile, telling me how hiding in the corn-field was his favorite pastime.

"It's like I'm inside a jungle, like an explorer and the animals are afraid of me and of what I can do. You wanna see?"

"Sure," I said and followed him into the field with the dried up corn plants.

Inside it was just like he said. The tall corn hid us and it was easy to imagine that, for miles, the only thing visible were tall hairy trees. He yelled from somewhere inside the field of corn and said, "Hey, are you also an explorer in these woods?"

"I sure am!" I said, laughing with him.

"Where are the dangerous animals?" He asked.

"Nowhere near us," I said.

"Is it because you've killed them all?"

"I've scared them off with my gun."

"I've scared them off with my voice!" He roared, a sharp roar. I laughed. He laughed too. It was the first time I'd heard him do that.

When it was time to leave I said goodbye to him and shook his hand.

I stopped taunting him and only watched him from a distance. He never tried to approach me at school or whenever I was with the other kids. He never even looked at me. In class he only spoke when the teacher called upon him and he sat in a corner, at the back of the classroom, invisible to everyone but Miguel, who, because he'd been held back two years, was in our class and sat next to Juvenal punching him on the arm whenever the teacher turned his back to us to write on the board.

Juvenal endured two more years of torture at the hands of my friends. When we graduated from fifth grade he wore black pants that stuck to his legs and a white long-sleeve dress shirt with sleeves that only reached halfway down his forearm and buttons that were stressed to their limit. Juvenal sat under the almond tree while we waited to march onto the stage. Our parents were gathered on the other side of the school. Miguel, upon seeing Juvenal at his usual place, decided it would be a good idea to throw small rocks at him to try to get him to stand up and leave his so cherished spot.

"Come on," said Miguel, "see if you can hit him from here."

I didn't try. I watched as Miguel threw small rocks that never quite reached Juvenal.

When a smooth rock the size of Miguel's hand landed next to Juvenal I said, "You should stop." Miguel looked at me, laughed and said, "Ok, one last one."

I followed the path of that rock with my head as it curved into the sky and found its way right to the middle of Juvenal's forehead. Juvenal was thrown back by the impact and began to cry, like he hadn't done in a long time. His piercing cry shattered the quiet morning and when his eyes met mine he shattered something inside of me. His eyes accused me of treason, of cheating at something. I watched him get up and clean his swollen, un-broken forehead. He wiped his own tears and watched us watching him.

The teachers called us to line up. We were ready to march onto the stage.

I stayed back a little. I wanted to check something. Hidden by the cloud of excitement, I walked to the almond tree and poked at one of the holes on the ground. There, inside the earth rested a yellow corn seed. I moved to another hole and felt inside and there too was a corn seed. I smiled and pictured the field Juvenal wanted, the jungle he desired.

Juvenal graduated with a large bump on the middle of his forehead.

"He looks like a unicorn," Miguel said as we walked toward the graduation stage.

"Anyway," my sister said, "I figured you'd want to know."

She hung up and left me wrapped in sadness. We exist as wholes only in our minds and in the minds of those people to whom we matter. To anyone else we're chunks of existence. I didn't know Juvenal in his thirties. That's not who will live on in my mind. He lives on as a kid, perpetually tormented. In his torment I found salvation and a lesson about the futility of compassion in the hands of cowards. He was the kid that kept the other kids from picking on me. He came in as a gift, a sacrificial lamb to protect me. Me, the smallest of all my friends, the slowest of all my friends, and the poorest of all my friends.

# Chrysalides

WHEN I WAS A CHILD I hunted butterflies when they were still not butterflies. They still hung from the underside of green twigs, glued there somehow. At six years old, I climbed the limbs of tall trees, sometimes in search of fruit and other times in search of the shiny cocoons. I'd stand on thick branches, my naked feet flexible, maneuvering the sometimes strangely angled branches to reach the not yet butterflies. Sometimes, the wind swayed the whole tree and I imagined myself an acrobat, a tightrope walker.

I was in one of those trees one day, perched on a bough, with a dozen or so cocoons nestled inside the pockets of my shorts. I could see the line of palm trees in the distance, dancing back and forth along the bank of one of the three rivers that crisscrossed Acajutla, that little Salvadoran town in which I grew up. I couldn't see the ocean but I could hear its breath, steady and constant. The leaves around me were sky and I, something light.

I knew I couldn't sit inside the tree for long. Adults didn't like us in trees. It was dangerous, they said. Many had forgotten the pleasure of curled toes on green branches. My dad was one of them, but his voice, unlike the others, forced me to uncurl my toes and slide down scaly barks of tall trees. He wasn't one to spend too much time with dialogue. His efficiency in curbing my behavior rested on his ability to inflict pain using various objects that lay scattered around the house: a leather sheath (home to his machete), shoes, electrical cords, belts, long thin sticks. My childhood was a jungle and my father was the wild animal that kept me from leaping freely from branch to branch.

I climbed down from that tree and sat underneath it with a handful of cocoons on my lap and a firm twig in my hand. I'd read about them in school, saw pictures of different types in a nature book the teacher showed us during science hour. I knew a caterpillar was inside, a wormlike creature, and nature was turning it into something else. The whole process was very strange to me. I didn't know by what biological power or physiological processes the transformation occurred. I imagined the white hand of a woman molding the tricolor larva into a bright butterfly. I'm not sure how I came up with that, since there was no picture of white hands in the book. Instead, chapter five began with the word *Metamorfosis* written across the page and three pictures underneath: one picture of a caterpillar, right next to it a picture of a cocoon labeled "*Crisálida*" and finally another of a butterfly.

I asked my teacher how the worm transformed and he said, "*Por la meta-morfosis*, Marcos."

I said, "*¿Pero, cómo?*" I wanted details.

He shrugged and said, "*Magia talvez.*"

Magic meant it couldn't be explained and so I was left ignorant of all that was happening within the soft walls of those seemingly dead cocoons. Either way, I was sitting under the tree that day with a plan to push the twig into and through each of the twelve cocoons simply to watch the chrysalis emerge on the other side, impaled on the end of my twig, writhing in confusion, wanting to be put back in so the white hand could finish doing whatever wizardry it had begun to do. It wasn't pleasing to me; it didn't bring me joy. But I also didn't feel sorry for the caterpillar.

Sometimes I'd put them against my ear and I'd hear the scratching of movement against the tight space within, as if the worm was stretching, already growing into something else. I told this to my father one evening while he slashed at some overgrown bushes with a machete, the all too familiar leather sheath dangling from his belt.

"That's impossible," he said. "They sleep the whole time they're in there."

"Maybe they're dreaming," I told him.

"They don't dream," he said.

I watched him while he worked, feeling admiration and fear. I wanted to hug him, to feel the warmth of his skin against mine. But, often, the leather sheath of his machete hung by his side slicing the space between us. It was such a strong need of mine to be touched by my father in a way that was gentle, so much so that whenever he did I would lean into his touch and take deep breaths as if I could inhale what I felt on my skin. It was confusing to love and fear the same human being.

"Maybe they're having nightmares," I said.

"Maybe," he said, never once raising his eyes to look at me.

Either way, there I was, sitting on the dirt, underneath a tree, the caterpillars in a pile on my lap. I was trying to decide which should meet its fate first. The fat one? The dark one? The short one? The sun cast shadows of leaves around me and in the distance I could hear the ocean playing on the dark sand. I stretched my legs in front of me, sank my heels into the sandy soil and the caterpillars were unaware. But maybe they weren't. Who knows? Maybe they always knew what was going to happen to them. Maybe the scratching noises were attempts to escape. Maybe their fate in my hands was their nightmare.

I was still trying to figure out which one to kill first when I saw my friend Antonio running down the main dirt road, the one that ran right through the center of town, past the whorehouses, past my house. He was running fast, faster than I'd seen him run before, faster then he'd ever run when we wore the masks of Amazon warriors, Thundercats, and G.I. Joes. He almost ran past me but at the last minute he saw me and brought himself to a stop right in front of where I was sitting. A thin cloud of dust stopped with him and hovered above his naked feet.

"I'm gonna get the beating of a lifetime," he said. He spoke with the wheeziness of last breaths. His belly and chest swelled and sank as he sat down next to me on the dirt.

"You were really running," I told him. I was surprised at his speed. He was the fattest kid I knew. He loved to eat. Sometimes I'd find him on a thick branch of a tree, his hands wrapped around a *bolillo* filled with refried beans. This extra girth made him the slowest of all my friends.

"Who's after you?"

"My mom," he said.

His mother was a scary woman who towered over many of the people in that little town. She was even taller than my dad. In my memories she lived enormous, with big brown flabby arms that swung back and forth like meaty hammocks. I saw her again many years later, after I'd left that little coastal town, and I couldn't understand how I'd seen danger in the calm eyes of a woman whose darkened and calloused face spoke of the sun, of standing for many hours above a hot *comal* while slapping dough into perfectly round tortillas.

"What did you do?" I asked him.

His eyes were watching the horizon, carefully, anxiously, waiting for his mother's head to begin its bobbing appearance on the other side of the small hill that shielded his house from our eyes.

"I think I killed my little brother," he said, his eyes on the ground, his heel digging a trench in the sandy soil.

"Jorgito? How?" I asked. I touched the cocoons in my pocket to see if I could feel movement. They were still.

"I was using my slingshot to shoot some rocks at those plastic bottles we found yesterday and he ran across right when I let go of the rock. It hit him right in the head. He just stopped running, right there on the spot and fell to the ground. My mom was right there too."

"Maybe you didn't kill him," I told him.

"It was a good shot, Marcos. It went right here," he said, using his index finger to press against my temple.

"Then maybe yes. Maybe he's dead."

He stared off into the distance, into and past the tall coconut trees that animated the horizon, a back and forth dance with the wind.

Antonio was silent and crossed his arms on top of his knees. He put his face in that shape he created. I imagined that he used that time to think about what the death of his little brother meant. It meant Antonio did not have to watch him when we were trying to play hide and seek or when we took the long trips to the river and Jorgito cried the whole time he rode the large rubber inner tube across the fast flowing waters. I imagined that in that moment of fear, in that space of time when Antonio's short seven-year life flashed before his eyes, reminding him of the fishing trips he often took, alone in the little raft he'd fashion out of a large inner tube he'd found at the dump, the trips he'd taken to the woods, the times he'd so carelessly ran on the sandy beaches of our town, or the times he so full of purpose perched himself on the pale colored wood of his porch to reach the mangos he voraciously fed on during times he wasn't placating his appetite with the beans inside white bread, he must have considered the possibility that he would spend the rest of his life in jail.

"What am I gonna do, Marcos?" he said, not lifting his face from his arms. "Maybe I can come stay at your place. We can spend the whole day in the branches of the *jocote* tree."

I considered the proposition briefly, thinking that it might be fun to hang out in that tree all day, picking the sweet round fruit off the branches.

"We'd get tired of *jocotes*," I told him. "Besides, I'm not in trouble. Maybe you can live in the tree and I can sneak you some food when you get tired of eating the same thing all the time."

He lifted his head and looked at me, his eyes glinting renewed hope.

"Your stepmom makes good *frijoles con huevos*. Bring some of those too," he said.

"I'll ask.

In the blueness of the sky above us vultures began a circular dance, a constant rotating celebration of death.

"See," Antonio said, his eyes dark again, looking at the sky. "They found Jorgito."

"They're fast," I told him.

We watched the circle populate with more dark wings. The wind picked up a little and the ocean's voice grew louder.

"I want to be a vulture," Antonio said. "They fly so high. Look. No one can catch a vulture."

I looked. They did fly high. I lowered my gaze to look at Antonio and that's when I saw her. Then Antonio saw her and then we both saw a crying Jorgito being yanked forward by his mom. She was walking so fast Jorgito had a hard time keeping up and he would fall here and there only to be, without pause, yanked up again by his mom.

Before I could say anything Antonio got up and ran toward them, apparently excited that he did not have to live inside the green branches of a *jocote* tree forever or that he would not have to wear black and white stripes for the rest of his life. He'd forgotten the approaching threat. The temporary effects of happiness smooth even the bumpiest scars.

I watched him reach his mother and little brother and then get on his knees to hug the little boy. His mom was yelling something but I couldn't make it out. Antonio held his little brother tight and Jorgito tried to push him off and the vultures still circled above and the chrysalides were probably scratching the walls of their home. Then, I saw his mother unravel a black electrical cord and begin to whip Antonio's back. The first lash caught him by surprise and, just like electricity forces the body to contract, he hugged his little brother tighter but the second and the third forced him to let go and that's when I lost count and I looked away to not let the image and the throaty moans awaken the ghostly shapes of the machete sheathes on my back. I heard muffled sobs. Antonio must have been covering his face with his hands.

When the sound of the ocean came back I looked in his direction. He was sitting on the ground. His mom was walking back toward her house, holding Jorgito's hand with one hand and the black electrical cord with the other.

I watched Antonio for a while, his shoulders moved up and down as he sobbed. I recognized that moment, those few seconds when the adrenaline has quieted the voice of the gashes and all that is left is a strangling emptiness. We shed our warrior masks during those naked moments. Our raw skins reminded us we were only children.

He walked back to where I was sitting and sat next to me, his knees against his chest, his arms wrapped around them. I tracked the border of one of his visible wounds with my index finger. He flinched a little. The old blind dog we knew as Cuta walked by us, its skin tight against many ribs.

Antonio found a rock next to him and threw it at her, hitting her on one of her protruding hips. The dog yelped as it ran away.

I found my cocoons next to me and I placed them against my ear. The chrysalides were silent, as if they knew what was about to happen. I offered Antonio the shiny bulbs. He took some, found a twig by his feet and without thinking about it shoved it into one end of the tiny home and pushed it through the papery material. The end of the twig emerged at the other end with a brown writhing worm impaled on its end. He watched it struggle some, pulled the stick back out, slightly pulling the worm back into its old home. The twig had cut the worm in half. It was still moving. He threw the writhing creature and the uninhabited house on the ground and crushed them both with his foot.

He grabbed the next one and he did the same. Then he grabbed another and then another and then another until all the ones he took were gone.

"Do you have more?" he asked.

I did.

"No," I said.

He said, "I need more." He got up, dusted the back of his shorts and he left.

I watched him leave, his wounds visible on the back of his legs, his arms and his neck.

That day, long ago in that little town, I played with the remaining chrysalides as I watched Antonio walk away in search of more little worms, and thought about my little insects in their warmth, maybe shifting already, their different parts forming, maybe a wing or brand new antennae. I picked up my twig. I wanted to check the progress of the caterpillar. I needed to know how long it took a thing that drags itself on the ground to turn into one that flies freely alongside vultures.

LORENA DUARTE

# *San Nicolás,* Patron Saint of Children

I can imagine her now
Kneeling in front of a small altar in her house
Photos, flowers.

*San Antonio de Padua,* patron saint of lost things
How long has it been?
Return me my most precious thing.

She was my 5th client of the day
From the same, tiny, miserable and defiant country as I.

Worn sneakers, kept carefully clean
Hardened hands carefully quiet on her lap
Carefully folded money order on my desk
One more immigration transaction—perfunctory.

Later read the file—nothing new or unexpected
One of the hundreds, the thousands,
Torture, disappearance, separation,
Your everyday case.
And only through strange fate was I not among them.

I imagine her now, lighting the candles

*San Nicolás,* patron saint of children
This is my deepest grief
Bring me my most precious thing.

Saw her two or three more times,
Laughed with her
She was funny and sweet.

This woman, who should have been a ruin
Who was ripped apart by flags and boundaries
Who was mute outside but
In my office laughed at my stupid jokes.

I imagine her now

*San Judas Tadeo*, patron saint of lost causes
This is the one thing I ask for
Return me my most precious thing.

It wasn't until the last time I saw her
That I understood—

She was there, that day, with her daughter
Her daughter, the one in the file,

Not seen for more than half her life.
A little thing with her mother's eyes
Left in the midst of a war
Left
Brought now, here, smuggled in
Because we choose to pontificate about borders
Pontificate when we, with our dollars and our guns
Leave countries ravaged.

Smuggled in for five thousand dollars
I understood then, the worn sneakers
Understood the three places of employment on file.

And her daughter, her daughter,
Dressed in perfect white dress
With crisp bows, shiny patent shoes
And the most beautiful ruffled socks.

I imagined her, buying them all, keeping them all carefully
Folding them softly, her calluses catching in the lace
Thinking of her daughter shining.

She had just arrived
And you could not tell where one began
And the other ended—

Grasping tightly
Ruffles and rags
Scuffed and shiny
Both sparkling.

I could,
A few months later
Only imagine what happened
When the daughter was sent back
Details were not known.
We only heard through the friend of a friend of a friend,

*Querida Señora*
*Se lo digo ahora, lo siento,*
*Lo siento, con todo mi corazón, le pido perdón*
*Por no poder hacer nada.*

I cannot imagine how your heart continues when
It beats thousands of miles away.

I could and can only imagine
I never saw her again.

Twenty years later,
I imagine her still
Hands pleading in the way all mothers do,

*San Cristobal,* patron saint of travelers
Who carried the baby Jesus on his back across the river
Return me my most precious thing
She crosses the border tonight.

LORENA DUARTE

# The Ocean

What I return to is the ocean.

Blue green deep, but mostly just dark. Meeting black volcanic sands, I come from a place forged by lava, earthquakes, with 7 hulking volcanoes, 7 million people, and I was 7 the last time I was not afraid of the ocean.

My mother stripping me to my underwear—laughing, dunking me, and I was not afraid, because she held my hand.

And these days, these days I must go in alone,
must face the waves and I feel empty, wholly battered and too unsteady,
don't trust myself to not just float away.

Constantly battered.
Being terrified of it.
I crave what I am afraid of, the ocean.

This bloody salty thing, the same salinity as our own blood, the bloody rivers of my country run to it and I, I run to it. Every lover that has stayed more than a night knows in case I die in the second night of our three night stand, you must know that I am to be taken there when dead and in ashes.

That I have to go home to it.
To the dark songs that suffocate me at night,
that makes me claustrophobic.
When I die, I want my ashes sprinkled in the ocean off the port of *La Libertad*,
which most appropriately, means freedom.

My paper boats will float there
over ocean wave lullabies.

The breakers that float along for thousands of miles

crash heavy into my little country,
come at me in my dreams
10 stories high, they crush me.

When I hear about the tsunami,
when I hear about Katrina,
I pray my pagan prayers for those people
standing at the bottom of the ocean
drifting, hearing the voices of their loved ones calling to them, come to us,
we will hold you.

In my dreams it is the same, the ocean's call is my family,
who wait for me at its shore.
My nieces I have not seen grow up, my auntie who waits to see me
one more time before she dies.

Shakespeare comes closest no doubt:
"This music crept by me upon the waters,
Allaying both their fury and my passion
With its sweet air: thence I have follow'd it,
Or hath it drawn me rather:—but 'tis gone." *

There I will return, without knowing why, to return to a place I barely know,
there, to the ocean, dark and dreary, fast and fury, beauty, deep the ocean.

Swim dive bottomless in this deadly place
I ask it, wash over me.

In the end,
I will come home to it,
will kiss the death in what I fear
will swallow it whole
put on my blue-green feathers
and walk in,
will answer the call:
come fast and then let go
here I am, waiting to hold you. **
(And rest here quiet, you are mine).

* *The Tempest*, William Shakespeare.
** *The Song of the Siren*, Tim Buckley.

DAVID UNGER

# La Casita

IN 1954, THE CIA ENGINEERED A COUP IN GUATEMALA WHICH OVERTHREW THE LEGALLY ELECTED GOVERNMENT OF JACOBO ARBENZ. THE INSTALLATION OF A MILITARY GOVERNMENT SOON THEREAFTER SIGNALED THE BEGINNING OF A 32 YEAR CIVIL WAR IN WHICH 200,000 GUATEMALANS DIED AND HALF A MILLION CITIZENS WENT INTO EXILE.

MY FAMILY LIVES in *La Casita*. It's anything but little. That's because it's also a restaurant, with eight wooden tables and lots and lots of overstuffed chairs. A vase with fresh flowers sits on a big fancy table under a crystal chandelier right in the middle of the restaurant. The whole room seems to glow, especially at night, when all the lights are on. And since the floor is polished like glass, my parents, Luis and Fortuna, insist that we walk one step at a time through the dining room.

*La Casita* has one window facing the street—I like to sit on the sill and watch people walking by on the other side of the iron bars. Sometimes they smile or talk to me. Once an Indian lady wearing a *huipil* gave me two *canillas de leche,* which I shared with my brother Felipe.

Everyone says *La Casita* is the best restaurant in Guatemala City.

\*

My favorite room in *La Casita* is the kitchen. It has two refrigerators—one cold, the other very, very cold—huge aluminum sinks and lots of shiny chrome pots and pans sitting on the gas stove.

Along one of the kitchen walls there is a big glass tank filled with lobsters— speckled creatures with long antennas and lots of warts on their hairy legs. They all have funny names like El Cid, Don Quixote, Superman, Hannibal, King Arthur. One by one all the lobsters except for Genghis Khan have disappeared and been replaced by other lobsters.

He is huge—Papá says he will never give him away.

When Felipe goes to the *Prepa* and my *niñera* Consuelo is busy, I like to go into the kitchen and watch Augusto, the cook. He puts on a big white apron and works so fast at the food counter that his hands whiz by, especially when he is slicing carrots and tomatoes.

*

One day I am left alone with Augusto. Mamá warns me to stay away from the stove because Felipe once tried lighting it with a wooden match and it blew up in his face and burned off his eyebrows and eyelashes.

Augusto gives me a stool. He knows I like watching the lobsters.

A little while later Otto, the waiter, walks in. He goes into a little closet by the back door and puts on a white shirt, black pants and a thin black tie. Otto is skinny like a cane.

Augusto is washing dishes at the sink. "Davico, do you like magic?" he asks me, drying his hands on his apron.

"I guess so. What's magic?"

"Tricks, you know, tricks—like when a rabbit comes out of a hat," he says, letting me see the two gold teeth in his mouth. "Would you like to see one?"

"Sure."

He walks over to the lobster tank and winks at Otto.

Otto starts whistling the Guatemalan national anthem. Soon I begin to sing proudly along with him words I don't even understand:

> ¡Guatemala feliz...! que tus aras
>
> no profane jamás el verdugo;
>
> ni haya esclavos que laman el yugo
>
> ni tiranos que escupan tu faz.

"Watch this!" Augusto suddenly interrupts.

He walks over to me. He comes so close that his perfume makes my nose itch. All of a sudden he whisks his hands behind my back. He has a surprise for me!

Augusto is shorter than my father, but wears lifts in his shoes. He has thick arms like a fisherman. Right now he looks very, very tall. I stare at the red pimples on his face. Some of them are turning white. He puts grease in his hair, which makes it shiny and holds its place.

Suddenly I feel something nipping the seat of my pants. Before I can turn around, Augusto yells out:

"Ta ta!"

He's spinning a giant lobster in front of my face.

"Davico—say hi to Genghis Khan," he says, proudly.

"I don't want to." I am afraid the antennas are going to poke me in the eyes.

Augusto points his chin at Otto and smiles as I run off. "Did you see his face?"

Otto has a mustache so thin it looks as if it were drawn with a pencil. His lips barely move as he lets out a squeaky laugh between his teeth.

Genghis Kahn has frightened me and I make a bit of *pipí*. I feel it warmly going down my pants as I gallop out of the kitchen and up to my room to change.

*

I decide not to go into the kitchen again when Augusto is there alone.

But when he is not there, I spend hours and hours watching the lobsters moving along the bottom of the tank, with their antennas and legs shifting and probing. They are as ugly as giant iguanas, except they live in water.

Genghis Khan is definitely the king. He climbs on the back of the other lobsters and sticks his antennas all the way out of the water as if to breathe. He does this three or four times a day.

If enough lobsters are in the tank he could get on their backs and climb out.

I hope that never happens.

*

The week after Augusto plays his dirty trick on me, I hear lots of airplanes flying low overhead. Yellow and blue papers drop down from the sky, twisting and spinning in the air like paper airplanes. They land on the rooftop and in the courtyard of the restaurant. I bring one of the sheets over to my father.

He reads the words in Spanish very slowly and angrily rips the paper.

"What is it, Papá?"

"Trouble," he says. "Trouble." And he shakes his head.

I know that the words on the paper have made him angry. I am a big boy, but I can't read. "What kind of trouble?"

"Politics. Why can't people leave us alone?"

*

The restaurant is almost always empty now. My father closes it as soon as the sun sets and the sirens start screaming. A few minutes later, all the lights go out and my mother brings out the candles.

"What are we going to do?" asks Mamá, one night.

Papá, who has gotten really good at shrugging, shrugs.

"We have to do something."

"Well, at least people can still come for lunch," Papá says, raising his arms in the air.

"Just the newspaper reporters from the United States. They never order more than a sandwich for lunch." my mother says, rolling her eyes. "If these blackouts continue, we'll have to throw out the steak and chicken in the freezer."

"I know that," my father says, sharply.

"Luis, please—"

"Yes, yes, I'm sorry. We have to do something," he repeats and then he hugs my Mamá.

She runs her hand through his hair. This makes me happy.

*

Guatemala City is so dangerous that Papá leaves at six in the morning to buy food for the restaurant in the market near the *Catedral*. He walks very quickly, hugging the walls of the buildings, just in case bullets begin flying. Once when I was sitting on the windowsill, he came back and showed me a flattened bullet he had found sticking out of a wall.

One night while my brother and I are playing pick-up sticks in our bedroom, we hear pow-pow sounds.

"Grab your pillow and blanket, Davico. You, too, Felipe. *Right now!*" Mamá says.

"Why?" he wails impatiently. My brother is winning the game.

"We're going to sleep downstairs in the restaurant."

Felipe grabs his brown dog and drags himself downstairs. He's not happy. I carry down the stuffed pig that spends every night on my pillow.

Our parents are upset about the bullets and they make beds for us underneath the big table in the center of the restaurant. To be honest, I am happy to have the whole family sleeping together, wrapped in blankets. I only have to stretch my arms to touch a warm body. Bullets and blackouts make my life more fun.

*

I think I could get used to sleeping like this.

I prefer sleeping under the table to sleeping in bed with my pig.

When the shooting stops, my mother has us go back to our room. We have to sleep with the lights out. I'm so scared of the dark my mother buys me a lamp with batteries so I can sleep with the light on. The lamp has a revolving shade—as it turns, the painted sun, clouds, and waves roll across the light. I love seeing the waves crashing on the beach and sending up imaginary sprays of water. Felipe hates the lamp because it keeps him awake. He says I'm a big baby.

I like the lamp even though sometimes Consuelo leaves a shirt hanging on my closet doorknob and I start seeing shadows. I can't control my mind. If the wind blows, my shirt billows out like a huge monster. Then I imagine that the dust under my bed has turned into a wolf and the scratches on the walls are spiders or snakes. If I hear whistling in the streets I'm sure that it's a bat trying to fly into our bedroom.

I can only sleep with the light on now.

*

Things are getting worse.

Consuelo doesn't take me to feed bananas to the elephants at the zoo.

The director decides to close Felipe's *Prepa*.

Consuelo stops taking us to the park after lunch to ride our bicycles around the fountains in the *Parque Central*. I miss the trees, the blackbirds, the sprays of water, the shoeshine boys. Even the dirty pigeons.

One night we are all sleeping under the dining room tables. My parents are whispering.

"Guatemala is too dangerous," Papá says. "What if a bullet…"

"Don't say it!" Mamá says harshly. "The children are right here."

I close my eyes to pretend I'm sleeping, but it's so dark you can't see anything anyway.

"People are afraid to go out. The government is going to be overthrown."

I imagine my parents are hugging each other the way I like.

"We have to be careful what we say," Mamá whispers. "Even the walls have ears."

*A wall full of ears.* What a strange and scary thought. I close my eyes, clutch my pig, and decide that this is a good moment to fall asleep.

*

The next day at breakfast, Mamá tells us that she and Papá have decided to go to a place called the United States.

"What's that?"

"*Where's that!*" Felipe corrects me, sharply. He is always angry at me now.

My mother touches my hair. "Far away. They speak English there."

"What's English?"

"It's a strange language," Felipe says. "I'm studying it in school. They say *table* instead of *mesa*."

My mother scolds him. "It's not strange. I speak it. So does Papá. You will both learn it so fast!"

"Well what about the *Prepa*? Is the *Prepa* coming with us?" I say, taking a bite out of my *pan francés* and *queso de capas*.

Felipe just shakes his head and pops another sweet roll in his mouth.

"No," my mother says. "The *Prepa* is a school. It stays here. Your father and I will go first to look for a new house."

"But what about us?" I'm afraid we will have to sleep alone on the benches in the park like the shoeshine boys.

"You will stay with Uncle Aaron," my mother says proudly.

The whole time my father is drinking coffee, reading the newspaper, and shaking his head.

*

Uncle Aaron is very tall and bald, has bat-wing glasses and wears a three-piece suit. His wife Lonia is very pretty, but she is always shouting at us— keep your feet off this, don't put your hands in that!

Who in the world would want to stay with them?

"Why can't we go with you?" I don't want my parents to leave us.

"We have to look for jobs."

"I can look for a job," I shout.

Felipe and Mamá are laughing at me. Did I say something funny?

"Can Consuelo come with us?"

Again they laugh that laugh which tells me that I don't understand.

"There's no room for her at Uncle Aaron's. Maybe later she'll join us in the United States."

I have never been there, but I am beginning to hate the United States.

*

The day comes when our parents bring us over to Uncle Aaron's house. They give us lots of wet kisses. Both Felipe and I are crying.

Uncle Aaron lives far away from *La Casita*. He has a huge wooden house, with a large yard, and two bulldogs that are always barking.

We can never go outside because the dogs might bite us. They have white foam around their mouths.

My aunt won't let us ride our bikes in the house.

"You'll break one of the lamps."

"We promise not to."

"No. No. And you will leave tire marks on the wooden floor."

She has answers for everything.

Felipe's red two-wheeler and my green tricycle have to stay outside under a plastic cloth near the garbage cans behind the kitchen. We can't even see them because the backdoor is always latched.

Everything is so different. I miss the shiny pots and the lobster tank. Even Genghis Khan.

From the back of the kitchen window I see a few days later that our bikes have become homes for spiders. One day I see a huge rat near my tricycle.

"Aunt Lonia! I just saw a rat chewing on my tricycle."

"Nonsense. Your bike is made of steel."

"On the tires."

"Tires are made of rubber," she says laughing at me.

I want to cry. Cry as loud as I can. But I feel that my heart is stopped up.

Felipe says that Aunt Lonia doesn't care about us. "I'm sure the rat is having more fun than us," he says sadly.

*

We stay at Uncle Aaron's house for over a month. For me, it seems as if two years—half my lifetime—has passed. I'm surprised that time can move so slowly, almost go in reverse, like when I run backwards and erase my steps.

Tina, the maid, keeps watch on us, scowling. I miss Consuelo. Otto. Even mean old Augusto.

*

It is the rainy season in Guatemala. Every morning we play checkers, pick-up sticks, and cards. We never go out.

Every afternoon, as soon as our aunt and uncle go to work after lunch, Felipe and I put on our record of Cri-Cri songs. Felipe's favorite is *El Burrito*, but I really like *El Chorrito*.

Part of it goes like this:

> *Allá en la fuente*
>
> *había un chorrito*
>
> *se hacía grandote*
>
> *se hacía chiquito.*

*Estaba de mal humor.*

*Pobre chorrito tenía calor.*

*Ahí va la hormiga*

*con su paraguas*

*y recogiéndose las enaguas.*

*Estaba de mal humor*

*porque el chorrito la salpicó*

*y sus chapitas le despintó.*

It's a song about a fountain that's in a bad mood. It feels hot. Then an ant walks by and gets splashed by the fountain. It also gets into a bad mood because the water makes her pretty makeup run down her little cheeks. I like the song because though everyone is in a bad mood, the music is happy.

Every day is the same. We play games. We listen to music. We are bored. It is very cold. I miss our parents.

*

One day Aunt Lonia tells us, "You're going to join your parents!"

"Where?" Felipe asks.

"In Miami, Florida."

I am sure I will hate Miami, Florida in the United States.

"Is it far away?" I ask.

"It's very far away. You'll have to take a propeller plane to get there."

"What's a propeller plane?"

"Like a car, but it flies through the air."

"A flying machine!" Felipe says triumphantly.

"At least you'll be free," my aunt says, "not like here."

I have no idea what she is talking about.

*

When we go to the airport, Felipe and I wear matching suits, shirts, ties, and shoes. Everyone thinks we're *cuaches*—twins.

Felipe and I sit next to each other on the airplane.

The airplane does fly in the sky and goes straight through clouds slicing them without getting hurt. How very strange.

Everyone treats us nicely.

We're given plates of food, coloring books, and even caps.

The stewardess gives a pin to Felipe. "You're the sky king."

She says to me, "You're the sky captain."

Felipe and I smile though we have no idea what she's talking about.

She's the first person of many we meet who thinks that everyone in the world speaks English.

*

Our parents meet us as at the Miami airport when we come off the airplane. They are standing on the asphalt. It is noisy and hot. We all begin to cry. I didn't know I had missed them so very much—my mother looks the same, my father older and tenser. He is wearing a short-sleeve shirt and slacks instead of his usual suit. I see my mother's legs—she is wearing shorts.

Florida is a strange place.

As we drive to our new home, we notice that Miami is flat as a pancake. No mountains!

It's very hot. I'm sweating as I sit, without even moving, in the back seat.

I realize that I will never wear the pants and sweaters I brought from Guatemala.

Everyone on the streets wears shorts.

*

People tell us there's a beach nearby—sand and sea. I have never seen a beach. I don't even know how to swim.

The clouds are different in Miami. Not as puffy. Everything is different.

We must ride bicycles to reach the corner store. We find boxes of candies called *Three Musketeers*, *Mars* and *Snickers*. And lots of bottles of Coca-Cola and Root Beer. We can't buy *roscas*, *espumillas* and *canillas de leche*.

We never eat black beans, yucca or plantains.

The avocados are watery.

No one speaks Spanish.

My mother says we have to learn English.

She hardly speaks Spanish to us anymore.

We will make lots of new friends.

You can't see any mountains or volcanoes.

*

I promise Mamá and Papá lots of things: not to speak Spanish at school, not to complain about the food, and to learn English.

Before long, all I remember of Spanish is

> *buenos días,*
>
> *tengo hambre,*
>
> *necesito hacer pipí.*

Forgetting Spanish—this is what coming to the United States means to me.

*

I miss *mi lámpara*. Even my shirt on the *gancho*.

*Mis padres* own a Chevy, but *mi madre* drives.

*Mi padre* says that when we get the *dinero*, he'll buy me a new tricycle and Philip a *patineta*.

I miss the *langosta tanque* in the *restaurante*.

I miss *dormir* under the tables when the *luz* goes out.

I miss the paper *azules* and *amarillos girando* in the sky and falling in the patio *de la casa*.

I miss Augusto and his *engaños*.

Skinny old *amigo* Otto.

I miss the *langostas*, with their *antenas* and hairy legs.

Especially Genghis Khan.

PLINIO HERNÁNDEZ

# Los Sheecago Buls

DEDICATED TO ALL THOSE CENTRAL AMERICANS WHO HAVE LOST THEIR LIVES IN
MEXICO TRYING TO REACH THEIR DREAMS IN THE UNITED STATES.

WILMER YORDEN MEJÍA had had a Chicago Bulls jersey since he was 12 years
old. It was his most prized possession. His mom had sent it to him in 2010
when Wilmer's uncle, who was the first in the family to receive permanent
residency in the United States, took it to Wilmer on his visit to the small
pueblo outside the city of Santa Ana in the western part of El Salvador. His
mom had supported the family for years with money sent through El Banco
Agrícola but this was the first physical gift Wilmer received from his mom.
The jersey represented his mom's hard work and love but also somehow the
love of a father he never knew.

Wilmer could still remember the bag the jersey came in, the new smell,
the hologram tags that authenticated it, the quality of the material. He be-
came the sensation in his village with that jersey and from that moment on
he took up playing basketball instead of soccer. As a result his nickname be-
came Yordencito and eventually he would help lead the *Instituto Nacional
de Santa Ana*, the high school he attended, to a national championship.

Yordencito never saw Michael Jordan play nor did he ever meet his fa-
ther. His father had left to the United States while he was still in his mother's
womb and was last heard of in Tamaulipas, Mexico. Yordencito's mother
named him after his father and his father's favorite basketball player, Michael
Jordan. His mother, Hilda Mejía Chacón, didn't know how to spell Jordan
back when he was born and like most English names given to his friends it
was done phonetically. Wilmer Yorden had three close friends in high school:
Jhonny, Jony, and Joni.

Before starting his last year of high school his coach did everything he
could to get Wilmer to stay in El Salvador and even got him a tryout with
the national team. He was invited back, but gently declined the offer. "I have
to reunite with my mom and brother," he told the national team coach.
Wilmer just wanted to leave all the violence behind.

He wasn't planning quitting basketball. In fact, Wilmer's best friend,
who had moved to California a few years earlier, told him that he could

come up to the States and play for community college and possibly transfer to a four-year school. Although he did not fully understand what his friend was talking about, this gave Wilmer motivation to dream and he would often lay in his room at night imagining himself going to college in the States, maybe to the university of North Carolina, making it to the NBA and playing on the Dream Team. A true dreamer. So he continued to wake up every morning to shoot hoops in a beautiful leveled dirt basketball court surrounded by cashew, avocado, and mango trees.

Many people tried to convince him to stay in El Salvador because of how dangerous the passage through Mexico had become since his father disappeared. But Yordencito saw no point to staying in El Salvador. He wanted nothing more to do with the violence and that had taken his older brother two years earlier as well as many of his friends. The death of his grandmother the previous year was the final straw because she was the last of his relatives in all of El Salvador. So halfway through his last year of high school against his mother's wishes Yordencito left Santa Ana and headed for the Guatemalan border, about an hour away on bus. He carried a small backpack that had a change of clothing and he wore the number 23 Chicago Bulls jersey for good luck.

Yordencito looked at the trip like an adventure but as soon as he crossed into Mexico reality set in. He was robbed of his money, backpack, and shoes. Luckily, he was able to get a meal and an old pair of shoes in a migrant house. With no money and no way for his mother to send him any (since he had no I.D.), Yordencito struggled and battled his way on top of trains through the southern part of Mexico, staying in migrant houses in Chiapas, Oaxaca, Veracruz, Mexico city, Guanajuato and Guadalajara. He improvised anything into a basketball hoop and used soccer balls or balled up socks or a shirt to shoot hoops and pass the time at different migrant houses.

It had been weeks since his mother last heard of Wilmer and her anxiety, she remembered, was similar to when Wilmer's father disappeared. One night while watching the *Univisión* national news broadcast she saw what she had been dreading for weeks. Partially censored images of migrants who had been found dead in Taumalipas. In the footage the bodies of five lifeless men were bound and piled on top of each other. The one on top had a Chicago Bulls jersey on. The next morning the family called the Salvadoran embassy. It would take the family more than a year to receive the remains of Yordencito.

A few years after Yordencito's death, his little brother Edgar, now a sophomore at UC Berkeley, called his mom frantically. "Mama, mama! I just saw

Yordencito, I just saw Yordencito!" When Edgar finally calmed down he explained to his mother that in his film class they had screened a documentary on Central Americans traveling through Mexico that had been filmed years earlier. Edgar sat there in disbelief, mouth open, tears streaming down his face as he watched an interview of a young man, smiling and talking about his dreams of reaching the United States, of his mother, his brother, his love for basketball, and the story behind his most prized possession: a Chicago Bulls Michael Jordan jersey.

JAVIER ZAMORA

# Anthem

*Cariño*, you've never lived my war—
    a glass of fresh water in the ocean.
Everything is mine
    on loan: the leaves I've combed out of my hands.
I want to mold what I cannot return to,
    let me say
palm, coconuts on palms, water. Let me say
    I know how to unsheathe husks to shut my thirst.
Know that I can't find the boy I threw rocks at fruit bats with
    or the cigarettes we lit
for their snouts to smoke. Let me say
    my poverty is a possum
skinned at the foot of fourteen families,
    it's a coastal barrio
where hooves carve cobblestones,
    where lieutenants order shots with shotguns,
and since then floors splattered with sorghum,
    fingers and ears since then,
and since then
    hurricanes. And yes,
this is all I remember
    and this is what my memory says:

*I know what it is to be a bucket*
    *of mosquitoes no one listens to.*

*Cariño*, I've lost count
    of the crosses I've painted
while whispering my name.
    I've lost count of the days
I haven't been
    my motherland.

JAVIER ZAMORA

# Pump Water from the Well

This is no shatter and stone.
    Come skip toes in my chest Salvador.
I'm done been the shortest shore.
    ¿And did you love all the self out of you for me?
I want you to torch the thatch above my head.
    To be *estero*. To be mangroves.
There are mornings I wake with the taste of tortillas in warmed up milk.
    There are pomegranates no one listens to.
¿Is this the shatter you imagined for me?
    Everywhere is war.
I want to scrape your hair as the wind begs.
    Hold my hands above mine.
Whistle the patch of dirt I pumped water from to bathe.
    Simmer down to chickens, dogs, parakeets.
This was my block.
    The one I want to shut off with rain.
Where I want to plant an island.
    Barrio Guadalupe *hijueputa* born and bred *cerote ¿qué onda*?
The most beautiful part of my barrio was stillness
    and a rustling of wings caught in the soil calling me to repair it.
Don't tell me I didn't bring the *estero* up north where there's none.
    I've walked uptown. I saw Mrs. Gringa.
The riff between my fingers whispered in whirlpools.
    Silence stills me. *Pense quedarme aquí,* I said.
*I don't understand,* she said. From my forehead,
    the jaw of a burro, hit on the side and scraped by a lighter to wake the song that
    speaks two worlds.
The kind of terrifying current.
    The kind of ruinous wind.

# Vuelo

las montañas
de La Conchagua
murmuran
en las mañanas
cuando despierto
en ciudad de
angeles soñando
llena de un
recuerdo
nublando entre
rios y volcanes
donde la luna
se refleja
en los ojos
de los cipotes
yo hija de
mi madre
ella un pajaro
amarillo
tomo vuelo
a medio dia
con bendicion
de sus ancestros
que anhelaban
la vida
fertil el campo
de su niñez
se cubrio de
guerra frio
ella con cruz
en su palabra
cruza fronteras

sus alas
aliento del sol
cinco estrellas
su destino
no hay distancia
en el corazon

# Descalsa

I step foot on the soil
of my mother's tongue
barefoot at ten years of age
the men with the guns
line the dirt roads to *abuela's* house
my eyes take in smoke
a memory has been burned into the air
I can breathe it in
a deep sigh for the decade
I heard the rosary turning from my mamas fingertips
as she faraway in the *ciudad de angeles*
lived the ravages of a war
that plagued her childhood streams
I stand muddy in the memory
of this El Salvador that is half of me

ALEXIS AGUILAR

# Labriego en Libertad

ERA COMO si el mundo se acabara. Soportaba impasible las noches cargadas de estruendos que conmovían con furor sísmico los cimientos de la vieja prisión y que la volvían mas fría y húmeda que nunca. Pero, ¿qué importaba si se acababa el mundo? si para Saturnino tenía mucho de haberse acabado. El tiempo ya no transcurría en horas ni en días pues esas medidas de tiempo habían perdido su sentido. Ahora sólo pensaba en meses, pero no en meses como enero y julio pues esos tampoco significaban nada, sino que en los meses calientes cuando el calor lo ahogaba y sentía que el cuerpo le iba a explotar, y en los meses fríos y húmedos—en realidad todos son húmedos pero la humedad fría es más atroz que la caliente—como el de esta noche en la que ya sólo esperaba que en forma proverbial lo partiera un rayo.

Habían meses bulliciosos como los de fin de año cuando se celebraba la navidad y el inicio de un buen año (o quizás el fin de uno malo). Esos meses lo entretenían pues miraba caras nuevas que llegaban a visitar a los demás. El ya no esperaba visitas, ni las extrañaba pues había dejado de recibirlas hace varios años—seguro que han sido años pues el año tiene muchos meses—y se conformaba con ver, aunque fuera de lejos, las que recibían los otros.

Los que más añoraba eran los meses abiertos. Era entonces cuando se colaba cierta claridad por la ventanita enrejada que lo convidaba a escudriñar el cielo en busca de aves que iban adonde querían. En los meses abiertos se abría todo—la ventanita era un ventanal y la serenidad de un porche que da a los cerros y al río, su catre sucio se ampliaba y se mecía con el vaivén de una hamaca, los insultos traían el canto de los gallos, las alabanzas de la misa, y los gritos de los niños, los pasillos se doblaban, subían y bajaban, y no lo llevaban al patio desgastado sino que a los frijolares y a las puertas de sus amigos. Los meses abiertos traspiraban olor a pino, tamal fresco y café dulce. Pero, por supuesto, a los meses abiertos les seguían los cerrados cuando no había luz que iluminara su celda, cuando sentía todo el peso de su existencia, cuando ni siquiera podía cerrar los ojos en las noches aunque hubiera querido poder cerrarlos para siempre. Fue en una noche de un mes cerrado cuando terminaron de desbaratarle la vida.

—Hey Saturnino te tengo buenas noticias. La juez dijo que quedás libre, que te podés ir mañana a primer hora.
El carcelero de guardia le descargó la brutalidad de esas palabras como una sentencia mientras intentaba alumbrarle la cara.

—¿Me oíste Saturnino? Ya no tenés que seguirte pudriendo en esta puta carcel. ¿Oíste Saturnino? ¡Saturnino!

Al oirlo sollozar el guardia decidió ir a jugar naipes con sus compañeros. Esa noche Saturnino se arrepintió de nuevo, como lo había hecho todas las noches por once años, de haberse robado una camisa en una tienda del centro. Había venido a la ciudad a buscar trabajo pero después de largos días de hambrear sin suerte pensó que con vender una camisa nueva iba a poder pagarse el pasaje de regreso a El Nancito.

Aceptó sin protestar y casi sin quejarse la golpiza de los policías porque reconocía que en su desesperación había hecho mal, mas nunca se imaginó que esa camisa significara tanta vida. «En otro país ya te hubieran cortado la mano con que robaste, cabrón. Suerte tenés de vivir aquí». Pero esta noche el guardia le había dicho que los once años habían sido un error, que se habían olvidado de él, que se alegrara que alguien al fin se había fijado que una camisa no valía tanto—pues que bueno que hoy me regalen su error para llevármelo para siempre con el mío de venir a esta ciudad maldita.

Al salir por la mañana pensó en su mujer y en sus hijos—¡cómo deben estar de grandes, cómo debe estar ella de linda! Pensó en El Nancito y sonrío. Luego, acariciando entre índice y pulgar los veinte pesos que le había facilitado la jueza más por vergüenza que por piedad, Saturnino se encaminó a su pueblo aunque sabía de sobra que nunca iba a volver ahí.

ALEXIS AGUILAR

# Este Lugar

Cuando volvió la vista hacia este lugar
dejó a un lado su belleza de abril
y recogió su belleza gentil vegetal.

Sus oídos se hicieron tocables por el rumor
ardiente de las arenas,
su voz se tornó larga y serena
y con ella logró formar un cerco
para proteger el temblor de las hojas
y el zumbido frágil de las libélulas.

Sus sueños se disolvieron en el lodo
al fondo de las lagunas,
y sus dedos se volvieron cauces de agua y luz.

Así reposó por años
hasta que un día,
como si no importara,
como si no hubieran miles de piedras
elevando sus ojos
suplicantes
hacia ella,
como si cada uno de esos cuerpecitos inertes
no hubiera encontrado ya en ella
su perfecto lugar,
se levantó,
sacudió con violencia sísmica la tierra
y partió sin volver la vista atrás.

ALEXIS AGUILAR

# Me Enteré Que Era Hispano

Al llegar a los EEUU
me enteré que yo era hispano,
antes, en Honduras, era sólo yo.
En los EEUU perfeccioné el arte de discernir
las más mínimas variaciones del color de la piel.
Hice, por ejemplo, una observación por años insospechable:
la piel de mi madre es más oscura que la mía.
Descubrí también detalles—como las líneas oscuras
en las palmas de mis manos—que de algún modo
habían logrado eludirme.

En los EEUU supe (no sin desconcierto)
que el español—igual a nosotros—es un idioma
subdesarrollado
y que, por lo tanto, comparte
la culpa de nuestro atraso.
Con malabarismos mentales logré entender
cómo en un país *libre*
es un delito no hablar inglés.

De igual manera, aprendí que *ilegal*
es sustantivo
y que cometía con mi propia existencia,
con cada sorbo de aire que tomaba,
un acto subversivo.

He aprendido mucho en los EEUU,
por ejemplo, que soy hispano.
Aprendí a vivir y a buscar mi hispanidad.
Aprendí que la puedo cargar con vergüenza
u ostentar con orgullo,
pero, sobre todo,
aprendí a llevarla
con amor.

GABRIELA RAMIREZ-CHAVEZ

# When Mamá Told Me

WHEN MAMÁ TOLD ME, I didn't understand how someone could just be somewhere and then poof away. I thought it was like when the earth opened up her mouth and swallowed bad people in the Bible, including the kids. Mamá would say, when I was disobedient and when she hit me lightly with a wooden spoon, how good I have it because I wasn't born in that time. My *tío* must've disappeared like that.

Or maybe it was like when I felt so small I wanted to disappear. Like when Ms. H asked me what Mamá does for a living and I told her I didn't know. She looked down at me through her brown oval glasses, blinking her little eyes, and said, "Well, don't you want to know what your mom does?" She waited a million and two years for a reply, and all I felt was the river running up inside, pressing behind my eyeballs, because I didn't want to say, "My mom cleans houses, big houses, not like the one-bedroom we share, where Papi was *this* close to being hurt by the *cholos*. She scrubs bathrooms and toilets on her knees, like a holy prayer, not like the other moms that stay home." I wanted to tell her I love Mamá, and I felt ashamed for feeling ashamed, but didn't say nothing because it was too late.

GABRIELA RAMIREZ-CHAVEZ

# Resistance Footage

THE FIRST TIME I see a disappearance is in a documentary. A silent clip in which a young man walks past a fenced building. A grey jeep pulls up, two figures jump out. One chokes him from behind, the other traps his arms. I wonder what the man is thinking, when a third figure with a black gun joins them. Passersby stand still watching the man shout and twist his body, except for his left arm, limp and broken. The one with the gun kicks his abdomen, sending him forward onto the ground.

I move the cursor over the video player, drag the white dot across the screen, to watch it all go backwards. Three figures help an injured young man lying face-down on the dirt. It could have been any of them, all dressed in bellbottoms, like a uniform. One clutches the man's arm and pushes it back into place. Together they struggle to pull him up, each relying on the other for support. One by one, they fly back into the jeep, and reverse toward a military base. I pause when only the man is left to air his thoughts in daylight.

# Oración

*"Que lindo, pero así no fue."* My mother rereads my poem on her smartphone, shaking her head. If it were on a printed page, she would hold it up to the light, flip it over, fold it up like a fan to see if the new lines tell the real story. Or else drown it in fire like the receipts that turned to ashes over the stove. The ones the *militares* left there after taking my uncle and everything from his home.

*"Él no fue."* He wasn't the one they left with ears, eyes, and mouth full of stones on the main road to San Juan. His body wasn't found like that. That was el Chino, or was it Manzana? It was one of the *solventeros*, the ones who huffed paint and sat near school corners waving at the girls. They never did a bad thing. Everybody has a nickname over there, not their God-given one, it's hard to remember.

*"¿Te acuerdas?"* she says. They were all *puntos*, little dots, erased from a sentence.

Or did she mean a prayer?

# 2

*En Voz Alta*

# El Salvador at a Glance

Area: the size of Massachusetts

Population: Not much left

Language: War, blood, broken english, spanish

Customs: Survival, dance, birthday parties, funerals

Major Exports: Coffee, sugar, city builders, busboys, waiters, poets

El Salvador
there are questions in the air about your character
they say you've dared to do the impossible
you've challenged the tiger to a wrestling match
you've decided that bullets hold the answers

El Salvador
little question mark
midget with a gun in his hand
belly button of the world

The only country in the world
known for eating its national flower

Little question mark that begins to itch

You were supposed to clean carpets
not ask for time out and dialogue

You were supposed to follow instructions
given in the english language
not go to the garden and write a song

It has been said that pain has the ability to travel

El Salvador's major cities:

San Salvador
San Miguel
Santa Ana
Los Angeles
Wachinton, DC

It has been said that pain does not know how to pose for a green card picture

It has been said that truth has the ability to happen
in the strangest moments
in the strangest cities
under the strangest circumstances

El Salvador in Washington
little question mark
little east of the border
migrant earthquake
wet back volcano
banana eating
tortilla making
mustache holder
funny dressing

forever happy

forever sad

forever wachintonian salvadorean.

# Latinhood

what does it feel like inside?
what color is this latinhood?
how does it do what it does?

what is it that makes it happen
in the way that it happens?
volatile
inquisitional
monolingual
with a yellow flower stuck in the braided hair

what language does it like to speak?
cachitquel
spanish
nahuatl
creole
or english?

does it know the rules to civilized behavior
or does it tend to go at your throat
when feeling threatened and cheated?

what color is this latinhood of mine?
is it black latin
brown latin
indio latin
white latin
latin latin
italian latin via buenos aires
latin with a tinge of whiteness
mestizo latin with korean roots?
is it straight a's

honor roll
hall of fame
welfare recipient
registered to vote
legal or illegal?

is it urinating latin
PhD latin
regular latin
or latin supreme?

is it mexican latin
salvatrucan latin
patagonia latin
latin with an american passport?

what does it feel like inside?
what does it feel like inside?

oh my god!
could it be that you feel flowery
hot and spicy
rio grande
bolivian lake
fm radio in a caracas afternoon
colombian capital full of parades

how do you know that you are a latin?
that you are not
a russian impostor with a peruvian accent?

what the hell is this all about?
is it about yellow rice
bean soup recipes
coca plants
garcia marquez
tourism
bananas
inflation?

is it about being weird
different
borracho
poetic
hispanic american with the sound of fiestas patronales?

what color did you get yours?
is it blue chilean
yellow asuncion
burgundy of st. croix
purple san jose?

who are you in this crazy web of latins?
are you a jimenez, an escobar
a maravilla, a scapini, a molina
a well of broken wishes?

who are you?
did I meet your mustache somewhere else?
are we related?

is it true what they are saying?
that this whole thing
is the simple ability
to swallow the world at birth

keeping it
 learning to chew at it
  letting it grow
   letting it grow inside.

GABRIELA POMA

# Las ofensivas

FOR GLORIA RASKOSKY

I remember being
Sent out to play
On the patio
Of my aunt's flat-line house
Outside Granada, Nicaragua.
The revolution
Had produced girls
Lip-synching ABBA songs.
*Chiquitita, tell me what's wrong?*

El Salvador too
Had a war next door
Where girls fell silent.
The houses were flat-line
And already gated,
Or had cardboard walls
That disintegrated
With the rains
That fell and fell
While the fallen
Kept rising and rising.

We hunted rats
With our fathers' slingshots.
The prized one was
As big as a rabbit.
We killed it
And placed it on a brick wall
That framed the arid patio
Of the house outside *La Sultana.*

Then the boys came looking
And told us it wasn't pretty.

We were the girls
Singing songs, *las ofensivas*.
Our father dies,
Our uncle dies,
Our brother dies.
The fallen, we know
They rise in Nicaragua,
They rise in El Salvador.
*Chiquitita, ¿dime, por qué?*

KARINA OLIVA ALVARADO

# On Parallel Lines

Crosshatched lives
        heading north because I have no choice

Sutures on the ground
        and the sky revolting into the night

The horizon forever at a distance
        with your memory foot-printing my mind

What hope do I have than nothing? The weight
        of your body others toss aside

My faith is everything I got; with index and thumb crossed
I bless myself at every stop to not forget
        I'm starving for a better life

To rise like a skyscraper
and shine like a hood ornament glinting in the sun?
        I'm willing to clear tables
        brighten toilets
to send you dollars across miles

Let's pretend I'm only visiting
        and tomorrow will return me back

When once I lived completely
        now in parts I'm left behind

In my heart you are the echo
                *Come home*
        your tender voice, the sweetness in my blood

Muffled by the train tracks

The northern rumbling: *Come*

And you calling, *Come back, come back.*

KARINA OLIVA ALVARADO

# Early Memory Of Light

To free her hands,
  mother places me on the alcove
by the dresser mirror where I sit like a baby Buddha
watching her paint her teenage face
arc brows like palm trees that bend forward
stroke lips, round and heavy
  like the sunset falling from the sky

In mother's shadow room, the mirror
spotlights her slim frame
  and she becomes another
of God's long and dusty fingers floating in
through drawn curtains that do not fully close
even when she attempts to overlap fabric against fabric

On the alcove, I watch without words
learning about the shape and color of love
feeling knowledge through a toddler's heart that coos

  *Mami*   *Mami*  *Mami*

I do not know specific words to know my loneliness
when one day she disappears,
  a small child that searches her out
in barren rooms like an empty gold locket

In great-grandmother's house, I roam
with bare feet on cold tile
scratching my naked tummy, talking to myself

148

*La Chillona*, cry baby, cousins yank hair
but it takes less to make tears spout
from eyes too wide for my face

Mama, come get me.
                    Mama, I love.
                                  Mama.

In school I learn words
and as children point and laugh: orphan
I touch the largest cloud, picture mother
     swaying in a dress of light as the sun bursts from her smile,
I swear stomp-footed and tear-stained, Mother
will fly home to hold me one day

After school, in blue pleated skirt, white shirt, and red tie
I toss red lunchbox on grandmother's teal wood bench
center thighs on just-mopped floor and pray to the TV,
    more than a friend with a voice,
        great-boxed God living in room
believing in its power and halo
believing in direct communication
I semi-chant love messages to mother,
      raise head to ceiling

                evoke Mother

direct cries of
      please, please, please
              to woman:

a golden outline of a lady that lives in a city of angels

a city of womb; city of wound.

KARINA OLIVA ALVARADO

# I've Been Told That Without You, I'd Be Nothing

That it's you who taught, fed, and clothed me
though I understand my privilege is not easily handed
in other lands, this is hardly an excuse
to keep plumbing and mining our bodies, scattering
my family like ashes to ashes
because you claim an inalienable right
since my own El Salvador tears its people apart.

But it is you who keeps us under threat and the stomp
of corporate invasions, whether here or there you demand
our happy silence, an oxymoron
quiet in our sweatshops, underpaid and overworked
domesticity to garden
your fountain of dollar bills that sustain our diabetes,
cancer, alcoholism, and rotting teeth, unable to pay for health
no matter how hard we work, our chests cave to keep us
one by one a nuisance, interchangeable
for the sacrifice of other replaceable bodies.

True, this country is the land of chance
like rolled dice in Las Vegas, and the possibility of stardom
while selling maps in Hollywood corners.
Truth is, your fist extends beyond your guarded borders
and what you do to a single immigrant, a single undervalued
brown body, bodies of women, you do to the world.
For some, you are the denials of a nightmare
like zombies entering foreign lands to seek the minds
of children, women, and men as the dead feed on the living
because you keep trying to return to the era when slaves
were born and died slaves—that Good Ol' America, the one

you want to "take back" and "make great again"
you tell me gives me my privilege
even as I struggle to pay for a decent apartment
try to rise from a hole of student debt, I am told
U.S.A. gave me this opportunity
to become educated, to seek education, to someday teach
but your star-spangled rings mute like a cracked bell
because it is not this nation that fed me. My mother fed me.
She bled dollar bills to feed our family.
There were days when all we had to eat were avocados
she picked from the neighbor's yard.

She's been the live-in, the seamstress, *maquiladora*
paid by dissected pennies, the desperate woman screaming
and pulling at her hair with nowhere to turn
to pay the rent.

An ingrate? No. I am grateful.
I am grateful to be alive and living,
chiseling words on stone towards a better life.
But enough has been taken
from El Salvador, from Central America, Latin America,
from immigrants,
why try to overshadow the heroic resilience of my mother?
Because I don't owe a thing to nations here or there governed by fists
greedily wrapped around dollars, but
I owe my life and the lives of my children,
everything that compels me forward,
to Carmen.

KARINA OLIVA ALVARADO

# Great Grandmother

Mama Tey walk with me
show me your imprinted steps
legs like yucca roots, feet
like paper bags stuffed
with soft and rounded stones.

You waddled to bathe our bodies,
hand pat *calabaza pupusas*, fold piles
of freshly washed clothes.

Your stories painted pictures
like bright dandelions and *flor de izote* in my mind.

Let me be so brave, Mama Tey
to not lose sight in my workaholic days
so that my own legs and feet guide me well,
to tell the stories
in following the memory
of your heart.

IGNACIO CARVAJAL

# Untitled

among the daily quiet of the sidewalks
i have begun to hear
a low, low murmur,
a tremor imperceptible.
it has a scent.
i pick it up sometimes
when i am falling
or thinking about punishment,
about damnation.
i imagine that it tastes
like water from the *caños.*
like a drop of *aguardiente*
that's been hiding,
underground, for decades.
it smells, i sometimes think,
like matches. not like a single
match or like those booklets
they give out at drinking establishments.
like whole boxes of matches,
matches made of actual timber,
whittled down and shaped,
not cardboard ones, burning—
burning somewhere far away, over a
hill or a *basurero*, mixing with the sea
and all the storms.
but that i hear it
is now
for me
most surprising,
for i never did before. never imagined
that something so seemingly
large

could go unnoticed
by so many people.
i hear it at night and when i'm dreaming.
i hear it in the morn. it sounds like pain.
but i am
somehow
able to tell
that this pain comes seeking.
it looks, it seems to whisper,
for the evil-doers.
i hear it—louder, every time—
above the vibrating metal of the fences
above the names mistaken
above the clink of coins
above the scribbling of laws
on nice, clean paper,
above the trudge
above the train
above the bullets.
"i'm on my way" it says,
and it sounds angry.
"the time is near," it says,
"*ya casi llego.*"

STEVE CASTRO

# Country folk in tune with the times

When I was a child, we owned a television.
It was mighty fine too. It was as big
as my imagination, but it was smaller
than our screen door. Our TV had all
of the colors of the rainbow. Well, it only
had three: black, white, and gray. But it
was a very bright gray and the black
that sprang forth from our apparatus
was blacker than a dead man's conscience
and the white that projected itself from
the screen into my eyes was so white
that if you took the color white
and washed it in the river three times
with Lava soap then you still wouldn't see
the whiteness that I saw.

We had so many channels, I could barely
count them all. Our television was modern.
It didn't run on firewood like our stove.
It ran on 100% electricity, which my mama
told me "was discovered by a man
who was born to die like the rest of us."

I used to think that if you broke the glass
on the front of the television, then you could
interact with whatever was happening on
the other side, but when I broke the television
glass with my mother's hammer to warn
Bugs Bunny of an ominous bullet headed
his way, I realized that I only saw machine
parts and wires inside the television's brain.
Within seconds after I broke the television,

my mother came into our television room
with a flathead screwdriver and some other
implements. I sat on our dirt floor and I watched
my mother for what seemed like days gradually
building a robot out of television parts and other
spare parts that she found throughout the house.

After her project was finished, I laid my head
on my mother's lap. She brushed my hair as I
watched cartoons in *Technicolor* that emanated
from our newly created robot's belly. "Let us name
our robot Leonardo," my mother whispered in my ear.

MARIO ESCOBAR

# Nameless

I was six when I saw her
nude like the open mouth of God
I was crossing a creek
on my way to buy lard
lard, lard, lard
repeating so I wouldn't forget
hands tied together
eyes wide open
I brought sugar instead
Two *colones*
weight more than the fear
of a child
My grandfather assured me
that idiots
burn in hell
I told my *tata*
what I had seen
He pulled my ears
and told me
not to say
a word
I cried
myself
to sleep
That day
she died
And I died
along with her

MARIO ESCOBAR

# An Apology to My Children

People I loved are buried
in the foolishness of a decade
and I breathe just to ease
this encrypted smile
to make the spirit glow
in the perfect snapshot
hiding tears
my children
know nothing of
Salvadoran rezos
prayers that won't give up
another flashback
pervades
I am not present
lost in the depth
of death
snap out of it
your daughter
is talking to you
my wife says
"Look daddy
I drew a smile
in the sand
just for you."

MAYA CHINCHILLA

# Solidarity Baby

I'm just a solidarity baby
don't know what it's really like,
played on fire escapes
danced on rooftops
made fortresses out of boxes and paper plates.

My first march I rode above the crowd
in a yellow baby backpack with a metal frame
quiet and observant
I didn't cry or complain
'cause Mami and Papi were planning solidarity, baby
organizing dreams, taking on telling the truth
running the Central American Underground Railroad
thru my living room
my second-hand clothes given third-hand with first-rate love,
giving the little we had to those who had less
this is my inheritance.

While all I did was play with office supplies
and draw pictures of ET with highlighters
and learn to breakdance in the halls
between the offices in front of MacArthur park on 7th
drawing aliens playing with friends with aliases
wearing *hüipiles* for solidarity baby.

*This one's for you Uncle Sam we don't want another Vietnam*
*This one's for you Uncle Sam we don't want another Vietnam* *

I'm just a revolutionary honee
a product of an international relation
imaginary Guatemalan, *porque Guate no existe*
mistaken identity:

undercover *gringa-chapina-alemana-mestiza*
coming from a long line of resilience.

*Mamá, Papá, compañeros de los Centros de Información*
extended family of activists
raising rebellious daughter
never doing as I was told.

*I understand now that you being ahead*
*of your time means much suffering from it.*
*But it's beautiful to love the world with*
*eyes that have not yet been born.*\*\*
I remember hiding under literature tables
listening to a proud Maya woman
*mujer de maíz*
using the conquerors language to testify
while Mami interprets.

I used to curl up on my father's lap while he
debated what lay between the lines,
*Chapín* Spanish booming from his chest, comforting.

I used to get names of dictators and leaders of the people mixed up:
Samoza and Sandino? Rios Montt or Otto René Castillo?
Banana Republicans, Cold warriors *Contras quien?*
Was Reagan a good guy or a bad guy?
Let me see if I can get this right:

A-B-CIA-GIC-FMSLN-URNG-UFW-XYZ

I'm just looking for my place
am I a CENTRAL American?
*Sí pues, soy del epicentro.*

So what have I ever done for revolution, honey?
But entertain thoughts of clandestine self-righteous
militant explosions.
*Si el poeta sos vos qué tengo yo que hablarte?*\*\*\*

I mean it's just a revolution honey,
why they getting so crazy?
I'm just trying to stay away from
letting them impose their guru on me.
Don't have to prove who's more down,
I'm just trying to keep my head up.

But, what have I ever done?
but survive race riots in high school
picking up the pieces using translator techniques
but get through college when the high school
counselor said it couldn't be done
but tell stories on a microphone,
possibly just touching one.

*Compañeros mios yo cumplo mi papel luchando*
*con lo mejor que tengo.* \*\*\*\*
With the best that I've got.
No one knows my secret plans
documentary days, radio nights, printed palabras
what I am capable of
practicing storyteller strategies and messenger *maneras*
holding the door open for the little ones who are coming thru
what I am planning to do
it's part of my dynamically (un)disciplined destiny
to observe what is not obvious
risking reporting truths untold
layering laughter between tears
campaigning and complaining for the silent
who carry this country on their backs!

Unless we document ourselves we are invisible!
there is so much left to do,
I'm taking on telling the truth
I'm just a revolutionary mama,
solidarity, baby.

* Song by Sabia
\*\* "Before the Scales," *Tomorro*w by Otto René Castillo
\*\*\* "Si el poeta eres tu" by Pablo Milanés
\*\*\*\* From "Viudo del mundo" by Otto René Castillo

MAYA CHINCHILLA

# What It's Like to Be a Central American Unicorn for Those Who Aren't

AFTER PATRICIA SMITH

First of all I am a mythical creature that is only mentioned
if at all
in relation to war, trauma, *maras*, revolutions, earthquakes,
Indians kidnapped by aliens, and the Guatemalan maid that never speaks
but has her own story to tell.

What happens if I never mention these things?
am I contributing to the loss
the silence
the gaps in historical memory
the opportunity for reconciliation
to make amends?

what if I never mention *pupusas*
or my grandmother's *pepián*, black beans and rice
or a *quesadilla* that's a cheesy bread,
or tortillas with melted cheese
or the million ways to fry *platano*
or Honduran *baleadas*, which I have yet to try?

What if I tell you that I am usually the only one of my kind?
that if I make up what it means to be Guatemalan-hyphen-American
no one in the room will be able to call me a liar?

What if I swear to all that is unholy
that if one more person shares that they went to study
Spanish in Guatemala and backpacked through the highlands without
ever mentioning massacred Mayans, the Quiché, the Mam,
the *Ix'il*, *K'achiq*uel…

Yes "modern day" Mayans not kidnapped by aliens,
the "absence of" that is Ladino, Mestizo
plus the Garifuna, the Mesquito, Pipil, Lenca…
not mysterious civilizations "disappeared."

Yes, thank you for knowing how *they* invented the zero
and no the world didn't stop in 2012
I don't want to hear about your trip unless
you are fundraising to get me and the diaspora
back on a regular basis.

What if I tell you I don't speak any indigenous languages?
except for the remnants of words that have crept into the Spanish
I re-learned in high school when I went to Guate that summer.

That my family denies any indigenous ancestry
though DNA and memory say different?
that we are an urban people who value engineering degrees
above all else?
that I haven't been "back" in ten years?
that there are silent wars among cousins and aunts and uncles
catholics vs. protestants vs. atheists vs. *cremas vs. rojos*
disjointed conversations of over here from over there and
over there from over here
and I can't go back over there in the same way anymore.
I can't go "back" there.
Over there doesn't exist anymore.

So I pack my Central American paranoia
that taught me everyone is shady until proven otherwise,
don't sit with your back to the door, don't count money in public,
leave your shoes next to the bed in case you have to run in the night,
remember walls have ears!

Mix in grains of sand from an imaginary homeland,
file them in plastic file box and ride off to the next adventure
leave a trail of glitter that smells of copal, banana leaves,
wood burning stoves and moist green earth
so that other magical creatures may find me.

MAURICIO ESPINOZA

# Childhood Home

This is where the days are long and summer never ends.
This is where I stand in front of a drafty window.
This is the window where migration-weary birds
come to feed on rusty bowls.
This is where my mother paints roosters on towel racks.
This is where my father always comes home too late.
This is where school hasn't started and cousins come to play.
This is where I hold a stick of chalk and write my first words
on splintered wooden walls.
This is where those walls are now gone.
This is where summer never lasts.
This is where the window is also gone
and the birds are only ghosts.
This is where the rain erased my words.
This is where my childhood home is no more.

ARIEL ESTRELLA

# Dead Baby Drop

Washed the stringy hair of a dead woman
On my first day with some pink fruity berry
Herbal Essences rip-off bought two dollars
Cheaper than the brand. Peeked into a bag
Of organs by my third week, knees stupid
From encountering that, my first autopsied
Decedent spun open. Still went back, J to A
To G to my stop. Went back after the owner
Called me all urgent-like from the backroom
Needing me to translate. He hadn't stopped
To consider my tongue second-gen deaddumb, useless
To tell a man *un ataúd de cedro para su ser*
*Querido cuesta $500 más de su presupuesto.*
Then they tumbled the baby. Under office lights
The cellophaned bundle abstracted the blanket
Into stretched asphalt whites and hospice
Blues and Looney Toons patches.     Cellophane
Wrapped bundles should not be in the office.
He fumbled the bundle, and as I finished the month
The backroom smelt of fuming chemical and ashy
Fruity berry sweet.

ARIEL ESTRELLA

# Crumble Red into Marrow

TO: 96 ST

Google Maps'ed the theaterhouse too late
To avoid the uptown 6, FB event already accepted.

The rhythm of stop names' an earworm I miss, but
Can't remember the order of 42nds and 23rds; I
Forget about 77th.

Hissing spit and tears walking to and from the play,
I squeal—piggish at the thrill and panic of placemaking.

It's been six years. But it was six years—nearly.
Six weeks from a diploma turned six months on my ma's
Red couch.

The go-to falafel spot with the too costly so tasty
baklava I penny-pinched for shut down so I

Chew on a gummy shark got from the bodega
Up on Madison, the area's second best.
Ate the head thick,

Building jutting up mauve on the avenue
As a brick pillar against matte felt grey.

Facade's clear of scaffolding, now. Now—
The long-shadowed, recycled set piece of
My noir night.

I slip my fingers into mortar and push in
To my second knuckles. Slice through putty.

Push in far enough to grab at it. Palm curled
Brick. Pull as hard as I pushed. I rip it out—every
Fucking brick.

The scaffoldinglessness in view. Blue gummy tacky
In cavities. Scrapes along fingers. The jut, the spit.

*the brick, the brick*

WILLIAM G. FLORES

# My Neighborhood's Approval

My neighborhood ain't perfect and this I can admit
But it's also full of people that survive and don't submit
These houses need some loving and we ask but they keep slumming
I think they want us out but they're happy checks are coming
Every year it's getting worse cause the rent keeps going up
Living here is like a curse but we refuse to give this up
When I say this I mean my hood cause my hood has been my home
No matter what the struggle it has never let me go
From the mothers down the street and the youngsters playing ball
And the Market on the corner with the sign that will not fall
The neighbors that took care of us, that seem to be on call
Cause when something needs a fixing you would think we do it all
So if people try to come to build a project in my hood
I would welcome it with open arms if they only understood
That our voices more than matter when you're building where we live
And you'll need my hood's approval cause if not we wont forgive.

CAMILA GODOY DELGADO

# estuvo "bien"

it was "okay," ending as it did, she asserts
"okay," in legible air quotes
as if to suggest it was everything but
"okay," she repeats
as she once prior explained
except, that explanation never truly occurred
and now it is doubly "true"
also with a lowercase t

"okay," like that shady store down the street
proclaiming a "sale" with prices reduced
but first raised
"okay," as when I "accidentally" ran out of gas
at *la Costa del Sol*
or bought that rancid "fresh" guacamole
at my local *taquería* (of sorts)
"okay," a writer short on words
resorting to apologetic quotation marks

and it resounds—to leave it, as it were, "okay"—
with every masked and cautious "hello"
traveling our virtual worlds
and it has worn, that "okay"
on moments shared
perhaps robbed us, even
of time spent

and since 2x it was "uttered"
in an alternative space
where I could not look into her
large and telling eyes

I am obliged to believe
"this too shall pass"—through

and I have "stopped"
and she has "stopped"
and, with time, it'll all "die down"
and, with time, we'll both "forget"
and, with time, we'll lie "peacefully" in our graves
and it'll all be just peachy

WILLIAM A. GONZÁLEZ

# Poor Westlake

Poor Westlake
My *corazon* burns
To know that you are
Disappearing right before
My eyes

You are the *Pueblo*
That made us
We played *canicas*
To dancing *trompos*
On sidewalks with unfilled potholes
You gave us the alley
In between Union Avenue
And Union Drive
Where we would box
Where we would
Play soccer
Where the LAPD
Would beat gangsters, *raza*
And anything with a heartbeat
Just for fun
Then would turn around
And hand us baseball cards

Poor Westlake
You're the heart
Of working class men and women
Connected to arteries from
Mexico, El Salvador, Honduras,
Nicaragua, and Guatemala, that
Is quietly being colonized—West of
Downtown Los Angeles as these
*Letras* kiss paper goodbye

Poor Westlake
You're that *pueblo*
That has been screaming
Forever but nobody
Has ever taken the time
To listen to your cries
You gave us *El Piojito*
The first El Pollo Loco
The Original Tommy's
Invisible city councilmen
Who bought crack at MacArthur Park

Poor Westlake
You provided
The battlefield of a silent
American inner-city war in
The 1980s and 1990s that
Never made the news
In almost every single block
Of your existence
A human being
Has been murdered

Poor Westlake
Gentrification is moving
Our *gente* to the valleys
You have become
Juicy prime real estate
Ugly rich souls
Walk their dogs
With hatred glowing
Through their pupils today

Poor Westlake
Even though capitalism
Is swallowing you alive
You will forever
Be embedded inside
Of our *corazon*

GUSTAVO ADOLFO GUERRA VÁSQUEZ

## *Hombres* who kiss men

*Amorcito corazón*
*Yo tengo tentación de un beso**
Busted!
While I was trying to target
my butch *hermana chapicana*
in a game of "you're out if…"
by saying "anyone who has kissed someone
of the same gender"

She called me out and forced me
to flashback to the days
when my father and I
would give each other
the most tender *besos* on the cheeks and
while nowadays
we don't kiss anymore
because in this country
men are not supposed to kiss each other
in public
I remember those days
*con mucha* nostalgia
the days when he and I would walk down the street
hand in hand
or him with his arm on my shoulder
until some guy in a 4 x 4 truck
with an "off-roaders for Reagan" sticker took it
upon himself
to bring my father and I further apart severing one
of the few umbilical strings that still bound us to
each other
by yelling the "f" word at us
and I don't mean the four-letter one

It hit me like a ton of homophobic bricks
*un balde de agua fría*
both at the same time.

*"¿Qué dijo?"*
My father asked wondering what he said

*"Nada"*
I say
holding on to the fleeting pre-pubescent
moment of father and son tenderness
before this country's gender regimes
locked us up like immigrants
without "authorization"
but where does the "authorization"
to kiss your father or son or uncle or anyone else
who is willing and able to kiss you back reside?

because if when Chente and Alejandro Fernández
kiss on the mouth
people wonder whether Chente's bi-sexual

then at what point
will my son sever a tie
that binds us and
deny me a kiss on the lips
*¿En la boca?* the *metiches* might gasp
Or will I be the one
to stop
to shield him
from those who will say
"you kiss your dad on the mouth? That's grosssssss!
Boys don't kiss boys…"

I mean
he already caught flack
from his 5-year old classmates
for taking a pink lunchbox to school
in not-so-kind kindergarten.

"That's for girrrrrls" the little boy said
so my son came home saying "ew, that's for girls"
when he saw something that he
wasn't supposed to like
*¿Cómo le doy la fuerza?*
How do I give him the strength to say
*"¡¿y qué?!*
*si las malas lenguas eso quieren"*
so what… if that is what they want?
How do I gather the strength
to kiss those I love
if they'll kiss me back?
How do we gather the strength to break those chains
that bind us
instead of breaking those ties
that bind us to each other?

*Amorcito corazón*
*Yo tengo tentación de un beso…*

* *"Amorcito corazón" is a Mexican love song with lyrics by Pedro de Urdimalas and music by Manuel Esperón. It was used in the movie "Nosotros los pobres" in which Pedro Infante performs the song.*

ROBERT FARID KARIMI

## *venganza* of the dream people

under the pillows
we lay.
>  (guatemalans are so much better when they are tiny
>  and can be put in a box).

we
have had our
skeletons taken from us
and replaced with United States wires.
our spines
make good hangers.

our new skin,
fabric from our land,
makes us portable
for tourists to place us
into their pockets.          *qué* cute, *no?*

all we are good for is          to carry dreams,
                            to carry memory.

we are ready
to dream for you.

bring us across the border,
place us under your pillow.
>  (guatemalans are so much better when they are tiny
>  and can be put in a box).

we are the cheapest trinket
you can bring home.
the cheapest piece of our mythology

you can sleep with.
no middle man necessary,
easily bendable.     *qué* wonderful, *no*?

all we are good for is                        to carry dreams,
                                   to carry memory.

don't forget,
buy a jacket!
buy a wooden trinket.
a painting *también.*

sell us,
so we spread across *gringolan...* we mean, *el norte.*

the fabric we humbly sell holds lives in its thread.
you are wearing history, misery, and lies.
the CIA never bargained that this thread
connecting us all would still retain its memory:

don't worry, we
will be civil in dreamlandia,
authentic we
practiced for over 25 years,
*no te preocupes.* we

are the dream people
underneath your head, we
are the spirits
of the long lost dead,
who are now found, we
now have a new sound
*soñamos*
inside;
inside
the waves of memory
never subside.
it is an orchestration
that combines

with the dust of the dead
as they decompose
and compose
a new wave of energy, we
are their carriers.

experts blame all your neurosis
on television and social media,
our night vision
will be your new truth.

*por* please
let us take away your cares.

close your eyes,
dream away.
we will take full responsibility
for your night-mar…
we mean, *sueños*,
at your convenience, *por supuesto*.

bring us
home.

place us
under your pillow.

     we
are ready

        to dream
        to remember          for you.

all we are good for is       to carry dreams,
        to carry memory.

you are too lazy to do it for yourselves,
you have lost your history and culture
and need ours to wear and carry to bed.

we will live forever inside your head.

remember:

      guatemalans are so much better when they are tiny
      and can be put in a box.
      easier to place         into your mind.
                  sleep…
                    sleep
                      sleep.
                          *buenas*
                            *noches*

PATRICK MULLEN-COYOY

# Where is Guatemala?

"Where in Mexico is Guatemala?"
The question hangs in the air,
                                        waiting,
For an answer that lies beyond your grasp.

How do you tell them where Guatemala is?
How can you give them a sense of a place, a feeling—
        a memory, really
—that even you barely know?

You start off easily enough:
            *What* is Guatemala?

It's *mixtas*, it's *rellenitos*, it's *shecas*.
It's *tiendas* selling *típica* and
Hastily-painted souvenirs
That you'll treasure for the next decade.

It's chicken busses and *tuk tuks*.
Carpets made of woodchips leading up to centuries-old cathedrals.
Smog mixes with incense and sawdust to create the sweetest scent—
            *aire chapín*.

It's conversations over dinner about family
Virtues, views, and values
            Not quite Ladino
            Not quite *K'iche'*
Not something the sociologist-anthropologist-tourist
Can easily catalogue in their guidebook.

And it *is* the poverty, the violence, the aching.
A rage against the governments—
      whether *de aquí o de allá*
—that hate your people.
Eyes washed out by red and red and red,
      and never quite finding the *líder* you were promised.

It's a family, a home, a life that's just $500 dollars away, minimum.
That longed-for motherland where you don't belong,
That all the photos in the world can't capture, can't consume, just
Can't.

It's kissing *abuelita adiós*
And the tears on the plane home,
Holding tight to those souvenirs that won't keep those memories
Already fading from sight.

Hard as I try, I still can't tell you where Guatemala is.

WILLY PALOMO

# Pupusas or Lucha

WITH A LINE SAMPLED FROM NEW YORK TIMES' RIDICULOUS FEATURE
"THE CORN CAKES OF RED HOOK."

They look like tortillas
& *yanquis* can't tell the difference

*entre mexicano y guanaco,*
*entrées como accents y pimienta.*

Call them tamale pancakes, stuffed
*masa frita*, the humble lovechild

of a *quesadilla y calzone*. The Spanish
couldn't pronounce *popotlax* either

—what we called *pupusas* before we forgot
the taste of *nawat y libertad.*

Take a knife to my skin
if you want to see what we're made of,

but real *guanacxs*, we ain't afraid
to get our hands dirty.

I stink *loco* with *lorocco's* reefer, slap
& massage *masa* until its ass-fat.

My father used to slap my hands
for squeezing *maseca* like play-doh.

*Making pupusas is women's work,* he'd say.
Call me a *maricon*. Once, he threw out

an entire restaurant-bought batch
*porque la salsa no era autentico*. Whatever.

Now, you can find pizza-*pupusas*
*y pupusas* from SLC. Now, I smack

fried chicken like God's Son
into *la masa* & watch it

pop & tremble *campero*
into a bassline of *humo y fuego*.

Call them what you like.
As for me, I'll call them domingos

where dinner sets off fire alarms
& the entire house smoked with *mantequilla*.
I'll call them midnights mama stayed up
to make enough to pay off

debt collectors, the way we gave our best
to survive & fill our children's bellies,

leaving them all licking their lips.

WILLY PALOMO

# El Hombre Machete

AFTER TÍA TERE

Tía Tere told me his real name
      was Daniel. *Ojos como las boquitas*
          *mojadas de botellas cristales.* Face,
             a chilled Pilsner with a cracked side.

Daniel, *un mano amputada, mitad*
      *de una oración callado en su puño.*
          Daniel, a bloody foot running nowhere
             by itself. Daniel, who split Usulután

into myriad directions with the slash
      of his machete: arm, leg, leg, arm, head,
          broken votive statues to a thirsty god.
             Whose horse hooves echo the gut-spill

smack of his blade and leave police
      with slippery limbs to gather and no
          liquor to bury them. Daniel, better
             known by locals as *el hombre machete.*

¿What else do you call a motherfucker
    who hacks apart men, women, and children,
        for the nickel-and-dime of their pockets,
           *cabeza por cerveza* and vice versa?

Everyone knows to run away from an indio
    with a name that ugly—everyone except
        for my Tía, of course. *¡Don't be a hero,*
          *niña estúpida!* cried *abuelita* in chorus

with all the other rational people.
>Naw. While mamas seized their babies
>>and grown men ran and left their balls
>>>at their tables, *niña* Tere held her *mesas*


down, just a teenage *campesina y cocinera*,
>a female David against midget Salvadoreño
>>Goliath, and she wasn't 'bout to let some
>>>crazy machete-wielding psycho-killer


chop her family into *chicharrones.*
>*¿Do you know who I am?* he asked her,
>>eyes squinting like a blade. Of course,
>>>my Tía gave him a side-eye twice


as sharp and spat *¡hell, I don't give
>a fuck!* She ain't move, not even
>>as he declared, *Soy el Diablo*
>>>and pulled out the gory machete,


face twisted with satanic laughter.
>Naw. *Niña* Tere laughed along cuz
>>she been already seen the devil
>>>and he ain't him. So he swung


his machete, a warning strike at the table
>and got it stuck. My *Tía* didn't hesitate.
>>Behind her back, she pulled a seething
>>>red poker from the fire. Said she stabbed


ese carajo in the neck as he shrieked
>like a butchered sow and fled, leaving
>>behind his machete, staggering back
>>>to his horse, never to be heard from again.

Tía Tere tells me all this as I help her
        prepare *hojas de guineo* for Christmas
                tamales, my punishment for snapping
                        the limbs off my sister's Barbie dolls.

Her hand a heavy slash across
        my cheek as she sits, humming
                softly to *himnos*, with legs not even
                        her diabetes could take from her.

I ask her if she's a murderer. Smiling
        a crooked old lady smile, she tells me,
                she would do it again to any man
                        who acts like he owns this world.

HAROLD TEREZÓN

# You Roque, Only You

You are the Roque toasted & grinded of my *horchata*

You are the sweet Roque whose crumbs I lick off my plate with each sip
of Nescafé

You are the Roque melting through my every *maize pore* sizzling on the grill
like my great grandparents' whispers

You are my plate of Roque fried, annoyed, with beans & cream before mass
every Sunday

You are the quintessence Roque loving underneath the ruin in which
we fell in love with

You are the most saddest Roque of the Roques in my garden

You are the Roque that punts and shoots the rose in my heart

You are once, twice, three times a wet Roque & I love you when we are
together in Guatemala, Mexico, Arizona, the moments shared with
every border crossed

You are the Roque I trust in, the blood of suffering people who implores
me, begs me, & orders me to stop the repression

You are the sonofthegreatRoque manifested in my language forgotten

You are the Roque that rocks my streets with swollen beats & black-eyed
rhymes

You are the Roque I will build dreams tragic nails will not puncture

You are the Roque of the Pacific that awakens the American dream

You are the Roque that battles my tendency to define myself as a nation

You are the Roque that invites the embracement of all the atoms battling inside me

You are the Roque deferred, festering like a sagging sore set to explode

You are the hidden Roque broken, exiled in revolution's thighs before returning home

You are not my first Roque. Or my last. What's there to say?

You are the Roque Ocean stepping out of my dream & into my 1993 Camry XL. Yeah I am talking to you, Roque

You are the very kinky kind of Roque you don't take home to mother

You are our Magical Roque ready to reverse the conquest back to its origin with bicycle kicks, jukes, & tricks only to be massacred when we step onto the fields again

You are the Roqueman, Roqueman, can do whatever a Roque can, spin a web in disguise, break a jail any size. Look out! Here comes the Roqueman!

You are the only Roque, & alone in loving you & reciting your name in all times of the night I forget I throw myself to drunkenness & perdition

# In Case You Forget

I did not give birth to you
so you could play all day
Oh no
you will not lounge around
like kings & queens of Spain
I don't care how cute & young
you think are
You will get off your lazy ass
& wash dishes
sweep the kitchen & living room
clean the bathroom
take out the trash
& cut the grass
even if you need scissors
to keep the grass short
You will not get
bad grades at school
because we did not cross borders
risking our lives
so you can chat all day
with your friends
& come home with a B
I don't care
& I didn't ask how high
you think a B is
You will go to college
You will not consider marriage
or have a boyfriend or girlfriend
until you graduate
Let me remind you that
if I say the sky is green
even if you see it purple

the sky is still green
Just remember
I got the iron's cord
your father's sandals
& a whole lot of olive branches
in the backyard
if you think to say otherwise
& don't think reporting me
to social services
will change a thing
because when I get out of jail
I will come back for you
because there's no way
you will end up like us

JANEL PINEDA

# How English Came to Grandma

English first met Grandma in her kitchen
as she cut and peeled mangos and
*sandía* and *mamey*

The Beatles blazing from her small radio
20-something-year-old Elba danced
to "A Hard Day's Night,"
singing English into existence
in a place it never should have arrived
(at least not
in the  v i o l e n t   way it did).

Like a work of *brujeria*,
English enamored her into
thinking the U.S.     perfect.
For grandma,
everything *americano**

*not synonymous with everything American
or even everything *estadounidense*
for her, *americano* was simply
everything she'd been taught to deem
"better"

was soaked in English
and she wanted to bathe
in that language's ocean—
no matter how bloody
she pretended it didn't look.

English first colonized her ears
then her voice
then her feet.
She fled El Salvador

in search of it—
*Los Estados Unidos,*
the obvious place
to go, the place where
everybody ended up
whether they wanted to
or not
'cause come on where else would they go but to
the place to which they all
belonged, no
I don't mean they belonged there
or that the U.S. wanted them to belong there
I mean:
the U.S. practically own/ed/s
them, whether or not on paper.
All this to tell you
the story
about how my grandmother
still does not speak English
how she tried wrestling it once
but it twisted her tongue
so instead she clings to her title of
Grandma and never *Abuela*
her I love you's instead of *te quiero*
her Beatles lyrics
her thick accented "yes ma'ams" and "right away, ma'am"
from her job cleaning houses in *wüdlan heel, paz á dina,*
sometimes even *beverlé heel*
her Spanglish
and her "I so sori"s
(because if she knew anything about English,
it was how much that language demanded
her to apologize)

MAURICIO NOVOA

# J's

I couldn't do Payless anymore—
no more K-Mart, Target, or anywhere else
selling cheap-ass knock-off, off brand,
looks-like-mama-sewed-em-together shoes.
When everyone else rocked the Air Force Ones,
I rolled in my white, $20 Shaqs
that the upper echelon in the hallways
of Parkland Middle School always stepped on
'cause they weren't shit anyways.

But when I saw those Red-Black-and-White
Air Jordans on the bargain rack for $80
in my junior year of college, I had to have them.

I walked through Glenmont still JC-Penny-bargain-bin fly,
feeling nice but still bottom dollar,
but with my J's on I could drift
through the same sidewalks Cuz stood on
without his fiends asking me for a dollar
for a McDouble then laughing because they could tell
I was as hungry as he was. I spent $80 so I could feel
like a baller, and I was so elated a 10 foot hoop
no longer seemed out of my reach.

My brother worked 30+ hours a week for minimum wage,
dropping out of high school so he could go full time
at the Shoe Dept., and every weekend he'd walk
to Foot Locker and drop $120 to $200 on some new
Foamposits, Jordan's, or anything else the North Faced,
Levi Jeaned, big money, small bank account teens wore.
He'd wait on the new Bred 11's that everyone saved their dough
to buy, that 20 people got stabbed for at the midnight release.

MAURICIO NOVOA

# Dandelion Graves

Kids of the forgotten refugees, soilless seeds
On the run from the barrel of a gun on their knees
Ducking immigration until they're stationed as far as DC
Or LA or the Bay, that was back in Reagan's 80s
When numbers shot up like a fiend, crack rock being steamed
In the apartment down the hallway from my mama's babies
But that wasn't the home that my parents made for me
Georgia Ave and Urbana in lily white Montgomery
Except the Glenmont section was brown as *Abuela's* coffee
And the smell of asphalt would never wash off *Papi*
A good day was a meal that wasn't frijoles and cheese
So my dreams were drenched in leftover Chinese
But pull yourself and you'll succeed is the bullshit they would feed
So everyone drank piss until they couldn't see
Cuz how's a kid like me supposed to think when it's engraved
That the only future that awaits is a dandelion grave

SUSANA NOHEMI AGUILAR-MARCELO

# Slam

YOUR MOM stares you down. Her eyebrows make mountains and her mouth snaps shut in anger—you weren't watching your little brother. Her eye bags look like tar pits and her jaw is tight. You should know better, she says. Because your father is always working and she's always working. She needs help but you're stupid. You useless, selfish girl, *a la gran puta*, what were you thinking?!

She hits you until time becomes a tornado.

***

Years later, you will sit in the kitchen of your mom's new house. You'll joke with your brother, who will then be a young man. After all it grew back, you'll say. But he will never let you forget it. With the poise of Johnny Cash, he'll play "Folsom Prison Blues" on his guitar. Your eyes will always travel to where he strains his pinky on the chords. Then your mom will nag you to drink your vitamins and Echinacea, because you must take care of yourself. And when will you learn not to over-pluck your eyebrows or wear heels with shorts? You'll tell her you are drinking your vitamins. But she'll laugh because you have eye bags like tar pits, and when will you ever learn?

***

But now you're mad. She said you can't watch *Tom and Jerry* until you wash the dishes. It's your favorite episode, so you make a face. Her hand sways back and forth in a threatening motion. You know what's coming if you disobey. But you'll go to the bathroom first. She can't prove you don't need to.

The bathroom door has no lock, and you have to slam it or it won't close. The apartment is really a slanted garage knocked together by the cheapest labor found squatted on Wilshire Boulevard. You dread how the walls screech. They remind you who you are. As if you could ever forget.

***

The landlord tells your parents that his dog, a Boxer, has his own space next to the garage. It looks just like him. Nobody knows you sometimes sneak into the dog house. The smell of cedar lures you in. You press your spine against the wall and admire how perfectly straight it is. Just like Spike's house complete with white paint and a red roof. The dog is our neighbor, your dad jokes. You laugh. Well, you do share fleas and a door you crack open at night because it's hot, though you can't sleep anyway listening to your mom crying, soaking her pillow with secrets and fears. At least the dog scares some of the mice, you think. Then you bite your tongue and pray for your mom and dad. They're too tired to pray for themselves.

\*\*\*

Taking baby steps to the bathroom, you notice your little brother walking behind you. But you ignore him—this is about you. You slam the bathroom door. A familiar shrill slices into your thoughts. Your heart beats in your toes. His hand is caught. Guilt rots your heart. There's blood dripping. The tiles quiver—your mom is coming. You wrap his hand in ribbons of toilet paper. On your knees, you hurry to wipe blood from the bleached tiles you've seen your mom clean time and time again. But all you see is blood. Your mouth turns dry. Your face turns red. You cry knowing you'll never be the same.

The door swings open. Your mom plucks the flesh of his pinky from the wedge of the door. This is why I hate you, she screams.

\*\*\*

It is this memory that will haunt you when he turns six years old. He will ask, Why is this pinky not the same? He'll hold up his hands, side by side, aligning both pinkies for you to see. One will always be shorter and slightly crooked with a hard, stunted nail. What happened to the pinky tip? he will insist holding up his hands closer to your face. His brown eyes wide, waiting for a response. And you, with a crooked smile, will tell him a mouse ate it.

SUSANA NOHEMI AGUILAR-MARCELO

# An Inchoate Symphony

WHEN I WAS YOUNG, I encountered God in the form of a question, but I didn't answer. So I spent my life calling him back.

Pray the rosary. Count ten beads. Repeat. Count ten tears. [Dear reader, insert what comes next.

I've been in the hospital every year since 2007. That year I cradled my premature baby in my palm. She opened and closed her fingers as if saying goodbye before she died. Our nurse said the baby's lungs are too tiny and there's nothing they can do. White linens soaked up my blood. I was pale like snow.

28th Street Elementary girls told me I couldn't be a "queen" because my parents weren't Mexican even though I watched *Carrusel*, the Mexican novela, just like they did, and I wished I was blonde, blue-eyed like our favorite character Maria Joaquina. You like the same things I like, I told them. But they said my skin wasn't white enough. But I had a solution: I ate rose petals, the red and white speckled ones growing in front of our boarding house, convinced they'd make me beautiful.

Red is my favorite color like blood, bricks, creamy red lipstick that smells of honey, and roses that grow from unmarked graves. We lived in South Central until I was ten. I helped my mother throw away the dead mice caught between the floorboards.

*To my brother and sister: I was nine. You were two and four, respectively. That means that as I learned to walk through fire, you learned not to walk too close.*

"*La siguanaba* is here!" I'd yell chasing after my brother and sister with my long, shiny black hair over my face. We'd run away laughing and crying.

I sprinkle salads with lavender and calendula. [Insert my fears, your fears, here.]

My mother, while cleaning, played her favorite love songs by Marco Antonio Solis. We thought he was Jesus.

God tells me not to open my eyes but I do.

White calms me like an all white room, like a white, cozy sweater smeared with red lipstick on days that feel like my bronchial tubes will tighten in Soprano 1 until my chest bursts.

Fireworks are pretty.

My sister played the violin when she was a little girl. Her long, black hair fell over her face as she carefully opened the case, took the violin out, and with a cloth cleaned it as if she were washing the face of the man she loves. Her teacher scolded her: "That's not how you play." My sister over-tuned the strings. They snapped.

My sister willingly checked herself into a mental institution in Texas for a few days to get away "from everything." She was surrounded by clear December ice. *I'm sorry I couldn't be there. I'd hold your hand, caress your face, comb your thick hair falling to your waist, and tell you everything will be okay. You never liked hair buns and braids because they were always too tight. We could pretend we're little girls again. We could lie silent in bed staring at the moon wondering what it's like to be queens. Then, I'd collect your tears in recycled jam jars and throw them in the lake.*

Whenever I'm stressed, I listen to Yo Yo Ma's prelude from Bach´s Cello Suite No. 1. It makes me want to crawl under a mountain of yellow leaves and hibernate.

My inner clockwork is busted. Fix me. Wind me up like a wooden doll.

I want coffee with Bailey's before my 7 p.m. class. But I already drank a venti Americano in the morning. The lady next to me in the coffee shop says I must be stressed. She eyeballs my Louis Vuitton bag, my anniversary present, with suspicion. "What could you possibly be stressed about?" she asks. "You're not playing the game of life right." I snapped. "What the hell do you know about crying in the rain and feeling so small you want to crawl in between the floorboards and die?"

Coffee stains are beautiful. [Breathe, please.]

Did Yo Yo Ma ever snap a string?

My mother had nightmares of guerillas and shadows almost every night. I prayed to God, waited for her cries, and then shushed her to sleep.

Jesus paid for our lives; he needs a refund.

Every day, I wash my face in a circular motion. I brush my teeth, clean the wax in my ears, pluck unwanted hair. I perform these ablutions convinced Emily Dickinson was on to something.

I want to fold into myself. Crease my limbs. Make me a graceful origami crane.

My father lives off coffee and cigarettes. He's a trucker and never gets sick. A six-foot cholo threatened my five-foot-five father with a gun. The bullet burst through the Pacoima house's wall, past my head.

My mother is always sick. I'm always sick. We're all sick.

I threw myself on the carpet and thought of the time my father taught me how to say "world" in English. My six-year-old tongue curled, and I said "worm" instead. We both laughed. And when my father came in the house, he stood while we were all on the floor. His ear covered in blood. The cholo jumped in his getaway car as soon as my father took his gun. "*No me convenía morir,*" he had told me a few years ago when I asked him what had happened. It wasn't convenient to die, he had said.

Count the many ways I love you, the ways I've let you down, am letting you down, will let you down.

In a hospital bed in 2007, my heart pounded from a high on postpartum drugs. In the dark, I counted ten rosary beads for ten toes.

Because this is how I count my way to God.

# 3

*La Poesia de Todos*

ROY G. GUZMÁN

# Midwestern Skulls for the Broken Latino

People who crave the jaw
& not the fox's gentle tail—
   his land mine

   of teeth; a temporary exit
for those who yearn to return to the coyote's
      tent to reclaim their belongings—
the chopped head, the neck
before it was plucked from the rest of the body
like a hen's for dinner. Antique shops

   for raccoons' clawed feet;
                  a necklace
for a woman in labor. After the snow melts
the dead return to their natural habitats—
eyes barely shut under the charcoal, whiskers
         trapped in the pinecones.
Some secrets are better rolled into the mouths

   of strangers
     when they sleep. A father can make up
suffering's seasons: leave in the afternoon,
then sneak in through a windowless frame—

though these, too, can be called winter & fall
    & held by a child's contemptuous hands
in a garden where only the wind
can be torn from branches.

       Did they really mean
to leave us shipwrecked—those sailors
who recognized flesh but not what the flesh
        can camouflage? People covet

the mandible as it's handed down
    for all to drink from. In his hands
I appear dead—
but here, here in my chest, is where my father
    finds the new continent


    of directions measured in forgiveness.
I sleep in the wilderness,
like a fox loitering in a frozen meadow,
                    & I'll feed him forgiveness
                      if he asks.

ROY G. GUZMÁN

# Amor Eterno

FOR WALTER ORLANDO TRÓCHEZ (1982-2009), HONDURAN POLITICAL
& LGBTIQ RIGHTS ACTIVIST

The gray, chipped wall you stared away at
murmured. Bruises

    you wore with honor,
          *verbenas*
      that encircled your abdomen.

        Lifeless frame.

Kidnapped by four men
whose masks were as old as their faces,

                             you escaped.

They brutalized you.
Men repeatedly disappear
             behind the faith

        of a brother's cruelty—

      in the rancid smell
of torture. Eight days later,
        shot
        as you walked downtown.

In the morgue for hours

before the police could lift the dust
      from under your shadow.

            Impunity.
At fourteen,

you contracted the virus.
The headlines said

the irony was that it didn't kill you,
                              but that bullets

at night
   emerge like shooting stars in need
                        of shelter.

            Homeless

with a father abroad—
because all our fathers dream
                     of misplacing us—

   you asked for asylum,

died
   before it was approved.

How many brown bodies will give up
                        their bodies

   so other brown bodies
           might live? In all the interviews

your mother said
you were not her biological son.

            But she loved you anyway

as if she had carried you
      in her belly

      just like her other two.

                    Where I was born,

corpses are left to bloat
            on examination tables. Justice

            is a blossom
from which roaches
                        crawl. *Our work*

*here is done*, they announce,


squirming like gods

            in despair.

They've learned one thing about nurture:

a wound is often the last thing
            that needs healing.

SILVIO SIRIAS

# Writing About Central America:
# A Translation of Love

IN MY JOURNEY toward becoming a writer, the most fortuitous curve in the road was my parents' decision to move back to their homeland: Nicaragua. I was eleven years old at the time and until then I had only lived in Los Angeles, the city of my birth. In California, since my mother's English-language skills were limited, whenever she and I would brave the streets without my bilingual father, she'd gently nudge me forward at every encounter to act as her translator. Although I found the experience interesting at first, after a few years stuck at the job, translating became a chore. But once we were back in her homeland, I ceased being the translator. The freedom was exhilarating.

Yet, ironically, today, as a novelist—and I suspect it's also the case with other U.S writers of Central American descent—I'm once again engaged in an act of translation, albeit a variant I find fascinating.

From the moment I first visited my parents' birthplace, at the age of seven, I became acutely aware that Nicaragua and Nicaraguans were a land and a people vastly different from the United States and its populace. I found the landscape of Nicaragua—physical and human—mesmerizing. Nicaraguans were open to an extent I had never experienced, and their joy for life was contagious. Yet at the same time there was an underlying sadness—manifested in an acceptance of their lot that I still find baffling—due to excruciating poverty and centuries of never-ending political turmoil.

During my Nicaraguan adolescence, I came to adore the country and its people—in particular the stories I learned while there. I shed my American skin and embraced a new identity as a full-fledged Nicaraguan. Before long I was fitting in perfectly and I ended up loving the seven years I spent in my ancestral homeland.

When I returned to Los Angeles, at age eighteen and on my own to attend college, I soon learned what I wanted to do more than anything in life: to describe the sights, sounds, tastes, relationships, and experiences of Nicaragua to anyone who was willing to listen. Of course, conveying these things over lunch was impossible. Within that limited time frame I could only produce a distant echo of what I wished to say. As a result, my tales were invariably lost in translation.

But I always knew, instinctively, that the best way to inform English-speakers about the lives of their Nicaraguan brethren was through the written word. My dilemma, however, was that I had no idea what I needed to do to achieve this. Blindly, I plunged into the study of literature—in Spanish, a language I grew to love while living in Nicaragua. Eventually I earned a doctorate, but that was of little help in bringing the Nicaraguan experience to an English-speaking audience.

That changed, though, and in an earth-shattering way, when I was introduced to U.S. Latino and Latina literature—a literature written mostly in English by authors with backgrounds similar to my own. Their works struck me like a bolt of lightning, and I started to read them voraciously because I knew they embodied the models I so desperately needed for telling my own stories.

But then I faced a more challenging hurdle. Several decades passed since I left Nicaragua. As a result, I was too far removed from the stories I wanted to tell. To translate these tales from Spanish into English with conviction, I needed to exist in their midst. I needed to fill every one of my senses with the experiences that had been haunting me since adolescence.

My quest to become a writer who translated stories from his ancestral homeland left me only one choice: I gave up my position as an associate professor of Spanish and U.S. Latino and Latina literature in North Carolina, and moved back to Nicaragua. Fortunately, my wife, Erinn, embraced my decision. In fact, it was she who first encouraged me to return to Central America. She believed in my dream. Our friends, on the other hand, thought that it was sheer lunacy for me to give up tenure and take a leap of faith for such a nebulous goal. But time has proven that I needed to be in this part of the world, first in Nicaragua and then in Panama, to become a novelist.

It has been seventeen years since we've moved to Central America, and time has passed swiftly. At first there were many trials—financially and, surprisingly, with my being able to readjust to a culture in which I once felt completely at home. But today I can honestly say that my life has never been more centered. I've learned to reside happily in a cultural and linguistic yin and yang. The only disadvantage I've encountered is that I am too far removed from U.S. readers to be able to promote my work in person as often as I'd like.

Regardless, thanks to my decision to return to Central America I've become a published novelist—in the United States and in English. The stories, as I suspected, are here for the taking. They appear as if by magic everywhere

I go. All I need to do is to keep my eyes, ears, and heart open. Bernardo and the Virgin, Meet Me under the Ceiba, The Saint of Santa Fe, and The Season of Stories stand as proof of that. In fact, tales that move me are in such infinite supply that I lament not having enough years left to tell them all.

Living in Central America inspires the Nicaraguan-American writer within me. In my novels, I appropriate experiences that call to me and attempt to render them in a manner that English-language readers can make their own. Thus, the circle is now complete. I am back to where I started as a child growing up in Los Angeles: translating for others. Admittedly, it's a different type of translation than what I used to do for my mother, but this time it's the kind of interpreting I truly love.

ORIEL MARÍA SIU

# Moridero migratorio

A LOS QUE MUEREN EN CAMINO HACIA ESTE NORTE

Decadente vida la que marcan los relojes
Opaca el minuto y los soles ya en la hoguera
Heridas abiertas desprendiendo sus hedores
Un gusano alegre; y las carnes descompuestas.

Las moscas en fiesta merodean el banquete
Las células que expiran y los gases ya en su baile;
Regocijo suelto en estos bailes de esta muerte
Hoy tu cuerpo inerte; estos bailes son tu suerte.

Suerte que viene de un destino que es condena
Condena cruel que en moridero te conviertes;
Moridero viejo, desde hace mucho milenario
Moridero nuevo, porque siempre te reinventas.

URIEL QUESADA

# Spoken Portrait

TRANSLATED BY NADIA REIMAN

I DIDN'T SPOT HIM until the moment he held hostage the only empty table at the café. I had just sat down as well, even though my spot was a pretty lousy one: right in the middle of the hall with my back to the door. Therefore every time someone opened it a current of air entered to beat me up while I held on to my cappuccino and cursed under my breath. Outside, New York remained dirty after the last snowfalls. Great pieces of coldness laid everywhere without melting. Hard, darkened, and trampled water resisted futilely the incessant paces. I had been wanting to write a poem the whole afternoon about this city which always managed to horrify me yet beckon me to return. I had walked around in search of a magical place, one of those unknown spaces that suddenly stay with you forever. After a few hours, what I had were chapped lips, an insensible nose, and an anvil of clothing that my body wasn't made to hold up. I was dreaming in Latin American that a good cup of coffee would cure all of my ailments and would allow me to open up a parenthetical space amidst the havoc of all that is materials and souls, a havoc that could not sit still even when the temperatures plummeted and the vespertine news forecasted another winter advisory.

I had entered the café following a current of people. Almost all of them approached the counter, ordered their drinks to go, and disappeared. When it came my turn to order, I hadn't made up my mind yet and thus, in a way, had exposed myself: only a true foreigner could take the luxury of wasting the employees' time, (probably political science, philosophy, or film students), the great names of tomorrow that needed to have patience today because the stranger required a few extra seconds to think even though behind him the line of awaiting customers consequently grew and lost their minds. I think I mentioned before that I sat in a bad spot. More than a table, it was a round chessboard held up by one central leg. Someone had taken one of the chairs. Without it, the board looked huge, desolate, like I could never be entertaining a guest across it.

People came and went, opened the door, I froze. I took a glance around the area in front of me, an inaccessible paradise made up of little square tables with their average, run-of-the-mill chairs. A woman read the paper. Two men laughed quietly and eyed distantly the movement around them. A group of Hispanics attempted to make themselves comfortable amidst large shopping bags. I felt again the impulse to write a poem rising. I scribbled down a couple of lines, but finally I crumpled up the page and dedicated myself to languor, one of my guiltiest pleasures. A few seconds (or centuries) later, the Hispanics began the rite of leaving. The instructions that they gave each other delayed even further the already lethargic process of bundling up for the cold. First, you had to put on the puffy jacket, close an endless number of buttons, zip up zippers. Then came the scarf, which was to be worn snuggly around the neck but not tightly. In order to achieve perfect scarf placement, it became necessary to unbutton the coat and start over again. The ear muffs followed, then the wool cap, and then the hat. Finally, the gloves. Once ready to leave, after making sure that all was done exactly right, they picked up the bags and began to walk between the tables like astronauts atop the lunar surface. "Excuse me," they said with an unmistakable accent. "Excuse me," they repeated as people moved to let them through without looking at them or abandoning their solitude.

At that moment, a ferocious face crossed in front of me. It spoke to the last of the Hispanics, but perhaps the Hispanic didn't understand him. The young man's face spoke again, this time pointing at the table that they had just left but that was still occupied by bits of their meal. The tired Latino attempted to summon his friends for help, but the look projected by the young man with the ferocious face didn't give him any sort of an opportunity. He argued something in broken Spanish and English, put his bags beside him, and began to pick up the cardboard cups and wipe the table clean with a napkin. Immediately after, the young man began to take possession of the place: he put his backpack on one chair, his coat, hat and gloves on another, he gave the table a final going over, and he sat down. He was tall and black, with pale eyes and wild hair. He had a sharply featured face and long hands with which he began to extract utensils from his backpack: a block of paper, pencils and pens, a magazine (actually, a clothes catalogue). With great care, he exposed each object within the limits of his territory. Then, he forgot about the world. Or at least that's what I thought.

I supposed that he studied Design. With his left hand, he kept the catalogue open; with his right he drew long strokes, stopped to contemplate details, created forms that I could in no way see. I decided that he was enrolled in Pratts and that he was a regular MOMA stalker. Five nights a week, he would bartend, he went to the gym almost on a daily basis, and he read mostly terror novels, a genre that was in after September 11, 2001. He would reside in Brooklyn, around the corner from school, or better yet, in the Lower East Side, which was closer to SoHo and the Village, not quite as artsy but with far more reasonable rent. His apartment would be located in a building built in the 19$^{th}$ century. It had to be minuscule, cramped with stuff, with posters inching all the way up to the roof, and it would have some chic detail. He would sleep alone (when he had no other choice) in an eternally unmade bed. He would eat at drastically different times every day, would usually consume more vegetables than meat and usually more pasta than vegetables. He would drink coffee to vanquish sleep and wine to regain it. He would feel like the king of the world. The rest was all about waiting for luck.

Once in a while he lifted his head, looked around without really watching, and didn't notice my impertinence in observing him even though I shamelessly followed his every move. I could get into trouble, but honestly, how often does one find a wonderful, wild face? They don't abound even in a city with limitless possibilities, like New York. The guy studied his sketch with much satisfaction, touched up a couple of details here and there, and then proceeded to tear the page out and crumple it into a perfect ball, which he then placed on the top right corner of the table. He opened up a clean page, caressed it gently with his hand, and this time, really and honestly looked around to notice his environment. For a second he seemed to lay his eyes on me, although actually, he was giving his utmost attention to something situated a bit further. Over my shoulder, to be exact. I turned to look at the cold that was coming and going without consideration, the cold that was beating my back and reminding me that I was but one more loner in New York. That's when I discovered the young girl who was huddling to keep warm under a light winter jacket. Her face was long and frazzled as if she had slept little. A small suitcase at her feet revealed her travels. The girl began taking off her winter wear, took out a cell phone from her purse, and began making some calls.

"Hey, Mike," she said the first time. "I waited for you at the airport for over an hour, and I haven't stopped looking for you since. I'm at the coffee shop in Union Square, but you're not here either... well, you promised to pick me up, Mike, remember? Let me know when you get this and come get me... Oh, and would you mind bringing my black coat? Love you, love you more."

She waited for a few minutes, perhaps with the hope that Mike would be home and simply couldn't make it to the phone on time. But Mike didn't call, and there were no available tables at the café until much, much later.

So the girl dedicated herself to finding friends. She asked everyone around if they knew where Mike was, if they had seen him, oh my God would he be all right… yes, a long trip, she explained, but she was back now. No, they had had no problems landing… do you know anything about Mike? She didn't even want to consider the possibility that he had stood her up. Again. This time it would be worse because she didn't have the keys to the apartment… he had gone to Kelan's in D.C. abruptly… always running toward the same arms… actually, my private life is not up for discussion, I apologize, I've made a mistake bringing Mike up, sorry about the inconvenience.

The drawer with the fierce face was working again. Inspired by the newcomer, I supposed, he slid his pencil frantically over the page. The moments seemed automatic, like copying spoken words. He no longer traced delicate lines; he now scribbled with anxiety, perhaps not to lose the essence of the scene. Page after page of the clothing catalogue began to close, and I could have sworn that he slid toward the corner where the crumpled first attempt laid forgotten.

The girl left Mike three phone messages. She then conversed with a so-called Rob. She sounded insecure, uncomfortable, although Rob didn't ask for any explanations. Briefly, she told him that she couldn't get into her apartment and that she maybe needed a place to stay for the night. She thanked him profusely: "You're a true friend," she said, hiding her anguish. Then she gave him directions to the café and they agreed to meet in ten minutes.

Almost immediately after, a table became available in front of the guy with the undoubtedly wild face. The girl took it, went to get something to drink, and in a second a man arrived who I assumed to be Rob. He was a little blushed by the rush and he had a paper bag with him. They greeted with a kiss on the cheek and sat down to talk.

She looked like she was about to cry, so Rob took her hand and held it in a significant way until the girl freed herself with a quick drawback of the hand, quick, but not so strong. At some point, the girl took out her phone. Rob let her check her messages but didn't approve of her making any new calls. In any case, the calls were short and actually depressed the girl even further. At that moment, Rob took out a box from the paper bag and put it in front of the girl. She hesitated, said a lot of things, but Rob didn't accept any excuses. He pushed the box toward her, asking her to untie the bow and look inside.

There was an orchid inside. The girl, with a very common gesture, looked at it doubtfully, held it up before her eyes, and was about to hold it tight against her chest. Like her, I would also have had a lot to say about such a gift. I would have liked it if the person made up a story for me, because actually, the worst one would be that Rob was saving the orchid in the fridge and had malevolently taken advantage of having it to overcome the girl's resistance. No, Rob, I'd rather you tell me that you hung up the phone, put your coat on in a hurry, and ran out to the street since you only had a few minutes to find something beautiful and make it to the café on time without risk of raising suspicion. Lie, say that you were cold, that you slipped on the ice and didn't notice the aggressive cars or people around you. There was a flower stand in the corner, behind it a little store with *norteño* music playing. You talked to the flower shop owner and she slipped to the back to find the most expensive flower in stock, a small, delicately lavender orchid. The woman brought the flower cupped between both of her hands like an offering. You didn't understand anything, Rob, but you thought that *norteño* music was the perfect accompaniment to the display of such a beautiful object. The song vaguely reminded you of some Germanic tunes that an ancient love used to loudly play on your stereo, which is why you asked the storeowner about what the lyrics meant. "It talks about the strawberry harvest of the South," she explained. "It's about the people that roamed around like gypsies around the Bible belt and didn't know how to read and write neither in English nor in Spanish." Reality has no right to spoil your evening, Rob. You reacted apologizing; but the girl was still impassible, trying to decipher in your eyes the reason behind so particular a flower on this winter night. "Are you in love?" she asked you. You stepped out into the cold without answering, with the orchid hidden inside a paper bag, shaking your head at the error of your ways, at the error of speaking too much to Hispanics. The important thing was the flower, that same flower that the girl now slowly caressed.

When the girl and Rob actually got up, they could barely hide their smiles. They both helped each other put on their coats and they left walking very close together although they didn't even touch hands. When they walked past me, she described something she had seen in a museum in Washington and Rob was carrying her bag. An eternity had traversed in front of me and I hadn't even noticed. By then my cappuccino was basically iced. Other people had left the café, so a few empty tables now encircled the guy with the unkempt face. I saw him perform the last frenetic strokes upon the page, and then crumble atop his project. In a very disciplined manner, he left his pencil to the right of the block of paper, he unmade the crumpled up ball that was on the corner, looked at it, added a little color here and there, and crumpled it up into a tiny ball again. He looked satisfied… No:

exalted. He was so sure of himself and his excellent luck that he sort of carelessly left the table and went to the bathroom without looking back. Of course I was there, vigilantly watching his every move, but he didn't have to know that. He also didn't have to know about the opportunity he was laying before me. The guy with the wild face would be back in a couple of minutes, but that was enough time for me to go up to his table and take a peek at his block of drawings.

When I approached the table, I found the blueprint of a comic in which a young girl left New York but before leaving she met up with a lover in a tiny city café. In their conversations there were no reclaims, but there were torrential tears á la Lichtenstein. At some point the male lover gave her an orchid that he had stolen. Thanks to the character's revelation (and a note at the margins), I learned that the lover was being sought after by some "Hispanics" who were going to make his debt payable through a beating. The conflict started to develop around the flower, the girl's fear and her urgency toward getting on that train. As the frames progressed, the drawings lost details until they became merely squares with scribbles. At the same time, there were more and more unattached phrases, merely suggested dialogues, and questions about what was yet to come.

It was then that I felt an urgency, a certainty that burned at chest height: the guy and I could run around that city all night until we turned the other one—the one awaiting the next winter storm—into a wondrous world of graphite and paper. I felt it so strongly that I abandoned Rob and the girl to follow the couple of lovers made desperate by separation, threat, and self-prejudices through those comic streets. I felt so close and immersed in their lives that I let time run free. Instead of listening for the young artist's return, I looked for clues about the lovers' destiny until the end. I finished leafing through the block of paper; I quickly leafed through the clothing catalogue. Then I noticed the forgotten crumpled up ball that was resting upon the right corner of the table. Without a moment's hesitation, I opened it.

I found a story previous to the two lovers fleeing into the night. When but a few steps separated its creator from me, a drawing of a man sitting at a small, round table clad like a chess board emerged from the wrinkled page and stared at me. The model was so shamelessly facing the spectator that it made a strange thrill rush through my body. Loose phrases and secret ideas encircled the sketch. And it was standing like so, with my eyes transfixed upon my paper self, that I heard a whisper over my shoulder, a sweet and fierce voice that asked me if I could help him find the ending to this story.

CHRISTINA VEGA-WESTHOFF

# from "*Suelo* Tide Cement"

Perceived as such, the voice carries—
forth—the cut/cat or the music/*culebra*.
The agony—the night entering
much too early without moon
with cloudless design—with
duct tape in recreation-izing
recolonization—new / neozonation
I am reading the words you are reading
snacktime creation. The
riff resonates yet we don't know why
or when or fonetic remembrances.
Across from


construction / quantities

been lifted from the notion of
breathless

yes, who cares, this is the
being (I) (we) create

you though understand the
future conditional

good day to each in
passing

*buenas*
   X
    cut short
hunger as an escaped entity
      foreign

# Juancito

HOW I LOVED coming out of my house in Zacamil at the hour of dusk to the calm of the setting sun and the illuminated volcano towering over the rooftops of the rows of small houses of many colors competing with the colors of the sky—a competition destined to fade into the dark starry sky without a winner. How I loved sitting near the almond tree with its big green leaves that seemed to dole out night dew slowly and steadily throughout the night, and talking to Juancito and the small cadre of friends who congregated to laugh and marvel as the stars blinked at us and shared the mantle of mystery that kept them cozy and distinct above.

There was Juancito, my older next door neighbor, with a name that fits his loving gentle light that poured though a face that seemed as smart as it was bright with idealistic youth, a round face with thin lips and wide almond eyes that smiled easily. He must have been 17 and I 10, and the others came and went through many evenings of what my older brother called bullshit conversations—useless and devoid of the adrenal flavor of *fútbol* and fights, of fashion and girls. Far removed from the expectations of our age and situation, we talked and marveled about the nature of the stars, the silent unknown around us, science, history, and the heart of humanity. We delved into topics that to this day grip my heart of hearts. Juancito shared with us his marvel for life, his hopes for a world free and true, his vision of a human race mature and just, and his enthusiasm for science and the future.

I was alone with him one night, leaning against my father's car in the parking lot above the row of houses of our neighborhood, after the other friends congregated around *"El Chele"* Medrano, the feared dad of a pretty girl who had been my playmate since I was 3, to hear him speak of sex and whores and why Jesus really sweated blood with Mary Magdalene in the desert. Juancito and I stayed apart, pondering hard on the infinite nature of the universe and the relentless nature of its laws, and came to that point where the mind wakes up into a sense of timelessness and ceases to be his mind or my mind, and it becomes a book of ideas that said that, out of the infinite number of solar systems, there had to be others with life like ours, or even life unlike ours but conscious and alive. The mind speculated that any mind which wakes up to the realization of its universality would wonder, perhaps at that very moment, if there was perhaps another mind pondering the same question about the existence of other minds like this one that is thinking right now; and just like that, we looked up to the night sky and realized that, at this very fleetingly eternal moment, another child like Juancito and me was looking up toward the infinite space above him and wondering about us. The mind who wonders seemed to breach the dark gulf separating one from another, and there was just the wonderment of having, for a moment, touched another.

After this and other conversations of religion, politics, philosophy, and things, life took over, and I lived the life for me, and he went on to his revolutionary calling. I overheard once that conversation when his aunt, the nurse, the one who took him in her home and once saved me from the toys I had shoved into my nose to see how far my hole went. It was that conversation where the mother figure tells him to be careful, that he is taking too many risks, that he could end up dead or tortured, that he should study and prepare himself for a good future and a good family, that he is smart and good and therefore must not throw everything away, that "be careful and think of us who love you and will miss you," and that the revolution he is struggling for will never happen and is all a farce and everyone is for himself and more good can be done by staying in school and raising a family. Yes, I heard that conversation, and I heard his response, loving and kind as when he talked to me, and just as full of splendor were his words when he told his aunt that what we are doing, this our thing, is not for us, that we will never see the benefits of our work, that it was for the future of humanity and that others in distant times will live the life that is right and just and good. This is not for me, not for us. It is for the future of humanity.

That was the last I heard of him. Juancito became a "disappeared"—a victim of a repressive paramilitary government for whom Juancito was a terrorist, a public enemy, the disease of the world coming from outside to disrupt their world of possessions and private wealth and the rule of arms. Juancito disappeared and was never, ever found. His happy, tender voice full of hope and smiles was never heard again.

There is a silent void where you used to be. I called you "Juancito" when you were older than me, and I call you "Juancito" now that I am older and you are still a very young man. It hurts, Juancito, to know you gone, to intuit you tortured and killed. I have kept our talks in my most intimate abode, and once in a while I look across the gulf of time and space and I see your face looking up into my eyes with a wide-eyed child next to you, wondering if I see you and if I am also thinking about you and know that there is another out there in this limitless, free, and revolutionary vastness.

SUYAPA PORTILLO

# Biography of a Hard Love

"La cobardía es asunto
de los hombres, no de los amantes.
Los amores cobardes no llegan a amores, ni a historias, se quedan allí.
Ni el recuerdo los puede salvar,
ni el mejor orador conjugar"
          —Oleo de una mujer con sombrero, Sylvio Rodriguez

"you are hard to love"

these words fall like concrete on me…
                    your face asks: "what is wrong with you people?"

            as in Honduran immigrant chicks in the US?
                    or do you mean Central American women…?
                            could it be queer women of color in general?

we are hard to love?

these words echo in my brain non-stop… sometimes daily like granizos falling
from the sky

and I think about the women behind me
those other hard to love women
            the single mother's like abuelita who made it so that one egg could
            feed many people in the house

*esa risa*… the smiles in those women's faces when the electricity was shut off in
the scorching heat of *la Colonia* Berlin
            … the fans were off and there we are in the stale air of San Pedro Sula,
sitting with candles, lighting the pearl white of our teeth, laughing like a circus
came to town
            my grandma's black eyes glistening with the candle light
                    her dentures flipping out of her mouth in laughter… I am not
                    sure what we laughed at so hard

my uncle's Honda motorcycle parked in the living room… a permanent fixture
he did not want anyone to steal it in the dead of night when the electricity was out

the lights were always out on our side of town

those dusty nights when we lacked basic needs, toilet paper, white sugar, electricity, eggs, water… were hard Cold War days that are etched in my memory
as times of laughter, discovery and love…

hard days that made love flow easy

my grandma died of two things: ulcers and bad men
you see, *ella cuido hombres*, she cooked bread and flour tortillas for workers
building the PanAmerican road that crossed Occidente
    … and ate the bread warm, right out of the oven, that earth oven that
looked like an igloo… if you eat the masa warm, sticky, and uncooked… it
could certainly make a hole in your stomach.

    … *lo de* bad men, well that has to do with loving the wrong men, from opposite
political parties
hard men that walked away for sport
grandma was a Liberal, as in *el partido Liberal, a morir*, her blood ran red she said…
        though biologists would challenge her
        who can argue with an obstinate Liberal party member who lived
        through Carías Andino and Lopez Arellano in the same lifetime?

But she never spoke of dinner and laughter with Farabundo Martí… when she
lived in San Salvador… *eso era peligroso* in 1960s, 1970s and 1980s Honduras…
*te lleva la DIN, te desaparecen…*
        … *como lo siguen a Marlito*… or remember when my tío, a photographer for *Diario El Tiempo*, was taken by *el DIN* for questioning…

How hard must it have been to have that in your heart and never talk about it…
As she lay in her dying bed she called out my name… to tell me these things…
stories about rape, political violence, failed marriages, injustice, loss… I was too
afraid to come and listen… it was hard to lose her love

It was hard to love when my dad got drunk, heard some *chisme* about my mom in the local *estanco*

> and came home and nearly beat the shit out of her… with scissors
> … while we were sleeping in her bed

those were hard to love days…

because what child can understand when they are awoken in the middle of the night to life and death fighting…

would it have been a *crimen de pasion*? or just *la condicion humana de la mujer, del hombre… en plena guerra fría*?

> *un militar* in green uniform and an *ametralladora* sling across his back took my drunk broken father away in the dead of 1979… who would take me to get pan dulce… and would I carry the *foco* to light our way?

We sat the *madrugada* on the red vinyl couches the living room was cold…
I don't understand why gentrifiers in Highland Park like to have them… reminiscing a past cold they did not live…

It was hard to love that old-school-bus-turned-transit bus that took us away caught in the rain, the chocolate milk water of the perfect storm reaching up to the windows… id the driver know how to get us out of this?

It was hard to know then,

because no one explained it to me, that this rush of dirty water would pass…
I imagined we were swimming in chocolate milk   it was so milky brown, sweet…
How it reminded me of *Quick Sabor a Chocolate*
deep down I was wishing the bus was maneuvering through *Quick Sabor de Fresa*
we never came back home after that…

> the rain stopped in L.A.

we came in hard buses…

> one after the other, one after the other, until we reached the borderlands climbed under a fence and got to *los Yunai*…

the little pebbles under our knees were hard and hurt as we knelt down in front of the INS official pointing a flashlight and a gun at us…

This is what my tías must have been talking about when they told us about their punishment in grade school for talking or giggling...
*"incarse diez minutos en un frijolito hasta que se le quiten las ganas de hablar"*

I did not speak.

a cold *madrugada* in Los Angeles my mother was kidnapped, in a 2-door car at gunpoint
       the car swirled from downtown up the 110 pasadena fwy
as she hit the concrete with her right hip... it made her hard

                       ... it still hurts today
           afraid to report it to the police
undocumented after all
lucky to be here... alive... in the cruel hard concrete

I can't even tell you anymore

I am hard
       ... and will require hard love.

SUYAPA PORTILLO

# 28 de junio

PARA MIS COMPAÑERXS HONDUREÑXS EN LA LUCHA


cada 28 de junio se me revienta una vena
es que se me hincha
    la vena que da al corazón
      que no aguanta y estalla

desde el 2009 tengo esta condición
          seguro que es la rabia
      que como un puño alzado al aire
rompe telarañas
    busca camino
gotas de sangre…. brotan por todo lados…
    salpicando las florecitas blancas del tabaco de
      un brillante y profundo rojo
marcando la tierra...

    como para no olvidar el camino

    …gotitas que forman charquitos de purpura
en los hoyos abandonados de tantos seres amados

gotas que como
    mi *lipstick* rojo, el que causa tanto rencor y repudio
      ya pinta el amanecer
pero no hay de que preocupar
    que el corazón todavía taconea
 de arriba hacia abajo....
    porque esta Honduras no nos la robaran...


28 de Junio, 2016
Los Ángeles, CA

KRYS MÉNDEZ-RAMÍREZ

# The Banana Files: Empire vs. Resistance

## Introduction

IT WAS 1983. The cold hustle and bustle of the world's people in the lobby of Tower 1 was at once intimidating and exciting, frightening and alluring. A diverse amalgam of mini universes zipping past each other, gravitating within orbits held together by neoliberal capital. It was a spectacle that even *Le Corbusier* himself could hardly have anticipated: a synchronous chaos that was, and was to be, erupting in a New York City moment. This was the spectacle that Maritza beheld, albeit briefly, as she emerged from the subway, a flicker of excitement momentarily breathing new life in her after an arduous day at a Bronx pizzeria. She rushed to deliver the bit of money she had saved for her mother, Berta, still back home in San Pedro Sula, so conspicuously distant from this city that had given her little other than dollars and winters. In spite of her exhaustion, she smiled as she thought about the packed envelope of cash she would hand to the mail clerk, feeling (finally!) somewhat vindicated for having made the biggest bet of her life.

As she rushed through the lobby, pretending to know where she was going, she was gripped with an all-body anxiety. She became preoccupied with finding the delivery place her friend had told her about. As she looked around, worrisome thoughts swirled against a backdrop of *gringos* in suits dashing past gawking tourists with bulky cameras and funny hats. And in a silent corner she spotted a curly-haired man in gray uniform, a mop and bucket at his side. In a flash, she was pulled in by an unknowable gravity. Maritza approached him and asked for directions, her anxiety fading when he responds in Spanish with a *boricua* smile.

## San Pedro and New York

The year my parents met at the World Trade Center, Cold War geopolitics and global neoliberal restructuring were transforming the relationships between cities and countries, spaces and places. The winds of a new-old libertarian ideology—one based on the incontestable supremacy of the invisible hand—had re-emerged in the creation of a new world order. And although merely a decade old, the Towers were already witness to spectacular changes, not only in the surrounding cityscape, but also in the circuits of commerce that ensnared cities everywhere.

Nowhere was this more evident than New York City, where several years of deindustrialization and suburban flight had nearly left the city bankrupt. Implementing a model of urban governance that was to characterize life under austerity, powerful investment banks like Chase and Citibank seized upon the city's economic woes to launch a financial coup, slashing funding for social welfare programs (including those used by impoverished communities of color) while diverting them into incentives for corporate investment and high-end real estate development. By the beginning of the 80s, the consequences of regime change were already palpable in the streets: the crumbling, graffitied edifices of neoliberal austerity juxtaposed against new glass high-rises and luxury condominiums. The new polarized geographies told not the story of two cities, but overlapping multiverses. Of course, one doesn't need to repeat the story of the Reagan years, so painfully familiar is their legacy. One need only recall vintage stock footage from the nightly news, their hallowed threats echoing across space-time: crack cocaine, AIDS, homelessness, communism. The ever-refined discourse of welfare moms and Black and Brown criminality.

At the same time, the world my mother left behind was succumbing to a different set of transformations. Far from being insulated from the revolutionary forces stirring up the rest of the isthmus, Honduras orbited a path heavily circumscribed by U.S. imperialism—a path dictated in large part by an historical legacy as the quintessential "banana republic." Interestingly, a proclivity toward liberal reformism within the Honduran military elite not only staved off the sort of popular unrest seen in Guatemala and El Salvador, but also created pathways toward civilian rule. Around the time Reagan assumed office in Washington, an elected constituent assembly was drafting a new Honduran constitution (to take effect in 1982). The election of Roberto Suazo ended eighteen uninterrupted years of military leadership. And an unshakeable recession throughout the country brought a virtual slowdown in the industrial capital of San Pedro Sula, quieting activity in the many banana plantations dotting the urban periphery. Yet none of these transitions were as impactful as what was to emerge from a collaboration with the American military, Honduras turned into Empire's launching pad for a paramilitary counteroffensive. As strategic piece in Reagan's checkerboard of war, Honduras was indelibly shaped by the mass influx of U.S. military funds, equipment, and training—including, most notably, an elite death squad (Battalion 316) led by a School of the Americas graduate. With the threats and intimidations, disappearances and drive-by executions, a different sort of coup—an imperialistic, military one—had descended on Honduras.

In my case, migration and the forces of political economy ensured that two cities in a Cold War universe—San Pedro and New York—would collide in orbit. As the product of a bipolar world come undone, I nevertheless sense Reagan's ghost. His message, crisp and callous.

## Chiquita and *Lempira*

I am always made aware of the layers of difference that separate me from the land of my ancestors, the several degrees of uprootedness. Growing up in the Brooklyn barrio, worlds away from the palm trees and earthy plantains of San Pedro Sula, my connections to a catracho homeland were sporadic, often brief, sometimes theoretical. Within the self-contained universe that is New York's unique form of multiculturalism, my Honduranness also functioned more as an accessory, a label of little distinction amid larger groups of *nuyoricans, dominicanxs, mexicanxs.*

In spite of all that, childhood trips made me who I am. In those years, we would drive to *Pollo Campero* or Pizza Hut, visit my *tíos* and *tías* in the *Fesitranh*, drive further out to Lake Yahoa or Tegucigalpa, or even further out to the Mayan ruins of Copán (a sacred childhood favorite). To be sure, those impossibly humid summers in the 90s were filled with memorable, awkward cultural exchanges, the impacts of which became ingrained deeply into a double consciousness. As a child, every return trip felt overwhelming as everyone in the Ramírez clan would come out to welcome us. In that amorous airport whirlwind of *tías, tíos, primos,* and *sobrinos* with names I couldn't remember, there was also my mother, the prodigal daughter returneth with wide-eyed *gringo* boys and a Puerto Rican husband. (Did it say something that my brothers and I were Abuelita's favorite grandchildren?)

Looking back, I can recall the relics of pro-American sentiment everywhere. My mother inherited the house my grandfather had built in his years as a carpenter for one of the infamous U.S. banana companies, Chiquita (formerly United Fruit). Even though my mother was the youngest of six, she was the only one to have to made it in the States—to have *aventurado*, as she puts it, by leaving her country. My curiosity was piqued by the hints of the *sueño americano* that floated from conversation to conversation, even on Honduran television. Being on the other end of that equation was nothing if not surreal. From my accent to cousins' expressed envy for my jeans, toys, and video games. Even in the pride my mother exuded in returning home with American dollars.

To this day, I recall a moment when my mother dragged me out of a car, only to exchange a $100 bill for *lempiras*, the man's eyes widening with ostensible awe as he smiled at Ben Franklin. Given that Honduran currency is named after an indigenous Lenca leader from the early years of anti-colonial resistance, the meaning of the exchange was also powerfully metaphoric.

The new millennium would change everything, of course. My grandmother, the Ramírez matriarch, would die just months shy of 9/11. My father would lose a job. And in our Brooklyn apartment, environmental racism would leave us with asthma, depression, and a variety of enigmatic illnesses between my brothers and me. And yet, *Lempira* and Chiquita has already left their imprints in my psyche: I am their mestizo banana child, an odd fruit and a fighter. And my roots are long and brown.

## U.S. Imperialism and the Original Banana Republic

If there is an argument I would want disseminated widely, it is the following: much of what we know about Honduras is misleading or categorically false. If mentioned at all, Honduras is rendered as characteristically 'poor,' 'small,' and 'violent.' Even well intentioned scholars and reporters, sometimes even *hondureñxs*, fall into the trap of referencing Honduras as a 'failed state' or a country in need of 'development.' While I can't deconstruct this language at length, I would say that it may help to re-orient our vision of Honduras, to see in it what Eduardo Galeano saw throughout Latin America: a cosmopolitan country rich in natural resources and histories of rebellion; a country that has been incessantly pillaged and ransacked, poisoned and corrupted; a country that has survived unjust odds and abuses of power.

A long history of U.S. intervention in Honduras traces back to 19th century commercial ventures. One well-known example is that of the New York and Honduras Rosario Mining Company: its owner, Washington Valentine, became so successful with the silver mines of Tegucigalpa that he was dubbed the "King of Honduras." It was the banana industry, however, that attracted the most U.S. capital investment, a process that helped reconfigure the Honduran agrarian economy into a monocrop exporter by the beginning of the 20th century. The transformation was such that when American novelist O. Henry first coined the pejorative phrase 'banana republic' in 1904, it was done in reference to his time spent in Honduras.

Banana companies like Samuel Zemurray's United Fruit Company gained significant political clout through economic imperialism: cajoling local authorities, obtaining generous land concessions, and securing special privileges and exemptions that eroded the country's tax base while deepening its debt. At the nexus of economic and military coercion, U.S. banana companies were also powerful enough to be able to launch coups against unfavorable presidents (including Miguel Dávila in 1911, and Francisco Bertrand in 1919) and then install successors who would provide more agreeable terms, including lavish land concessions and control over docks, service facilities, and other infrastructures.

The relative failure of coffee in Honduras resulted in an almost complete monopoly of foreign-controlled banana industries—particularly, the big three of Chiquita (United Fruit), Dole (Standard Fruit), and Del Monte)—in shaping the country's internal political economy. With banana imperialism at the heart of unprecedented degrees of land dispossession and wealth extraction, very little of which remained domestically, Honduras became a theater for mass labor unrest and union organizing. In fact, the famed Marxist writer Ramón Amaya Amador beautifully captures this drama between exploited *campesinos* and *gringo* capitalists in his novel, *Prisión Verde* (1950).

Although coups and military dictatorships were also rampant in the history of Honduras, by the 1980's, civil unrest was largely contained by a military reformism and U.S. Cold War imperatives. As it is widely known, the Palmerola Air Base in Comayagua served as the central base of operations for U.S.-trained Contras against the Sandinistas and Salvadoran guerrilla forces. However, the local impact of U.S. military assistance—reaching a peak of $77 million annually—is rarely ever discussed. While not as severe as in its neighbors, U.S. complicity played a role in the Honduran state's repression of everyday civilians, including the disappearances and tortures of communists and left-leaning activists. Some of this funding helped develop an infamous elite death squad, Battalion 316, responsible for the killings and disappearances of hundreds of hondureñxs. Unsurprisingly, Battalion 316 was initially led by General Gustavo Ávarez Martínez, a student of the infamous School of the Americas (now Western Hemisphere Institute for Security Cooperation) in Fort Benning, Georgia.

With the end of the Cold War came a brief reduction in U.S. military aid to Honduras. However, the triumph of the neoliberal model foregrounded yet another war against the Honduran people initiated during the Reagan years—that of widespread poverty, accelerated now by free trade agreements and structural adjustment programs. One cannot underestimate the extent of the destabilization produced with market deregulation and the privatization of social services in a country with crushing poverty, exceptional even in the context of Central America. Anthropologist Adrienne Pine, for instance, notes how the IMF and World Bank strong-armed Honduras into reducing its economy to two tracks: export agriculture and *maquiladora*-style industry. The signing of CAFTA-DR in 2006 has only accelerated many of the same destabilizing market dynamics, including a deepened economic dependency on the United States. Given particularly that the U.S. continues to be the primary market for Honduran exports, what one witnesses with such trade agreements is much of the same asymmetricality that has characterized over a century of U.S.-Honduras relations.

More so than overt state repression, the economic violence exacted by foreign multinationals and U.S.-led neoliberalism is difficult to qualify, so extensive are the ripples across Honduran society. Typically forgotten are the diverse consequences of persisting poverty and joblessness, the loss of land and autonomous livelihood that Amaya Amador captured decades ago. One of them is mass movement to cities like San Pedro Sula, whose unplanned, rapid-fire growth epitomizes the disruptions in a country once traditionally rural, now one of Central America's most urbanized societies.

Finally, one cannot understand the contemporary situation in Honduras without engaging the issue of violence and gang warfare, also facilitated in large part by U.S. imperial relations. Since the mid-90s, the deportation of (suspected) gang members from U.S. cities was implicated in a renewed terror across Central America; in Honduras, where civil conflict had been avoided, gang warfare was complicit in the worst insecurity problem in recent modern history. Between 2001 and 2010, U.S. Marshals transported about 130,000 convicts to Central America, over 40,000 of which were returned to SPS and the capital. (This is not to suggest that gangs were the source of the problem in themselves, since a context of neoliberal austerity, joblessness, and state mistreatment of racialized immigrants are arguably more culpable.) Ironically, under the auspice of combatting drug trafficking and terrorism, Honduras borrowed many of the same punitive strategies deployed in North American cities against communities of color—except with more catastrophic results. Anti-gang legislation and 'Mano Dura' policies targeting delinquency also became means to curtail civilian rights, a demonstration of U.S. influence in the age of the Patriot Act.

This was what the Honduras President Manuel Zelaya inherited when elected in 2006. While highly imperfect, his administration did make laudable attempts to lift Honduras from poverty and deplorable dependency, including lifting the minimum wage, mandating free, universal education for children, and providing subsidies to farmers. Zelaya was also in the process of implementing other liberal measures that were ended with his ouster, including legalizing the morning-after pill and incorporating Honduras into

Hugo Chavez's ALBA. Given these conditions, it's easy to see how his presidency threatened to the status quo.

## Honduras: The Militarization of Everyday Life

Year after year in post-coup Honduras, countless numbers of indigenous, LGBT, and environmental activists have been killed or disappeared. Honduras has become one of the central hubs of a multi-billion dollar enterprise in narco-trafficking, and San Pedro Sula momentarily acquired the notorious label of being the 'murder capital' of the world. The English-language media is full of sensationalized reportage of a country that is otherwise conveniently forgotten—even when the emperor's hands are so clearly filled with blood.

When an indigenous environmental activist, Berta Cáceres, was assassinated in March 2016, international attention had once again spotlighted the violence and insecurity reigning in Honduras. Cáceres, alongside members of the organization she co-founded—the National Council of Popular Indigenous Organizations of Honduras (COPINH)—had been battling the construction of the Agua Zarca Dam, a hydroelectric project that was to be built on a river of spiritual significance to her Lenca community. While her death sparked mass outrage and highlighted the very real threats faced by Honduran activists, it also pointed to a culture of impunity that cast militarized murder as natural. Moreover, few reporters have been able to contextualize the extent of military domination in Honduras and its deep roots in U.S. training, assistance, and patronage.

While I cannot speak from the vantage point of everyday experience, I only needed to consult family to sense the reality of the violence. In the years I witnessed airport-style security and stop-and-frisk policing change the daily rhythms of New York City life, on the other end of a cordless landline I'd hear of a different reality, with *tíos* and *primos* casually discussing kidnappings and robberies at gunpoint in SPS and Tegus. Those who could afford it would move into gated communities. No one would leave the house at sunset. When visiting a dying aunt who lived just a few blocks away, my cousin insisted on us taking a cab. It was a lifestyle my mother couldn't stomach, having lived away so long. She would sell the house for a fraction of its worth.

Some years later, while living at a Rhode Island college, my radicalization brought me back to Honduras. I remember the morning in late June when I'd jump out of bed upon seeing the online headlines, incredulous: a military coup? There was something surreal about reading how a president had been arrested in his pajamas, and within a matter of hours, flown to Costa Rica and kept in exile. It was 2009, and Americans couldn't give a damn. My family didn't care either. So in the ensuing weeks and months, I had to wade through contradictory reports from biased news agencies (those I'd learn were owned by one of the country's leading families, and allied with the post-coup Conservative party), as well as independent radios and online periodicals fiercely broadcasting the resistance in the face of death threats and state repression. As I scrambled—and failed—to find solidarity groups to organize with, I was disheartened by the U.S. media circuit, which had agonizingly little to say. I watched as Obama dragged his feet, and then-Secretary of State Hilary Clinton refusing to denounce the coup.

During the ensuing years of mass-scale, non-violent resistance to the coup—and the violent military repression that executed an untold number of civilians—the Obama Administration conveniently turned a blind eye to the mess it helped foment. Honduras became a problem to quickly dismantle, quietly bury, even if the solution came at the expense of human dignity and livelihood. Years later, in an interview she conducted with an Argentinean news agency, Cáceres herself would point fingers at Clinton for the years of brutal, post-coup state violence that killed off her *compañerxs* for defending their land rights. Incredibly, in her book, *Hard Choices*, Clinton even claps herself on the back for helping restore democracy—an example, she claims, of her "pragmatic" foreign policy approach.

While the coup wasn't the start of daily urban violence and militarism, as sometimes suggested, it certainly accelerated many of the processes of resource extraction and land dispossession that had been initiated earlier under banana imperialism. We know, for instance, that Honduras's legacy of pandering to U.S. foreign policy and land-guzzling multinationals was given a powerful boost in the post-coup governments of Pepe Lobo and Juan Orlando Hernández—both of whom 'won' highly contested elections under the threat of military force. With the full backing of the Yankee military, the post-coup administrations fulfilled the demands of global capital and local oligarchy by selling off Honduran natural resources and green-lighting environmentally destructive megaprojects at the expense of local *campesinxs* and indigenous sovereignty.

The reinforced alliance between foreign capitalists, agro-oligarchs, and a state-military apparatus resulted in an all-out war against left-leaning activists of all stripes. However, with the passing years it was made clear that a broad cross-section of Honduran society had become susceptible to threats, disappearances, and cold-blooded executions: from indigenous and Afro-indigenous communities, to environmental and LGBT activists, to *campesinos*, street children, students, reporters. Through it all, in a cycle of violence breeding ramped-up security measures breeding more violence, what has emerged is an unprecedented scale of U.S.-sponsored militarization.

There is no question that a startling pattern has emerged vis-à-vis Honduran insecurity: what in the 80s was justified in Cold War terms of toppling communist subversives (threats to the new world order of unfettered markets), is today carried out under the auspices of fighting gang warfare and drug trafficking. While the complicated relationships between poverty, gang involvement, and illicit drug economies are indeed difficult to disentangle, U.S. imperial response has been one of confining or deporting as many of its problems to outside its increasingly militarized borders. When an unprecedented number of child refugees attempted to seek asylum at the U.S.-Mexico border in 2014, Clinton's response—that unaccompanied minors 'should be sent back'—failed to acknowledge the causal roots causing the crisis, exacerbated in large part by *her own* actions. In a similar lack of accountability, when an expanding narco-trafficking industry disrupted life among indigenous communities in the Western rural region of the Moskitia (including demolition of their ancestral lands), U.S. DEA agents and U.S.-trained military police failed to acknowledge, let alone make amends, for the murder of innocent civilians.

While it is daunting to think of the many communities that are today impacted by the ongoing re-militarization of everyday life, it is much easier to trace the different, often overlapping, forms of U.S. assistance. It is perhaps unsurprising that security models originally implemented by U.S. Empire domestically and abroad have filtered into Honduran streets, *maras* and *delincuencia* now covers for unchecked state violence and repression. Hoping to keep some of the chaos from spilling over into its own backyard, the Pentagon has quietly enabled a number of paramilitary-like initiatives in Honduras in recent years: millions of dollars funneled through bilateral or multilateral defense agreements, such as the Central American Regional Security Initiative (CARSI); the development of inter-agency task forces like FUSINA; and training for militarized police units, like the infamous TIGRES. The U.S. blood trail is particularly evident in these last two agencies: As scholar Dana Frank points out, FUSINA was initially headed by a School of the Americas graduate, German Alfaro, commander of a battalion implicated in dozens of extrajudicial killings of *campesino* activists in the Aguán Valley. Moreover, a local committee for disappeared family members from the 80s (COFADEH) has even denounced the Tigres as a "crude resurrection" of the political disappearances and executions performed by the U.S.-trained Battalion 316 death squad.

I have no doubt that much of the violence strangling Honduras today is directly rooted not simply in distant legacies of U.S. imperialism, but in active and ongoing security interventions. Recent movements showcase the resilience of *catrachos*, now absolutely fed up with the culture of impunity that has reigned in our country between local autocrats and exploitative foreigners. In 2015, when it was discovered that millions of dollars had been embezzled from the Honduran Social Security Institute (IHSS) by the president's National Party, an unprecedented number of Hondurans took the streets, week after week for several *months*, carrying torches and demanding an end to the administration's corruption. Still yet, in the following year, Berta's assassination brought out even more people from the international community, a chant of "*Berta Vive, La Lucha Sigue*" reminding everyone of the ongoing life of Honduran resistance. As with the many other martyrs who have died in battles in the Aguán, Moskitia, San Pedro, or elsewhere in the diaspora, they are reminders not just of the sacred precariousness of life, but also a collective calling to fight for our freedom. It is the revolutionary spirit of Lempira echoed in the aspirations behind the country's motto: *Libre, Soberana e Independiente.*

CLAUDIA D. HERNÁNDEZ

# Santiago Atitlán, Deciembre 1990

Has venido a mi tierra, al Lago de
Santiago Atitlán, para ver una puesta de sol

Que solo se puede vislumbrar entre el
Volcán San Pedro y el Volcán Tolimán.

A tu llegar, los guías te arrean a la
Presencia del infame Santo Maximón—

Todos claman tener en su hogar
El verdadero Santo Maximón:

*Rilaj Mam*—Abuelo Nuestro
 ¿Le llevarás su tabaco y su ron?

Has venido a mi tierra a vagar por
Sus senderos enlodados, desgastados,

Pero aún no has visto lo que tienes que ver

La corriente del lodo no ha velado los catorce
Desplomados que esa tarde protestaron.

Hoy, se contempla un sol sonrojado,
Escondido tras volcanes     callados.

CLAUDIA D. HERNÁNDEZ

# Santiago Atitlán, December 1990

You have come to my land
To visit Lake Atitlán:

To see a sunset that can only be viewed between
*Volcán San Pedro* and *Volcán Tolimán*.

Upon your arrival, the guides herd you
To the foot of the infamous *Santo Maximón*—

(Everyone claims to have the real
*Santo Maximón* in their home)

*Rilaj Mam—Abuelo Nuestro*
Will you bring him tobacco and rum?

You have come to my land to wander through
Her muddy paths; her tired paths.

But, still, you have not seen what you need to see

The flow of mud has yet to veil the blood of the
Eleven who collapsed in their uprising.

Today, we contemplate a crimson sun
Hiding behind silent volcanoes.

CLAUDIA D. HERNÁNDEZ

# *Kim Ayu* (Come Over Here)

My insides contract
It is my breath that escapes
It goes in search of my people

I hear an echo that resonates
Sweet voices, tender tongue:

*Kim ayu*—Come over here

A wind of incense grazes my core
The marimba's keys
Chime in the distance

It is the moors, they have come
With their ancient deer dances

I hear an echo that resonates
Sweet voices, tender tongue:

*Kim ayu*—Come over here

The clamor of the bells
From the temple resound
That melody can never fade

On my flesh I feel a wax burning
It leaves scars that teach me
To appreciate my new existence

I hear an echo that resonates
Sweet voices, tender tongue:

*Kim ayu*—Come over here

My fierce soul no longer trembles
I have found my new *Edén*

(*En Poqomchi'*) *Suk Nuk'uxl*—
My heart is content.

# Frijoles

THE STAINLESS STEEL POT sat on the *estufa,* and as the water started to boil and spill, Flaca could slightly hear the *clack clack* from the lid lifting and *spzzzzzzzz* as the water slithered down the side and evaporated at the touch of the flame.

Sitting on the torn-leather discolored sofa with a cushion molded to her *trasero* (because after all, that was her spot) with only one sun ray peeking through the beaten door window, Flaca watched Animal Planet in *Español.* After a rushed morning of taking *las niñas* to school, she would finally relax, indulge, and watch attentively, as if she too were in school learning an important lesson— on survival. On the flat screen TV, covered with fingerprint trails from all her daughters' *dedos,* she saw the *vibora,* black and deep green scales, slowly slither across the arid ground and attack the naïve, multicolored frog.

*La rana* reminded her of her *pueblo*—Concepción, Honduras—but more than anything of her *niñez,* especially when she ran after them once the rain had passed through. She chuckled at the screen and shouted "*¡Sonza! ¿Cómo no la vistes?*" as if the frog could hear her. She stared at the screen, *pegada al televisor,* and watched the snake swallow the frog whole—slowly.

*Spzzzzzzzzzzzzzzzz*

"*¡Ay los frijoles!*" exclaimed Flaca, a heavy-bodied woman whose *chanclas* slammed loudly against the wooden floor as she rushed to the kitchen from the living room, extending her thick brown arm toward the stove onto the sticky knob to lower the flame. The top handle had fallen off making it difficult for her to immediately lift. Only two holes for the screws remained. Naturally, she opened the kitchen drawer and pulled out a fork with bent prongs and inserted it into the holes and swiftly lifted the lid.

*Fwaaaaaaaaaah*

She watched the bubbles collapse to the bottom of the pot and could see the brown objects soften. Her eyes, aged with heavy eyelids and etched with sadness, mirrored the color of the beans.

She set *la tapadera* on the coral tile counter, using the free fork to pierce a *frijol* with the bent prongs. She guided the fork into her mouth and pulled the bean carefully off the hot prongs and chewed it.

"*Hmm… les faltan poco*," she whispered and thought they needed more *sal*.

As Flaca opened the cupboard, a loud *sqeeeeeeak* filled the kitchen; she could see all the containers that held her secret seasonings to her mystical *sazón*. Amongst all the jars, she identified the unlabeled, lidless container, applied all her weight to the ball of her feet, and stretched just enough to grab the salt. Her fingers sunk in and reached for the rock salt at the bottom. Her fingertips held the rough textured substance and then sprinkled it into the pot, as if summoning the beans to sprout.

With a large wooden spoon, she stirred slowly, watching the beans swirl to the motion of her hand, creating an endless vortex that reminded her of the volatile green and brown leaves swirling midair when the *huracanes* hit her *pueblo*. After the turmoil, the snakes would appear in large numbers. It seemed as if they were coming together and creating new fibers for a carpet that ran all across the ground.

She placed the lid back on the murky steel pot. As she walked over to the living room to continue watching her show, Mari appeared quickly braiding her hip-length hair.

Mari, Flaca's eldest daughter, had recently returned from college—an all-women's college (yes, the ones that "turn" them into lesbians or so all her cousins and even her sisters thought.) Little did they know she already found other *mujeres* attractive, even before she left out-of-state for school, but with the constant homophobic remarks her family made, Mari found it impossible to ever spill that *secreto* without any direct damage to her family's *reputación*.

During her college years, she slept with a few women, became a *feminista* (you know, with the body hair grown out and all) and a revolutionary (or so she thought). Despite having a few partners, she could only ever recall Rita's full lips kissing her neck while her soft hands ran down her waist. She became her *compañera* for all her activist work—immigration, reproductive justice, LGBTQ movement and even would sit next to her at the end of the night and read (*disque ella*) "revolutionary" literature, while playing Karla Lara in the background.

Initially, they bonded because both had parents from *CentroAmerica*, but after night-long conversations about the revolution, feminism, systemic inequalities, their bodily autonomy and their families, Mari knew that she wanted to introduce Rita to her parents—even though she knew that meant never exchanging a word with them again.

Yes, indeed Mari was an idealist who actually believed she was the "down" revolutionary that could start the next wave of feminism in her hometown in Pomona, California (that no one had even ever heard about) and somehow get all the *madres* to join her in the movement to bring down the patriarchy. Can you believe it? And after all this—only one question remains—*Ay, Mari. ¿Y que se te metió en la cabeza?*

As Mari headed toward the kitchen and finished braiding her brown hair and secured it with a *liga* she inquired, "Mom, *¿ya mero están los frijoles? Ando con filo.*"

"*Si les acabo de poner sal. En unos diez minutos están listos.*"

"*Ah, okai pues. En eso saco las tortillas y el queso.*"

Mari opened the fridge and cringed at the smell of a rotten something she couldn't immediately see or detect. She was the shortest of her sisters, standing at only about five feet, which was even more apparent due to her long hair. As she moved a few items around—*el tenderete* of sour cream that actually contained *habanero salsa*—the rainbow-patterned bracelets Rita gave her jingled. Despite their abrupt separation, she could never bring herself to throwing them away, especially since she thought about her often, and how they both should have been living in Southern California.

"Mom, *el refri ajiede*," said Mari angrily.

"*Ya sé. Luego lo limpio*," her mother replied, with her usual tone of apathy.

"*Tengo tiempo, si quiere ahorita lo limpio*," Mari said as she shifted her eyes with uncertainty from the fridge back to her mother.

"*¡Ay no! Siempre me botan la comida que todavía está buena,*" her mother responded as she shook her head.

"Mom, that's not true. *Y además usted es la quien compra de más y cocina para todo un pueblo,*" Mari chuckled as she stared over at her mother, noticing that her eyes developed more creases around them and her *canas* were more prominent at the front of her hairline. After being away for 4 years, she realized that her mother had aged quite a bit since she first took off. Her eyes seemed hollow—detached from her sockets, suspended from above.

"Oh Mari, *hablando de pueblo, a ver si me vas buscando boletos para ir a Honduras en diciembre. Creo que por fin tendré suficiente dinero para viajar,*" requested her mother gently.

Flaca did not work and her only source of income was through a *coperacha*, where she picked a number and then agreed on an amount of $50 to give every week for each number of participants—all *mujeres* who were in a similar financial constraining situation. For this one, she had been given the last number—13. *¡Qué relajo! Y pa' cabar unas mujeres eran pero bien conchudas*, so the money didn't always come in on time, but she knew that after this one, she would finally have enough money to buy a round-trip ticket to Honduras and spend time with her *hermanas* and finally meet all their children.

Mari peeked her head over the fridge door and said, "*¡Por fin va ir a visitar! Claro, mom. Luego busco. Después de comer.*"

Mari still cringed at the marinating scents released from the fridge that were now stuck in her nostrils. It then occurred to her that she had never asked her mother what she missed most from home. She had not been able to return to Honduras for over 20 years. (Mari could not even begin to imagine what that felt like. She was only away for four years, and she cried so many weeks because she missed home and her mother's cooking.) When Flaca first arrived to East Los Angeles in the early eighties, she lived undocumented for a few years, incapable of learning a language that left a bitter aftertaste. Her older sister, Amparo, took care of her when she first arrived, and soon a *suave pachuco*-like Mexican man promised Flaca *la luna y las estrellas* and after nine full moons, she gave birth to her first daughter, Mari.

"Mom, *y ¿qué extraña más de Honduras?*" Mari finally asked, waiting attentively for the answer.

Instead of sitting down on the sofa, Flaca glanced over at Mari and then stared at the gloomy ceiling, as if she could see the answer floating above her, as if she knew the answer many years ago, waiting for someone to ask her. She released a heavy sigh and softly said, *"Pues, no me lo vas a creer, pero los frijoles."*

As Mari grabbed the bag of tortillas *de harina* and the mozzarella string cheese, she shot a quick glance of disbelief at her mother and laughed, *"¡Mom, comemos frijoles casi cada día! ¿En serio?"*

*"Sí, ya lo sé, pero aquí solo comemos frijol pinto y yo estaba acostumbrada a comer frijol rojo."*

*Pumpumpumpumpumpumpumpumpumpumpumpumpumpumpumpumpumpumpum*

Flaca heard the intense drum playing and turned her head and saw a lion on the screen—rushing towards a zebra. Her attention diverted for a few seconds, while her eyes now reflected the image of the lion ripping the neck open, and then proceeding to chew right below—directly at the zebra's chest. Quickly, the drums became softer; the zebra's black and white stripes became drenched with the color *rojo*. The narrator described the bloody scene—a victory for the lion.

"Really mom?" Mari continued to laugh, doubting every word her mother just shared with her.

*"¿Y apoco saben tan diferentes así pa' que los extrañe? ¿Y por qué no cocinamos los rojos?"*

*"Sí. Bueno, no. La diferencia es poco, pero suficiente pa' que uno distinga el sabor. No los cocinamos por tu papá. ¿Que no vez que a él solo le gusta el frijol pinto?"*

On the screen, Mari could see the lion's satisfaction while ripping the flesh further, ripping the valves and arteries—straight to the heart. The narrator no longer spoke, the drums no longer beat—the silence permeated beyond the screen into the living room and the kitchen—muting Mari momentarily...

"Wait—*¿qué?*" Mari managed to whisper as she pushed the fridge door, making it tremble afterward. She dropped the tortillas and cheese on the table and placed her hands on the edge, suddenly feeling nauseous. She glared at her mother not believing that even the fucken *frijoles* she ate almost every day upheld some patriarchal bullshit in their household. (*Y disque la Mari se creía muy rebelde.*)

"Mom, are you serious?!" shouted Marie as her eyebrows arched, resembling the peaks of the San Gabriel Valley Mountains.

"*Si, Mari. Cuando recién llegue y luego que me junte con tu papá, me dijo que no sabía cocinar y—*"

"*Ama, ¿porque no me lo dijo antes?*" Mari interrupted.

Her shoulders sank—she felt the punch pound her spine—snapping it into irreparable fragments. She felt anger rush over her and unexpected demise fill her eyes with moisture. Mari felt her animosity for her father exponentially multiply and immediately hated herself. She could not find the strength to move or react. Her head dropped and loosely hung off to the side, as if her neck snapped, too.

*Claro,* at this point Mari thought to herself what *had* been the point of leaving home to go and pursue a degree at a women's college if her *madre* still remained trapped in the house—not even having the liberty to cook *una olla de frijoles rojos*? How had she not noticed? How could she not have asked before? For the first time, Mari doubted whether she was a feminist. How did she come to *even* believe she would start the next wave of feminism, if she couldn't even start at home? How could she share all the knowledge she acquired without making her mother question her own self-worth and value tied in with the household space?

*Spzzzzzzzzzzzzzzzzzzzzzzzzzzz Spzzzzzzzzzzzzzzzzzzzzz Spzzzzzzzzzzzzzzzzzz*

She felt the pressure of the pot of beans fill her throat—ultimately knotted—unable to spill them.

"*Bueno que importa, además solo son frijoles—la misma chingadera,*" Flaca said indifferently.

"No mom, it's not just about beans. *Usted sabe cocinar—*" Mari could not finish her sentence.

"*Sí, claro que sé, pero a tu papa no le gusta la comida hondureña. Así que le llamó a tu abuelita en México y le dijo que yo no sabía cocinar y que me mandara sus recetas para que aprendiera cocinar al estilo mexicano—y bueno aquí estoy,"* her mother chuckled, but it was seasoned with nostalgia, desperately trying to hide the taste of loss and agony.

Flaca walked back to the kitchen and could see that her *hija* was upset, but did not understand exactly *why*. She had partially completed a third grade education while in Honduras and around the same time, at age 7, her mother passed away, succumbing to breast cancer. When she arrived at the States, she wasn't even thinking of having a family, but when you have no one talk to you about *cómo cuidarte* then you find yourself counting the full moons left until your first newborn is welcomed into this earth, stressing about how you will make ends stretch to have diapers, formula, and clothing, even if it means skipping two meals a day and filling up on crackers and water. At times, she wanted to go back to school, but then thought, *¿Qué va hacer una vieja como yo allí de metiche?*

"*Mari, ¿que tienes?*" her mother asked as she reached for her slumped shoulders.

Mari could not respond—she knew that the moment her mouth opened, her eyes would close and release the tears she'd been holding in for years. She wondered how much longer this could go on for—if she could ever look her father in his eyes and forgive him for erasing her mother's culture from the household that she worked endlessly to create.

"*Solo son frijoles,* Mari," her mother whispered as she gently swept her left hand across her back, as if attempting to heal and restructure her broken spine. There were no rings in her hand, just a rough texture with the skin peeling off near the nails from all the accumulated years of washing dishes *a mano*. Mari felt the warmth of her mother's hand soothe the cold air building up throughout the years stuffed in between each vertebra. She felt her eyes swallow her tears and felt their saltiness in her throat. She felt defeated—she wanted to hug her mother with such a time force capable of somehow transporting her to a point in her life that was not dictated by a man—a time when she savored *los frijoles rojos de su país*, a time when she was free.

But she couldn't. Mari simply remained immobile—unable to process what had just been revealed to her.

*They are not just beans—they are much more. She is much more than this.* She looked around the kitchen, at the fuchsia, lime green, and bright yellow walls, the window her mother looked out every time she washed dishes, and she wondered how often her mother had hoped for something different—something more.

Mari couldn't even understand how her mother had been deprived of tasting her home. Unable to move, she told herself to not let one tear out—for this was not her suffering, but her mother's; nonetheless, she felt herself grieving, as if this pain were shared—a pain she did not know how to explain to her mother—a pain passed down to her—a pain that made her mother less *Hondureña* than her siblings.

Without warning, Flaca's eyes filled with tears once she noticed her unresponsive daughter.

"*Mi'ja que tienes? Hablame,*" Flaca whispered and felt *mal* and still did not quite understand how *frijoles* could be more than just that. *¿Por qué le importan tanto a Mari?*

As Flaca faced her daughter, she could see the moisture in her eyes. A small strand of Mari's baby hairs hung loosely by her eyes. Her mother gently tucked it between the crevice of her eyeglasses and ear. Mari's vision became blurred and she could only see the pink-pixeled tile floor below her. She remained there—breathing. Soon, she noticed her mother's breath synchronized to hers, and this put her at ease. She realized that the last time she cried was when she ended her relationship with Rita—but could not recall at this moment why she had done so. *Why had she done so?* She missed her, and needed her to hug her. She felt her eyes overflow with tears, and suddenly a few dropped and met the floor. Her mother slowly pulled the chair out and sat her down.

Flaca grabbed the tortillas and cheese and walked over to the stove. She set the worn-out *comal* on top of the flame and gently opened the pack of tortillas. Afterward, she grabbed the individual string cheese packs (they had ran out of *queso fresco*) and then placed the tortillas on the *comal* to warm up. Simultaneously, she pulled two bowls from the dish rack and with *la cuchara* scooped beans out of the pot and into the chipped ceramic bowls. She pulled the string cheese and added it to the bowl, watching it quickly melt to the heat of the beans. The bubbles began to form on the tortillas, so Flaca quickly transferred them onto the bowls. She held the two bowls and placed them on the table where Mari sat.

Her daughter still did not move, so she decided to place some beans on the tortilla and hand it to her to take a bite. Mari feebly raised her arm and grabbed the bean and cheese stuffed tortilla. A few beans managed to fall out, but despite that, Mari took one small *mordida*. Already, Flaca had taken a couple of bites from hers.

Not able to withstand the silence anymore, Flaca diverted her attention to the screen—the remains of the zebra now picked by vultures.

Hesitantly she asked her daughter, "*¿Como están los frijoles, mi'ja?*"

As she released the last word, the door knob shuffled a bit and Mari shifted her head quickly to the door—alarmed, like a wide-eyed deer.

The door cracked open and she instantly recognized her father's work boots.

Mari stared deep into her mother's eyes and noticed they smiled back at her.

"*Estan salados.*"

FRANCISCO ARAGÓN

# Blister

*THE NOUN*


A disease
of the peach tree
—a fungus

distorts leaves.
The first time
I was taken

to see him
I was five
or six. A vesicle

on the skin
containing
serum, caused

by friction,
a burn, or other
injury. He lived

on Alabama Street
next to Saint
Peter's and wore

a white t-shirt,
starched and snug.
A similar swelling

with fluid
or air
on the surface

of a plant,
or metal
after cooling

or the sunless
area between
one's toes

after a very
long walk.
Don't ask me

how it is I
ended up
holding it.

An outer
covering
fitted to a

vessel to protect
against torpedos,
mines, or to improve

stability. My guess
is that he
brought it out

to show me
thinking, perhaps,
I had never

seen one
up close,
let alone felt

the blunt weight
of one
in my hands.

A rounded
compartment
protruding

from the body
of a plane.
What came

next: no
image but
sensation of

its hammer
(my inexpert
manipulation)

digging
into but not
breaking

skin—the spot
at the base
of my thumb

balloons,
slowly filling
with fluid...

In Spanish:
*ampolla*
—*an Ampul*

*of chrystal*
in the Middle
Ages could be

a relic containing
the blood
of someone

holy. I'm fairly
certain it wasn't
loaded.

FRANCISCO ARAGÓN

# Dogs

Or the one Maria found, trotting
along the banks of the Yuba—
named after the river, red

scarf around the snowy neck
that week of camping, coaxed
onto the backseat and home…

He mentions one—*de raza alemana*, he says
and I'm almost charmed by the voice:
telling how he'd tie his German

shepherd to a pole, escort her
to church: Plaza Santo
Domingo flanked by the park, kiosk

beside the roasting beef, pleasant
*olor de carne asada* wafting
to the bench after mass

where they talked—she mostly:
her sewing, her trip to Panama
in search of wholesale fabrics

—I'm trying to picture it: Managua
in the fifties, around the time
my father's plane lifts off, touches

down, sending for her months later,
big with Maria, as I'm also
trying to picture him

on the other end of the line: in his
sixties, portly, sugar
in his blood, a whiff of something

on his breath as he speaks
of the Sacramento
River: pole and gear, sixpack,

Rocky and Comet slinking behind
—*but the car's busted now*, he says
basting in gravel

near Chico. He gets to bed
past three, watching *Cristina,*
the Tuesday Night Fights, sunk

in a beat-up armchair:
replay of that memorable bout, Aaron
Pryor delivering a blur of shots

to the head, Alexis Arguello absorbing them...
During the phonecall
we talk dogs. He had three,

we had two—something
I suppose in common;
this talk of ours

a first.

FRANCISCO ARAGÓN

# January 21, 2013

IN NOVEMBER OF 2012 ARIZONA STATE UNIVERSITY ISSUED A PRESS RELEASE
ANNOUNCING THE ACQUISITION OF A PRIVATELY-HELD COLLECTION OF MANUSCRIPTS
CREATED BY NICARAGUAN POET RUBÉN DARÍO, WHO IS WIDELY RECOGNIZED AS THE
FOUNDER OF SPANISH-AMERICAN MODERNISMO. THE COLLECTION CONSISTS OF 900 OR
SO HANDWRITTEN PAGES OF POETRY, ESSAYS, STORIES, AND PERSONAL LETTERS, NINE
OF WHICH REVEALED FOR THE FIRST TIME AN INTIMATE RELATIONSHIP BETWEEN DARÍO
AND THE FAMED MEXICAN POET AMADO NERVO. SHORTLY AFTER ASU MADE ITS
ANNOUNCEMENT, THE NICARAGUAN NOVELIST SERGIO RAMÍREZ PUBLISHED AN
ARTICLE IN WHICH HE RENOUNCED THE LETTERS AS FAKE.

Dear Sergio:

Your depiction—in *Margarita,*
*How Beautiful The Sea*—
of my homecoming to León in 1907

once again filled my arms with bouquets
that dampened my silk suit, baskets of flowers
and fruit, which I accepted with a nod

though leaving them in the hands of my entourage,
a cambric handkerchief wiping the sweat
dripping down my face and neck.

And as I opened a path for myself, village
folk pressing around, their lips at my sleeves,
a little boy with curly hair led the way

clutching the flag of Nicaragua.
I loved how you had Momotombo,
years later in 1916, blow—

moments after I drew my last breath,
the volcano producing a deep rumbling,
sending people into the streets,
 a spatter of sparks lighting the sky.

I wasn't aware (of course) of what came next—
your novel placing me there, in that room:

the doctor's scalpel blinking like a star
in the moment it traced the incision
on my forehead, my scalp folded back, the saw's

fine teeth biting into cranium, he
feverishly snipping ligaments, holding in his hands
my brain, seconds later proclaiming:

"Here it is—the private vessel of the muses!"
More than cringe, I blushed
at being handled with such care.

Perhaps you're surprised by this letter?
You shouldn't be. Anything is possible
in this racket of ours. But artful

is not how I'd describe that piece
you penned last November. You see:
those letters to Amado were real.

I bargained with myself, rewrote them
to preserve them, precisely because I knew
what would happen—you know

as well as I: he would have destroyed them
after reading them: *What will people say?!*
(he with wife and children) held sway…

I *was* in New York shortly after New Year's
in 1915 heading home, when I wrote to him
one more time. But you were right

and I'm mildly embarrassed to admit it:
I told a little lie on those sheaths
of Hotel Astor stationery in Times Square:
 the poem I enclosed wasn't composed
in Barcelona

expressly for him:
it was a piece of *juvenalia*, I know, but one

I had a soft spot for, and which I re-titled
and dedicated—to him. It was a running joke
between us: sending each other our fluff.

And yet, it's ironic, Sergio: thank you
for being complicit, for hinting at
my understory. How did you manage to nail

those final hours? I was indeed lying curled up
on my side, wrapped in a thick, gray blanket, snoring
lightly, my mouth slightly open as my fingers gripped

the silver crucifix that Amado—yes, Amado Nervo—
had given to me in Paris
when we shared that apartment

in Montmartre, and that I always carried
with me. I'd like to think that, somehow,
you knew—and know—this truth.

I'm waiting for the day when you,
the world, stop fighting it. I am
dead, and the dead are very patient.

Love,
Rubén

CLAUDIA CASTRO LUNA

# The Stars Remain

*Of what came before and nights were white*

**1.**  1970. Everything I know about the church, God, the devil, and the spirit world comes from my *abuelita*. She gives me instructions to ensure that my *alma*, my soul, finds its way back into my body after its nightly excursions, teaches blessings, shows me an altar's essential components: water, a candle, incense, and whenever possible, a clump of rue. All of this knowledge she passes down to me hand over hand, word over word, the way she learned from her own *abuela*.

As soon as I'm old enough she teaches me how to cross myself. "*Por la señal de la Santa Cruz...*" she says and I quickly stumble after her like a kid trying to keep up with a rushed parent. The words are matched step by step by a repeated pattern of hand gestures making the sign of the cross. She places my thumb over my index finger and guides me, pausing first over my forehead, then over my cheeks, then to navel and shoulders finishing on my lips. "Kiss the cross," she says when we get to my lips. And I do. I kiss it and say a reverent "Amen."

Abuelita takes her time with me even though patience is not her virtue. By necessity she is a woman of swift action. Widowed in her early twenties, determination, grit, and an irascible temper exemplify the breath of her emotional repertoire. In a fraction of a second she can go from laughing heartily to reaching perilous levels of anger. One of her searing and creatively strung lists of insults can flat out shake down all the leaves of a mango tree leaving bare branches with birds cowering at her words.

Lucky for me my *abuelita* loves me, her oldest grandchild, and so she works hard to share with me the array of amulets, prayers, and rituals known to her so that I may live a long and fruitful life under the winning patronage of all the saints and angels in Heaven.

**2.**  1971. Again and again Papá declares that things of the church are "*Puras babosadas*." Religion is the opium of the masses, Papá says, and says it without any hint of pretention or cynicism. Mami is not as strident in her opposition to church and spiritual things, but her silence lends a tacit agreement to Papá's more active opinions. In a country 99% Catholic, I belong to the 1% of families that reject any type of organized religion and deplore penchants of the spiritual kind. Religious anything is strictly forbidden in my house.

My parents are young teachers, raising two young daughters. As members of the country's teachers' union they focus their energy on fighting for better salaries and with improving the squalid living conditions of the students they teach. To them, understanding the social and political conditions under which we live, and doing something to change them, is all the religion we need.

**3.**    When the heat of the day lays languid in the crowns of the tallest trees, Abuelita takes me down the length of our long cobblestone street to the town's square to hear Mass. We return in darkness and find *Papá* pacing back and forth enrobed in the dim light cast by the lamppost in front of our house.

"*Dónde estaban?*" he demands in a rough voice. "*Las busqué por todos lados!*"

"*En la iglesia,*" answers Abuelita, unconcerned.

"*Què, què?!!!*" Papá can't hide his annoyance.

"*Que fuimos a la iglesia, hombre, solo por un ratito…*" Man, Abuelita says, we were at church just for a little bit.

"*Pues, no quiero que la este llevando a la iglesia. Entiende?*" Papá snaps and his eyebrows meet smack in the middle of his forehead. If he were an animal he would have growled and snarled, but given that Abuelita is his mother, he offers a warning instead: Don't take her to church again!

Abuelita looks back at him with heraldic bearing, with one look she lets him know that if she wants to she will take me to Mass any day of the week she damn well pleases.

**4.**    1976. One day Papá appears in the doorway to the bedroom I share with my sister. He is just out of the shower; water still trickles from his wet hair.

"*Qué esta haciendo esa mierda allí?*" He demands.

I look up at the "shit" he's pointing to. A small bust of the Virgin Mary hangs from the wall, her face tilted downward. An identical figure rests over my sister's bed. I grow cold. When my sister and I decided to put them up, we knew we risked a confrontation that could end up settled with a belt, but the little busts were too beautiful to keep in their newspaper wrapping under our beds and they matched perfectly and Tia Vivian said they would prevent evil spirits lurking at night from snatching our souls and Carmen and I don't want our souls snatched.

I stare at Papá staring at me. I have been on the receiving end of his searing belt enough times to know that tears don't make welts go away. "*Nos las dió Tía Vivian la última vez que visitamos. Abuelita las compró en el Mercado,*" I say and glance at my sister playing with dolls on the floor between our beds. "*Son para velar los sueños,*" I add. Safe dreams or not, Papá stands under the door's frame; his jaw locked, his mouth considering something. A grunt escapes him. The doll's hair winds around and around Carmen's fingers. I wish that whatever is running through his mind, please, be it not to hit me.

"*Quiere que las quitemos?*" I ask ready to spring up and take them down.

"*Solo son babosadas ustedes!*" he says, then spins around and disappears down the hall. Nonsense he calls it, our gesture to hang the Virgins.

"*Nos salvamos!*" says Carmen and the suggestion of a smile registers on her face. We are saved indeed. Though I cannot see it, I know, a smile also registers on mine.

**5.** February, 1977. Presidential elections. General Carlos Humberto Romero from the PCN (*Partido de Conciliacion Nacional*) is declared the winner. Widespread accusations of voter intimidation and ballot tampering ensue. The outgoing President, Coronel Arturo Armando Molina also from the PCN and also made winner in 1972 through egregious electoral fraud denies any wrongdoing. Eight days after the election a group gathers in San Salvador to protest the results and national security forces open fire killing hundreds—between 200 and 1,500—no official figures are ever released.

**6.** 1978. Señor C, another of my parents' friends and fellow teacher, is killed while reading the afternoon newspaper. The killers leave a hand imprint on the wall outside his front door. The level of violence and terror erodes the objections Papá harbored against my religious inclinations. One day Mami tells him that I attended an Evangelical service with a neighbor. He stares at me and laughs.

**7.** 1979. Since our move to San Salvador the sound of gunfire is as familiar as the sound of roosters breaking dawn was in Atiquizaya. My legs twitch every time a convoy, teeming with heavily armed soldiers, crawls along as I wait afterschool for my bus. I dread getting hit by a bullet. But what scares me even more is that Papá may disappear and not return home one day. To disappear is to suffer the cruelest fate. Some of the disappeared are left on the side of roads dismembered and tortured. Others are kept tortured but alive as political prisoners and others are never found.

**8.**   1980 is a terrible year. Terror and silence are the baseline of our everyday. I pick up and paste together scraps of information from what I hear on the radio and from slogans sprayed on walls. I scavenge for drifts of overheard conversation in buses or when adults visit our house. No one ever considers sitting with us children to tell us what is going on. Few dare talk about it. Silence becomes an acknowledgment of fear. Fear an indication that death roams hungry day and night.

**9.**   *"En nombre de Dios, en nombre de este sufrido pueblo…*
*les suplico, les ruego, les ordeno, que cesen la represión."*
—Monseñor Romero, Bishop of San Salvador

The war makes people do the unthinkable. Papá has taken to tuning his transistor radio each Sunday to hear mass. Mami, Papá, Tío Jaime, Carmen, and I, even the dog, Monina, huddle on the stairs leading up to the second floor to hear Monseñor Romero deliver Sunday's homily from the National Cathedral.

Monseñor Romero's voice rises and falls, fills the air with urgency and hope and we cling to his every word. At thirteen I understand that to call out the injustice and repression, to speak against the military, is to risk your life and it is clear Monseñor risks his a lot. I guess Monseñor is the reason behind Papá's new attitude toward the church, but also something else is at play, something I cannot grasp, and won't understand until decades later.

**10.**   On March 26<sup>th</sup>, Monseñor Romero is murdered while officiating Mass. On December 2<sup>nd</sup> three American nuns and a lay missionary are killed on their way from the national airport in the outskirts of San Salvador. No one is spared. Everyone is suspect: the old for old, the young for their youth, students and teachers for their knowledge, women for accomplices and children because they get in the way.

**11.**   On a windy afternoon Mami comes home and tells us that our petition for U.S. Resident Status has been approved. To leave means survival. Following the news of our departure hope crawls back into our lives. I skip more than walk. Only *Papá* drags his feet. I've heard his concerns about leaving: how to survive in an unfriendly place without speaking English, how hard to leave everything. "Everything" is code for the political movement he believes in and risks his life for.

At night Papá stands in the back door's threshold looking up as if waiting for the stars to spell out a message just for him. Despite grim days, the stars fierce brilliance dazzles us night after night. I know they would still shine if Papá disappeared. It would make no difference to them if we left or stayed. Suddenly, I glimpse the choice Papá needs to make: to abandon his comrades and convictions or to protect his family, to take a step off a ledge or to walk straight into darkness.

*Of what came after and days were blue*

**12.** 1982. Life in the U.S. is safe, yes, but also small.

We are each other's only reference points in the absence of our large extended family and my parents' network of friends and work colleagues. Our world dulls in stark contrast to the tropical sun that suffuses everything in El Salvador. Concerns are of a different kind: finding jobs and schools, learning English. My parents struggle to make ends meet. Mami cleans houses and works an assembly line checking transistor parts. Papá washes dishes, mops floors, and mows lawns. They struggle with their marriage. They struggle to give us as much comfort as their pockets can afford and as much warmth as they can find in their wounded hearts.

Little by little Carmen and I swap Spanish for English. At first, we practice single words with each other.

"Battery," I say in my thick accent.

"Battery," she repeats in her nascent American one.

School, The Brady Bunch, Happy Days, and other T.V. shows propel us into fluency. We go from words, to phrases, to sentences, and the day arrives when Spanish is no longer necessary, or wanted, between us.

With a university degree in English from El Salvador, Mami reaches fluency. Papá struggles. Washing dishes and doing janitorial work require minimal English skills. He spirals downward—the less he is able to communicate in English the worse he feels about himself, the bigger the gap between him and Mami. English fills our world the way a cotton ball inside a glass absorbs water. There is less and less space left for him in our narrow glasses.

**13.** 1985. With time the Spanish words that contain our experience and that might help us make sense of our exile get covered with thick dust, idling messages inside glass bottles bobbing at sea. We drift apart. We retreat into ourselves and let sorrow, loss, fears, guilt, navigate unresolved and unchecked in the tunnels of our subconscious.

**14.** 1990. One morning, after 24 years of marriage, Mami leaves for work and never comes back. My sister is away at college. Papá and I, and our shared sadness, are left in the apartment. I go to bed and leave him, sitting on the floor, his back against the bed frame, knees to chest. I wake up to find him in the same position—frozen in place.

**15.** As a university student I travel to study in Europe. Years later back in the United States I reconnect with a young German doctor I met while visiting exiled relatives in Holland. He visits and along the coast between L.A. and San Francisco he proposes. Eager to move on, to have a home again, a family, I say yes.

My marriage lasts almost three years. I call Papá from Germany and ask if I can move in with him. Mami is remarried and living in Costa Rica. Papá lives with Tía Sonia, her two sons and Abuelita, who came to the U.S. to support Tía Sonia while Tía works long days to establish her fledgling Salvadoran restaurant. Papá and I share a room and the single bed in it, and since we have similar habits quickly fall into a routine: we read in bed and when each is satisfied with the night's reading we turn the light off, give our backs to each other and fall asleep.

**16.** 1993. The best part about my return is reconnecting with Abuelita. She is older and weaker but has lost none of her luster. She still laughs her full belly laugh and uses the same irreverent language. "*Chimado! Venga para acá!*" "*Hijoeputa!*" "*Que mierdas son estas?*" She sprinkles her days, and ours, with shits, whores, asses and worse. After all the years she has not lost her spiritual compass. She still wears a scapular doused in holy water around her neck, still leaves a glass of water by her bed to ensure that her soul never thirsts during the night. On Sundays I take her to Our Lady of Guadalupe Church in El Monte to hear Spanish Mass. For an hour we enter a borderless space. Next to Abuelita, I'm home. The rest of the time I'm dislocated: my body in California, my mind in Germany, and my heart, torn, somewhere in between.

**17.** My birthday arrives. Tucked in bed, Papá recounts, with as much detail as he can recall, the day I was born. After all the violence, the material lack, the loss of country, the weight of silence, the failure of his marriage, the failure of mine, the demise of family members, friends, and colleagues, after all this, he finds the memory folded tenderly, like a perfumed handkerchief at the back of a linen drawer. Papá is not a warm man. That night, his words bloom in the devastated terrain we share. I am loved, his words say, always have been.

At dawn I open my eyes to find Papá standing in front of his dresser. Shadows grip the room, clothes piled high on a chair, and in a corner my two suitcases gather dust. The cramming all around makes the darkness more encroaching. Through the chaos I feel Papá's calmness. He contemplates a framed image of Saint Jude, Patron Saint of lost causes and silencer of demons, a gift from Abuelita he told me when I commented on it upon first entering the room.

I pretend to sleep, but my heart gallops. In shock I realize he is praying. That morning I learn that Papá is my abuelita's son after all. I learn that he is small, small like I am. We are both finding our way in the world, starting over again and again. Through him I recognize that to reach the fullness of light after deep darkness, requires both bravery and humility. Like the thawing after winter, the softening that allows tiny crocuses to cut through soil, something melts inside me.

**18.** 2004. I am married again and the mother of two little girls. Twenty-nine years have passed since my sister and I took down the Virgins above our beds. Now, a framed icon of Monseñor Romero with the inscription, "*Mi amor es el pueblo,*" hangs in my small office. Next to it, images of Our Lady of Guadalupe fill all available wall space.

One December afternoon while on vacation from El Salvador, Papá visits me in my office. I sit at my desk; he stands in the doorway and points with a bony hand to a framed photograph of the Virgin. Where did I get that one? He wants to know. His stance gentle and inquisitive. A gift that my husband bought for me in Albuquerque, the photo is of Guadalupe painted on a garden courtyard wall.

Etched on face is the topography of time's passing: the shores of an arduous life visible in his hollow cheeks, the meadows of forgiveness around his softer eyes. He is no longer the man I feared.

"*Esta bien bonita verdad!*" I say, holding his eyes. I don't defend my actions; don't explain that I find solace in prayer, that in her image I find my compass, resilience, and hope.

"*Asi es*," he says nodding softly. The suggestion of a smile registers on his face and though I cannot see it, I know, it also registers on mine.

CLAUDIA CASTRO LUNA

# Meditation on the color purple

The last few plums of the season
dangle at the tip of soft branches
swaying to wind's song
dressed in garnets and ruby pinks
most were swiftly snatched in early summer
now the remaining few hang
black-purple enrobed

They remind me of the widows of my childhood
women dressed head to toe in mourning
flesh dangling from bare arms
their weathered skin wondrous and resilient bark
their rheumatic hands softened
with secret unguents, coconut oil and honey balm
wrinkled women, closed shapes
walking over Barrio El Angel cobblestone streets

The final Santa Rosa plums
look like Doña Elvira the last time I saw her
she held herself up, her gaunt figure pushed
against the threshold of her house
thin arms wrapped around each other
her husband long dead, one daughter fallen in war,
the other exiled far away, and Yolanda
wielding will, her worn machete, providing for her own clan

Doña Elvira blended with the wall smudges
turned dusk from mud, sweat, poverty and war
I walked slowly toward her reeling in
the thirty years passed in each other's absence
the ridges on her forehead, the channels in her cheeks,
the faint light of her eyes more purple than black
bitter root the fear in her body
terror of falling—shriveled, and alone.

JESÚS FIGUEROA RUSSELL

# Holidays For Martyred Saints

Like holidays for martyred saints
we carry the weight of remembrance on our shoulders

Like holidays for martyred saints
we walk in processions heads held high
announcing our presence with dignity

Like holidays for martyred saints
we continue the journey as homage
laying carnations in our path
leaving consciousness in our wake

Like holidays for martyred saints
we light candle after candle in rows
praying, resisting, hoping that tomorrow
the path is smoother and less narrow
for the ones that trail behind us

Like holidays for martyred saints
we call on our predecessors to intercede in our favor
sending smoke signals that they might not have approved of
calling them, defending them, embodying them

Holidays for martyred saints
for every breath for every lash for every gash ever inflicted

Holidays for martyred saints
for every tear shed in the distance
for every unknown who grew to know the ground too closely

Holidays for martyred saints
for every arched back and sweat drop
running down the rivulets of furrowed brown faces
for every hand worn smooth by cleaning chemicals

Holidays
for every stabbed knee
for every killed dream
for every single mom crying on the kitchen floor
imploring of her god to send her more
for every broken home
for every cereal bowl with orange juice
for every deception told

For everything that doesn't fit inside the boundaries they've drawn for us

JESÚS FIGUEROA RUSSELL

# Lala in LALALand

*Lala suda y su dolor sale en forma de lagrimas de sal*
*Caen sus gotas en el inodoro*
*Que se vaya todo todo todo*
*Marjaba escapó la opresión*
*Y recuerda su tierra, tierra llena vasta*
*Volcanes sultanes desierto de jungla mixta*
*En su memoria mezcla*
*el istmo con su tierra natal de Beirut*
*Triste recuerda su niñez*
*Hija mercadora de bazares hundidos por granos de memorias*
*Ahora está en nuevas tierras*
*Lala suda duda y reza plegarias para no volver*
*Socate la galleta máma que aquí no hay marcha atrás*
*Pringas de sudor golpean el piso frío*
*Se estrellan al impacto y en sus trozos se refleja el estado del alma*
*Lala la paca*
*Lala la mala*
*Lala la prieta de los chele Figueroa*
*Lala la que*
*nada no hace para mandarle a sus hijos*
*Lala la que*
*llora por las noches al escuchar los aullidos de medianoche*
*El diablo andante, siempre*
*Cruz cruz*
*Lala en Los Ángeles*
In Los Angeles Lala cries
She misses her kids, her home, her old country life
Central American Latin American living in Los Angeles
Lala in LALALand
Trips to Disneyland with the fam
But the family isn't hers, although the kids are more attached to her than
their Mother

Don't play with Lala
The mother warned
She speaks weirdly and is from El Salvador
But I like the way she talks
Don't go into her room anymore
Ok mommie
And Lala is alone once more
And she remembers her land
Volcanoes
Lakes
Soft flowing rivers that braid their way through the earth
*Tierra de ella*
Home is where the love is
But her loves are 3 thousand miles away
With Mama Tila and Tía Conchi
Lala cries on the bathroom floor
Lala cries remembering Lebanon
Lala cries remembering Chalate
Lalas' cry in two separate instances of space and time
Shared pain across different spatial realities
And in comes Margarita
Mommy said I can't speak to you no more
And Lala cries remembering her youngest born
Sun colored hair on rose tinted cheeks
Margarita pats Lala's back
And for a second her dolor subsides
Lala in her native land
Lala in a new land
Lala in her land
Lala in LaLaLand crying for a past told in fluttering vignettes
*Abuela y nieta* crying for what was left
Both in new lands
Their land, new land
*Lala la que dejó su tierra en busca de tierras ignotas*
*Aventurera Caprichosa luchadora*
*Cachimbona*
*Lala en tierra de nadie, Lala en busca de algo mejor*
*Lala la reina*
*Lalalala*

ANDREW BENTLEY

# El Gringo Chapín

"EL SALVADOR? Is that a lot like Guatemala, Daddy? Is it neat?"

"I'm sure it is!"

On my father's lap with a book in my hands, I traced the strangely-shaped contours of my country of origin and its neighbors while simultaneously observing pictures of people with baskets on their heads. From the moment my parents told me about my identity as a Guatemalan growing up as an adopted American, I was hooked. I was seven years old in second grade, and they told me everything they knew about Orbinda, my twenty-one-year-old birthmother, who lived in a violent but beautiful country dealing with an unfair war. Sixteen years later, never losing sight of my beginnings, I majored in Latin American Studies as an undergrad, ignoring small-minded people who rudely asked what I was going to do with that or how I was ever going to find a job. I entered college thinking I wanted to be a high school language teacher and began learning Spanish as a way to connect more intimately with my country. After I read authors like Gabriel García Márquez and Mario Vargas Llosa, studied abroad in Ecuador, and began learning more about my roots, I fell in love with Latin American cultures, especially those from the "mysterious" isthmus in the middle, Central America. What did Arturo Arias call it, again? "The invisible hinge between north and south?" That's *real*. Of course, I have received a lot of crap from "real Latinos" for calling Guatemala "my country," but there is a sense of belonging in my heart that the critics will never fully comprehend.

In 2013, armed with encyclopedic knowledge of, *damn it, my country of origin*, and with the belief that we were going to be okay, I boarded a Delta flight in Albany with my parents. We were to stop in Atlanta and arrive in Guatemala City by early afternoon. In the final approach, I saw the volcanoes from the window and felt myself getting puffy-eyed as Dad said, "Wow, this is cool. This is where your life started! You were born here!" I was scared and excited at the same time. I had been preparing for this trip all along the way, but I couldn't kid myself. My naïve seventeen-year-old self had read about violence in Guatemala through a Google News search and wondered, *but the war is over, isn't the violence over, too?* Maybe that was my innocent Americanness emerging from its cocoon. I remember a news report of two transgender women who were gunned down in front of a bar in broad daylight. I had read how American tourists were robbed at gunpoint on the road leading from the airport into town right after they arrived on a long-haul flight. But we were going to be okay. God would not be so cruel.

That week was the happiest of my life. We visited Guatemala City, marveling at flashy billboards and glitzy malls that could have easily been at home. "*Guate*," as the locals call it, evoked feelings of excitement, curiosity, sadness, and disappointment as we saw street children juggling at red lights beside rich ones in BMWs with tinted windows. It was so unfair. Was this my Americanness shining through once more? We had the chance to leave the capital for the beckoning countryside, something my parents had not been able to do in 1990 because they were so fearful that they lived off of vending machine food during their stay. We visited tiny villages on the shores of Lake Atitlán, which my seven-year-old eyes had only known through pictures on that night in second grade. We rode a tuk-tuk down the main street of Panajachel as I searched for, yes Dad, *another* quetzal trinket. We also went to the market in Chichicastenango to find more treasures. Mom and Dad were nervous there at first, but I reassured them that it was okay. Sights of cute children who giggled easily and babies being gently bounced in their mother's slings to stop the crying made Mom feel better and Dad got a kick out of the persistent boys who wanted to sell him handmade flutes.

"Tell them '*no gracias*,' Dad!"

"Your boy is crazy!" (Yes, the K'iche' boy said it in English!)

The day my parents returned to reality in the States was sad. I drove with them to the airport at five o'clock in the morning. It did not even hit me that they were gone until I came back to the empty hotel room with three beds. All of a sudden I was completely alone in the place that was supposed to be my country of origin—I insisted upon it—but where, somehow, I knew nobody. It was the most unbelievable feeling of complete emptiness and solitude. That night, I did the whitest thing ever and went to a McDonald's around the corner to make myself feel better with crappy comfort food. It didn't feel right eating it with marimba music playing in the background. Little did I know how in a few weeks' time, my life would be turned upside down and it would never be the same again.

Sergio was a nice man with an interesting life. He had studied ornithology and we shared a love of birds and Guatemalan literary figures like the famed Miguel Ángel Asturias, whose statue we passed a couple of times. He drove me to a small hostel where María, the lady at the front desk, took good care of me. She took me out to eat and encouraged me to open up about my trip to Guatemala as the *Gringo* and the *Chapín*; I was both, hence, the term "*Gringo Chapín*" was coined over a plate of salmon sushi. Perhaps it was because she had young sons, but María just seemed to get me. With extremely mixed feelings, I told her that I wanted to find Orbinda. My Mom and Dad were not hurt by my desires to find her; they have wanted this for me all along, otherwise they would have never been so open with the inquisitive seven-year-old with tanned skin. I knew her age as of 1990, which would make her either forty-four or forty-five years old. Perhaps most importantly, I was armed with her *número de cédula*, her identification number, which she will have probably registered with the Guatemalan National Registry of Persons.

The next day, I took a number at an office of RENAP, *el Registro Nacional de las Personas*. We were right next door to Guatemala City's own version of the Eiffel Tower. My heart felt like it was going to beat out of my chest. It also felt like an eternity before they called my number 707. When I got there, they were in the 300's, and each time, someone would head to the window for information and take an eternity, as things tended to do in Central America when you're in a hurry. I was too nervous to even play with my phone. What if she were dead? What if she had been murdered in the state-sponsored violence that took so many people away? *Damn it, God would not be so cruel, Andrew.* When my number was finally called, I gave the briefest version of my story that I could think of given the situation. My emotions were all over the place, and I was not even sure my Spanish was coherent. The man told me that I needed to visit the RENAP office closest to where I was born.

After some research and negotiating with Sergio, he sent another driver to bring me to the RENAP office on the fringes of the capital. As we drove the next morning, I clutched the blue folder with all of Orbinda's important information. This RENAP office was different because instead of pulling a number like I was next in the rack at a meat counter, there was a long line snaking its way out of the building. The people in line, mainly indigenous with traditional garb, looked weary of my presence. I was the tallest of them, a feeling quite unlike anything I had ever experienced. After what seemed like an hour in the hot sun, an armed security guard with a machine gun went to lock the gate. Without fully comprehending what I was doing or what prompted me to act so brashly, I pushed my way to the front of the line and faced the man with the weapon. I explained that it was imperative that I get in the office, that it was an emergency, that I was searching for a family member I had not seen in twenty-three years. For a moment I thought he was going to shoot me as my eyes met his smaller, mysterious, black ones, as if they held many secrets. He let me pass. Incredulously, I edged down the row of seats as each person was called to the front desk. Many of them did not even have shoes.

When I was called to the desk, I handed the woman Orbinda's name and ID number, and without daring to believe what I was witnessing, I watched as she went to the backroom and opened a drawer. She came back to the desk with an encyclopedia-sized book filled with photographs and information about people. At this point, my heart felt as though it was going to explode. Could this really be happening? I remember the most indescribable joy when the woman turned to Orbinda's page. There was her name, her date, and place of birth. She came from a tiny village near the Mexican border. Her parents' names were there, Belisario and Dolores. Her picture was there. Her picture. For the first time in my life, I saw what she looked like. I had her eyes, mouth, shape of face, and prominent ears. All that wonder since I was seven, put to a halt. Tears streaming down my face, I asked the woman if she could make copies. As Sergio's friend drove me back to the hostel, I called Mom and bawled as I said, "MOM, I look just like her!"

Perhaps the most shocking element of this successful RENAP trip was the fact that they gave me an address, in Zone 18. They cautioned me to be careful and to never venture there alone. Before going back to the hostel, I had Sergio's friend help me find the address. A confused and scared-looking young boy answered the door and told me he had never heard of the woman I was seeking. The next few days are like one big blur. I returned to the hostel and María clutched her heart as I shared the news. I waited in a few more lines at RENAP offices dotted throughout the city. I was desperate to find an updated address, a phone number, anything. I thought for sure I would have luck at the office on the Pan-American Highway, but when the woman behind the counter just stared at me like I had fallen out of the sky from another planet, I ran outside and hailed a cab. Two taxis attempted to pull over for me, one cutting off the other and nearly forcing it off the road. Ignoring him, I went for the less aggressive taxista and asked him to drive me around the city, anywhere, Zone 10 even. I needed some time to think. He jiggled the rearview mirror to get a better look at me as we inhaled the black smoke coming out of a red municipal bus. He asked me if anything was wrong, and I told him not to worry about it. He could tell I was distraught. Forgetting about the traffic or how much money I had, I told him the condensed version of how I wanted more than anything to find Orbinda, to even talk with her for five minutes. We reached a red light when he turned around and promised that we would find her together.

Gustavo became a friend when I needed one more than ever before. He accompanied me across what seemed like the apocalyptic ends of the earth, to parts of Guatemala City where humanity and any hope for a brighter future have been washed away. At this point, I don't even know where I got the courage and persistence to keep going. I had to somehow become more *Chapín* and less *Gringo*. We returned to that house in Zone 18 and interrogated more neighbors. An old woman sitting on her front step had *heard* of Orbinda but didn't know anything else. More office visits; more sleepless nights; more knocking on random doors hoping the house didn't belong to a serial murderer, all with Gustavo at my side. A tip from one of the workers at the hostel whose name I never discovered saved my life— "Go to Metronorte," he told me, the business center in Zone 18. They had records of people. Completely ignoring the armed guard with an AK-47, I barged into a cramped office with nicely-clothed workers as Gustavo waited in the parking lot. I could tell they took me seriously when they found a phone number in a computer system. I shook uncontrollably as I dialed the number. The man on the other line wondered why I wanted to speak to his ex-wife. Holy shit… could this be my birth-father? He gave me another number, this time for a landlord. Gustavo spoke to her, and she informed him how Orbinda lived in a house *with her two daughters*. I had two little sisters all along, and the landlord, a Nicaraguan lady named Anabela, gave me a cell phone number, which she insisted belonged to Orbinda, along with yet another address.

Gustavo and I had a hell of a time finding it. We did find an elementary school, more neighbors, and a hot dog vendor (which I later learned was a *shuco* vendor). A powerful thunderstorm interrupted our search. I crouched in the car—something told me to crouch because of all the horror stories I had heard about this notorious area—watching the heavy rain obscure my view of candy-colored squatter settlements hugging the side of a hill. A bolt of lightning nearly missed us and instead struck a bright pink building on the other side of the road. As the storm lifted, I got out of Gustavo's taxi and thought pensively. A woman crept up to us in her car, driving so slowly that I felt suspicious. It was Anabela, and she knew it was me just by glancing at my bewildered expression. I hadn't called Orbinda's cell phone number because I didn't want to scare her, but Anabela handed me her already ringing Nokia with Orbinda's name on the screen. She answered, and the following conversation transpired in Spanish.

"Am I speaking with Orbinda?"

"Yes…"

"I want to start by saying I don't want to scare you. I've come from far away to meet you; I live in the United States.

"Who is this?"

"I don't want you to feel frightened, but I believe I am your son."

"My son? WHO IS THIS?"

"Do you remember the date, January 10th, 1990?"

Silence. Static. Honking traffic. A loud half cry, half gasp.

"Are you still there?"

"MY SON. You're alive! Where? HOW?"

"I'm here in Guatemala City."

"HOW?"

"I'm here in Zone 18, in the Atlántida neighborhood with Anabela. She says we're right next to your house. Can you see me today? *Do* you want to see me?"

"Of course! I'll be there in fifteen minutes."

They were the longest fifteen minutes of my life. As we waited, the unthinkable happened. A girl dressed all in black walked by slowly toward the bright pink house. Anabela told me that it was my sister, Jenny. Resisting the overwhelming urge to approach her so as not to sabotage any possibility to see Orbinda, I asked Anabela how her car was so dry after such a powerful storm. There was no storm. Even the *shuco* salesman told us there was no storm. There was no thunder and lightning, even though Gustavo and I had seen how it struck right in front of the bright pink house where Jenny had entered. Either it was a deceased loved one trying to guide the way, or magical realism really did exist just as Gabo had taught me. Before I could make sense of *anything*, Gustavo nudged me. A short woman, also dressed in black like Jenny, was waving from the other side of the street. We knew who each other was instantly. Without even looking both ways, we each made a beeline for each other. She was carrying groceries, which fell to the ground, sending onions and potatoes rolling in every direction. She was carrying her purse, which also fell to the ground in a sea of hand sanitizer. Her phone was ringing in her hand but it didn't matter. When we reached each other in the middle of the road, Orbinda embraced me as she collapsed to the ground, heaving, crying, and laughing all at the same time. She hugged me so tight I felt as though my ribcage were going to break, as she touched my face. "You look just like…" but she could say no more. Even Gustavo was crying as Jenny reached the scene, followed by Wale, my other sister.

Thus began the relationship with the rest of my family. I was happy, my parents were happy, my Guatemalan family was overwhelmed but happy, and somehow, everything seemed to finally make sense for that seven-year-old boy on his father's lap. Orbinda had given me life and sisters and Mom and Dad had given me their hearts and souls and literally everything else I have, and, most importantly, the will and volition to keep going as the *Gringo Chapín* in the United States, in Central America, in the universe.

ADELA NAJARRO

# Early Morning Chat with God

THIS MORNING I'm back to asking for patience.
With my cup of coffee I sit outside to say Hello
to you God, my Jiminy Cricket, my salsa
dancing quick-with-a-dip *amigo*. We have
a very collegial relationship. I laugh
at all your jokes and praise the wonders
of a sky's watercolors. I know you like me,
a benign affection and tolerance as I run
around like a chicken with its head cut off,
a truly gruesome image, nevertheless
hilarious like a grisly cartoon. The blood splurting.
The body winding down to zero. The crashing
into unforeseen objects. I think if I
were back on my great-grandmother's farm,
the farm that I know only through stories
my mother tells of Nicaragua, Bluefields,
a tortilla filled with just enough, and I saw
the long scrawny neck and the axe,
I would be sick to my stomach: the aimlessness
of her final strut, the reality of blood
loss, her claws scratching the dirt, kicking up rocks,
a panic. But when she stops, into the pot
she goes. A meal, what we need to continue,
her flesh simmered off the bone. Truly delicious
in a tomato sauce flavored with green peppers
and onions. Transformation. The feathers
plucked. Soil and dust washed away. The table set.
Goblets of red wine, white china plates,
a cast iron pot twirling a bay leaf
scented steam. Then a prayer and gratitude
that we have enough to make it through
another night alone, a night filled with longing
whispers and the turbulence of dreams.

ADELA NAJARRO

# After the 1979 *Revolución Nicaragüense*

My parent's history was erased. Their Nicaragua
gone forever. My mother believes

I will be assaulted if I return to Managua. My father
refuses to go with me.

They wrestle memories

of what was playing on the radio
and a humidity that did not cease. I wonder

about evenings where green parrots
fly into an overbearing canopy,
while iguanas sit low and watch.

The iguana knows how to run
when shadows arise
loose from bodies dormant and dead.

In 1920, after Rubén Darío's death,
the entire nation agreed to rename

a city in his honor. His birthplace,

Metapa, became Cuidad Darío,
poetry being the national pastime.

But then Somoza, armed men in jeeps,
ghost shadows dancing on skin,

all too often.

As Nicaragua's poetic sweetheart,
Darío conjured mermaids
diving deep in lake Managua

and swans sailing slowly on the ponds
of a golden palace.

He set a lyrical backdrop
for a land where my mother's
hair was tied up in ribbons
as she skipped past a garden
where a peacock spread
royal blue and a rose was cut,
only to droop
in a vase by the window.

Sometimes,
imaginative sonnets
by long dead poets

allow us to escape

bone skin children, bloated seagulls,
cathedrals where incense burns shame.

As the revolutionary hurricane swept
coffee plantations clean,

green humidity clung at right angles
on reptilian scales,

while Darío's mermaids

choked in the fresh air.

ADELA NAJARRO

# Star Variation in Blue

if the world is fracture and uncertainty
          let us take comfort in the unknown

if the world is fracture and uncertainty
          let us take comfort in the unknown

rainfall collects then rushes through
          a bend in the river
          a gutter in an alley
          stars in a night sky

          let us take comfort in the unknown

once concentric spheres made the sky

once God wore a beard and sandals

once we were      water    sky              stars

let us take comfort in the unknown
          if the world is fracture and uncertainty

          a bone can fracture
          a body bleed
          that is certain

when a bone fractures
          guttural vowels howl

when a body bleeds
          consonants cannot stop the pain

it is certain that vowels escape

       chaotic
       hard

into what cannot be written

       as bones fracture
       as bodies bleed

let us take comfort in the unknown
the world is fracture and uncertainty

in the beginning
       a woman loved the stars
       a man loved God
       both loved rainfall rushing

through concentric spheres in the sky

it was known the Goddess

       had thick breasts
       belly and thighs

and that we are brought to life
       through  water    sky        stars

let us take comfort

the world

too often

is fracture and unknown

that is certain

ANA PÉREZ

# Dust Angels

"WHEN I LOOKED into your eyes, I knew what being in love was all about and now you will know that love too," my mother told me when I told her I was pregnant. And it was not until I had a child of my own that I truly understood what she meant.

Unconditional, complete, and uninhibited love is what my mother has given me. My father is just a blurred memory, so my mother's love saved me. I was born in the state of La Libertad and the city of Santa Tecla, a place where most people "had": had toilets that flushed; had light switches to flick on and off; lived on streets that had names and addresses. Yet I was born on the outskirts of my city, the part of town where the streets were not paved, had no name, no electric light. Unlike most people around me, we had little.

I am the daughter of a woman who was sent to the city to work as a maid when she was twelve. Shoeless. I'm told that her body then was much like my own at the same age: long, skinny legs, with round, knobby knees, flat-chested, and with no hips to speak of. Just like I did at that age, she must have had to push her hip out sideways to create a resting place for the children she cared for. Women naturally have protruding hips, but my mom at twelve had to improvise and leave her child's play behind. She was an indian and a peasant girl who casted her eyes to the earth most of the time and who could barely write her name, forced to grow up and be a woman way before her time.

I'm the daughter of a man who was the master of the house she worked at, an upstanding man who headed a household with many children. Children I have never met. And like most servants of that time, and of all times, my mother's story is of conquest and resistance.

My skin tone comes from my mom's side of the family—the earthiest browns, mixed with the luscious red clays of my family's land. La Libertad. The land of liberty. My mother is the third child of ten children my grandmother raised. "Thirteen if three hadn't died," brags my grandmother with a high-pitch chuckle at the end. "In those days, there were no hospitals and no doctors. All I had was a bottle of *aguardiente* and my mother to catch the baby."

I'm the bouncy child—the one with loose curls in her hair in a family of straight-haired children. I'm my family's rich soil—the soil in which many hopes have been entrusted. I'm the pretty little girl who dressed in the pleated Catholic school mini-skirt uniform. I'm the curious wide-eyed child who learned to get on a bus by herself at the age of five. The girl neighborhood women liked to share their seats on the bus with when they were on their way to the market.

The only thing I know about my father is his name. But I can claim to be the first in my family to be born in a hospital. Until my mother made the journey from her home in the hills of coffee plantation, everyone was born in the main room of the house. It was the only room with a dirt-floor, packed mud walls, and *teja*-roofed house. Yet that room was large enough to hold up to seven beds, large sacks of supplies, an altar, and a couple of trunks that held everyone's belongings.

The seven beds were well used. No one ever slept alone. For a while, I slept with four other cousins in the same bed; they lined us up horizontally so we could all fit. And like my grandmother, my mother's older sister Emma gave birth to her children screaming and swigging shots of a sugarcane based alcohol, lying on a *petate*—a mat made out of bamboo threads.

The smell of wet earth fills my lungs even now. Sometimes after a long run, I smell the sweat under my armpits and get my fill of the musky scent of the earth. During births the floor swallowed the rich waters from deep inside the female members of my family. But on regular days, the water came from my grandmother's daily cleaning. She would bathe the floors with handfuls of water from a plastic bowl to have the earth pack itself neatly. Sometimes when rain starts to pour and I'm standing in a large dusty field, I transport myself back into my grandmother's house. As a child I would watch my grandmother intently as she carried out this daily ritual. Sometimes if I looked close enough, I could see little angels rising from the dirt, their little wings flapping to escape the large droplets of water that were meant to trap them.

When I close my eyes and take a deep breath I can feel my grandmother's fingers through my hair. "¡*Hay que pelo*! (Oh what hair!), *Niña quedate quieta* (Girl stay still)," she would say to me as she combed my hair into two neat braids. I have always had long hair—except of course for the time when my mother left. Then I chopped it off. Once my hair was gone, I thought so too would go the feelings of being lost without my mother's hands scrubbing my body in the sink as she attempts to "take off the stains" from my elbows and knees. I wanted to chop off the feeling of the tasteless food sliding down my throat. Stop the nights from passing, since they would slowly take away her scent from our bed. Stop the screams of men being dragged out of their homes after curfew by soldiers in their attempts to end the uprising and of me lying with no one to comfort me. The hair was off. I was eight. But the feelings have never left me.

The dust, the sadness, and the little angels trying to escape stay with me—as does my daily ritual of trying to scrub "the stains" off my knees and elbows. Sometimes when the scrubbing isn't enough, I swab on a little lemon juice and I sunbathe. But the stains never get lighter.

I don't know if the memory I have of my mother leaving is real, or if I am just piecing together the stories I have heard. Some of my early memories are of sleeping next to my mother and grandmother, of them sneaking out of bed when it was still dark out and lighting a kerosene lamp. I would wake to the smell of kerosene and the murmuring of prayers as the women chanted the rosary kneeling on an altar with pictures and statues of saints and virgins next to my grandmother's bed.

When my mother was there, she would wake me long after all the morning meals were prepared and everyone who worked in the field or in the Patron's ranch was gone. We would sit and eat together—freshly made tortillas, a bit of beans, a cup of coffee, and sometimes cheese. When my mother was not there, I would be forced out of bed as soon as my grandmother lit the fire in the kitchen and started to make tortillas.

Like everything else in the house, the kitchen was simple and made mostly of creatively transformed brown earth. The stove sat on a raised wooden platform. It was an oval shaped out of clay with a ridge open on one side where firewood would be packed in. On top sat round clay *comal*— a flat surface where tortillas were cooked. Next to the *comal* was another small fire pit where one by one beans, corn, eggs, and sometimes vegetables were cooked. Those terrible mornings when my mother was not around, I was expected to get up, brush my teeth, comb my hair, and get the baskets ready. Then I would walk behind my grandmother as if in a trance, for what seemed like miles until we would arrive at the coffee plantation. I always knew we were getting close when I could smell the sweetness of the red cherries ready to be picked.

I had my own little basket that fit perfectly in the front of my body and was tied to my torso with a strap that allowed the basket to float like a tray to collect the cherries as they dropped from my fingers onto it. I started working in the coffee plantation alongside my family when I was six. The coffee trees are three to five feet tall. As grownups picked the cherries on top, children worked the under-branches. Younger children, three or four years old, were given the task of picking the beans that had fallen to the ground. We often turned this task into a game and a competition to see who could pick the most beans.

At the end of the day, after all the families packed their pickings into large sacks, everyone gathered in the large courtyard of the plantation to spread their beans on large mats—then the sorting process began. By the end of the day, with my little fingers stained black and sticky from the beans, I would sit on my knees and sort through as many as 5 sacks of coffee beans.

Unlike the other children that worked around me, coming to the coffee field and working alongside my grandmother, aunts, and uncles was almost a treat for me. Unlike them, I came only a few weeks during school vacation, and I always knew that I was a visitor. I always felt a little weird befriending those children, since my friends back in the city would laugh about those poor *campesino* children with bloated bellies and skinny legs. I guess I saw myself as different, and I constantly made a point of showing I was better then they were. I did not realize then how similar we were. Those kids were who my mother had been only 25 years earlier. I was one of them deep down.

My father got tired of having a second family and of my mother's attention when she was pregnant with my brother. Before his birth, he stopped coming and stopped supporting us. It was then that she became desperate and started to cook and sell food on the streets of our neighborhood and in the coffee plantations on payday. Payday was always festive. The children got their treats, and the women put aside the money they needed to buy the basic needs of the household and sometimes even managed to buy a pair of shoes for their kids. And some of the men took the money and got themselves drunk out of their minds. It was common to hear men who got into machete fights and would end up losing an arm or an eye. I can still see them in my mind, shiny unblinking eyes, arms raised as they circle in for the kill. Thinking back, I don't remember seeing men with missing limbs back then. It was not until the late seventies and early eighties that men with fewer limbs became a normal sighting.

Given that our visits to my grandmother's house became more regular as my mother grew more desperate to make money, I can't quite recall if the vision of her standing over us is a memory of the many mornings we spent there or if it's really what I remember of the morning she left. I was eight, my brother five, and my sister two.

That morning the sound of crickets was loud, and the stars were shining bright. My grandmother was chanting her prayers, but this time my grandfather was kneeling by her side, and my mother knelt in front of them. My grandmother crossed her thumb over her index finger and drew crosses first across my mother's forehead, then one large one from shoulder to shoulder and belly to mouth then a little one over her mound.

When my mother tells the story she always cries. As a teenager, years later during our difficult first few years of reunification, I would yell at her, reproaching her having left. It has taken me having my own child to imagine what it took for her to leave us. Now I imagine her standing over us. She was very thin then. I know it because when she came to the U.S. she had her photograph taken and she would send it to us. I can imagine her pain at knowing that the journey ahead for her had no guarantees. "People die in those journeys," my uncle told her. I can imagine that as she kissed us good-bye she was scared she would not see us again. Just like when I travel, I get scared that I will never see my son again.

Yet the courageous little girl inside her must have told her that if she walked out of the hills to go work in the city back when she was twelve, then she could surely walk away again and this time across many countries.

The first morning came for me, and many mornings after without me knowing how far she had gone. Maybe no one told me anything because no one knew how far she would really walk and if she was destined to cross that final border—the thin veil between life and death. For weeks my grandparents kept telling me lies. First that she had gone to get supplies from the city. Then that she had gone back to her old job living inside a rich family's home and that she only had one weekend a month free. She would come then, they said. Weeks turned to months. Finally the rainy season came and with it the steady sound of raindrops on the *teja* roof. It was also time for us to go back to our house in the city. So I went with a little bit of hope that maybe she would be there.

But in our home her absence was more pronounced. Her things were nowhere to be found. She did not have many things back then. None of us did. Then my uncle told me the truth, "You should be happy. Your mother will be sending you beautiful things from the U.S." But with my little knowledge of geography and having heard other children in my neighborhood talk about their mothers working in the states, I knew that no pretty dress would ever make my heart feel any better.

I looked at my uncle and walked away. I would not let my sadness show. "*Esa niña es tan lista*," I heard him say. I knew then that my long curls had to go. I knew then what I had to do. I took all the money I had saved. I went to the hairdresser and said, "Chop it off."

I'm a mother now. Marcelo, my nine-year-old boy, is tall and strong bod-
ied, not skinny like I was. But he did inherit the barrel chest of every male
in my family. He also has my mother's and my broad lips. When he was
born, my mother came and stayed with me for two weeks and taught me
about caring for a baby. She taught me the importance of bathing—of how
to be gentle with the sensitive parts of the body and about preventing dark-
ened elbows and knees.

Even now, I occasionally walk into the bathroom and ask Marcelo if he
wants me to scrub him. As I kneel, scrubbing his knees with a loofa sponge, I
see browned water cascading down his legs. I see the angels floating in the
water, their dampened wings not able to take flight. I see the earthy browns
and luscious reds draining. I see my knobby knees in my son's knees, and I
now understand that no matter how hard I scrub or how many times I put
lemon juice on my knees and elbows or on his, the stains will never get any
lighter. As the angels disappear down the drain, the weight of my mother's sac-
rifices dawns on me. I wonder what it would take for me to be willing to leave
my son, and I understand her desperation and see that she had no choice.

RAQUEL GUTIÉRREZ

# Sleepy Amber

These borders are porous, a parasite in our bodies, water and oxygen in surplus;
hover, these symbols diagram another matrilineal existence above our heads

the borders of 1941, or how the line crawls. How soft is its underbelly in the
Honduran breeze, or does the refreshing coolant belong to El Salvador? The border
was soft once,

the throat is responsible for our mobility through its mountains. They suffer
the burden of personal satellite dishes, assets slowly rising in values, mercury, and
awareness that

the coyote apologists and aging punks and other cautionary tales of contrarianisms
made no plan for who is going to take care of you when you're fucked. Catalino, the
toothless.

A grandfather, wiry and turtlenecked. The last time he stood, gold pocked molars,
the only remaining in the back of his mouth, glittered when he laughed.

The border is tender, raw to the touch. We are coarse with our soccer wars, seething
quietly northward. A *comal* burning during the rainy season, a humidity that deadens.

And you, the town alderman with the sleepy amber eyes, hearing cases involving *ma-
chetazos*; the smell of blood on the small of backsides already broken by oligarchy, the
smell of blood

too wild for your daughter, barefoot and curious. You drank and you were abusive.
You drank and you were abusive. Obtusely. I refuse you even though I have your eyes.

RAQUEL GUTIÉRREZ

# There is a moth in my lazy pompadour,

driving around and around avoiding happy hours
    for ancestral gestures in the microwave majesty
another commute formal communing in the zone that says the night's veil has thinned,
fractals fracturing factual capitulations the fragile chapter
    that erupts with humvees and custom hues careening against the daily dying latitude,
a day against consumptive views imbued with not even you can take this panoramic
away from me.
Even when you're not here.          You are mine.

A diuretic prophecy beauty golden and while paling, this sun was temporary,
    assuring me that it was once real.
The axiom tempered by its potential for secret latrines and dirty convivial greet me
    with grin and groin. Such gusto. *Con mucho.*

Shout all you want me down,
lover.
It is how I tread light.

RAQUEL GUTIÉRREZ

# she was my laid eyes upon it

stone turns birthing canals filled
with lava swelling
engorges sputtering volcanic prancing liquid metal

she used to let me cut her hair
little purple flower ring finger
a gorgeous engorged atoning
a gorgon once named
far-roaming, forceful and ruler      was she even mortal?
corpulent trenza cannot contain her, Babylonian hard-on whirlpool
a butter abyss an ocean an infinite inferior for the imperial, impervious ass
the crushing metronome swells, where every minute is accounted for overflow
how do you do so much each day, every day she is beheaded
bane that tired old-money minotaur can't be around brown people
    without buying the
every day she grew back, every day she poked out of her pants
the cat has his own condo laundry burgeon these are the burdens battle
    marathon
it's hard to beat back the West so we settle for the crux and a coin-op
*cruzando* complaints.      she hands over serpent her reign      milk skin *lengua*
when my back is turned      but even handfuls can learn from the arid *madrecita*
and she wouldn't recognize me, fingers too blind      soft matter too soft
    to turn stone
forget the interrupted      curse the gregorian dictate of the tower ahead
where she always
lived before she lived
sometimes I look back at her      was she a temple or a grave?

ÉRIDA MARIELA

# Her Blood

*Mamí* killed him with a prayer

Cleaning his filth for a final time
She decided death was preferable to his
Unholy life. She stared into eyes that were
Already dead and demanded his demise.

*"Te prefiero ver muerto que así"*

He, her brother, died the next day.
She was the only one without surprise. Or regret.

Twenty-five years later she looks at her
Son knowing he is also captured by the
Same capricious spirits. Why are all the men
She loves enticed by an intoxicated death?

Sometimes, *Hermano*,
I sit and pray that this time
*Mamí* will refrain
From killing
You.

ÉRIDA MARIELA

# Shells

i have seen men
turn women into shells
scatter them across the beach
burying them under
wet heavy sand
reachable but
out of sight
unable to feel the ocean calling
ready to be pocketed
another
disposable
treasure

ÉRIDA MARIELA

# The Opposite of Docile

she learned from fighting women
punch, scratch, draw blood women

hide the kitchen knives women

cut you with a shard
of their broken heart women

cats backed into a corner
bite first, cry later women

panthers on the prowl
eat you and smile women

broken women
who made sure they broke
what broke them women

LUIS OVIEDO

# Forward

SHE CRACKED OPEN EGGS and rubbed the whites on my knees, "To make them strong," Marcos said. When I fell and tore open my forehead as I ran down the patio corridor to watch Spider-Man on TV, she was there to pick me up and wipe the blood, and call my mom at work. She fed me *sopa de res* and tortillas when I was sick. She made sure my hair part was neat, and my little white shoes were on right. And when my preschool closed early because the guerrillas put out word of an offensive or bomb threats, Marcos picked me up and darted with me down this street and that, to get me back home in one piece. Maybe she would have taken a bullet for me. She was young enough to move that fast, but old enough to carry ancient wisdom.

Marcos, like the soccer greats, had no last name that I knew of. When you are 4 years old, and in distress, there is no time for last names. I was equally oblivious to any blood relatives she had elsewhere. She was part of our family. Yes, I had grandmothers who loved me, and aunts who fussed over me. But they had to, because they were related to me. Marcos chose to love me.

Just like many others throughout San Salvador, Marcos arrived from one of the far off villages in the more rural parts of the country. She had a room somewhere in the back of our house. I recall glancing at the room once or twice. Once a month or so she would visit her village and see her own family. Her absence was seamless; I barely noticed she'd been away. It wasn't until years later that I realized the realities—economic stratification, civil war, racial lines, urbanization—that brought her to our doorstep.

Similar realities caused us to leave our home around 1979.

It was October when then President General Romero was overthrown in a violent coup supported by the U.S., although the pot had begun boiling long before then. The next year, the Salvadoran National Guard attacked and killed upwards of 50 people participating in a peaceful demonstration. Offenses and defenses, paramilitary killings, disappearances and the forced recruitment of child soldiers all followed. But, by 1992, the powers that be proclaimed peace and the end of a neatly packaged 12-year civil war. Estimates say that of the then existing population of 5.3 million, some 1 million were displaced.

Even as a five year old, I knew that when Marcos had me hide under the bed from flying saucers coming one particularly dark night, that we were hiding from something else. UFOs don't have firecrackers, silly.

Dora Alicia, who came after Marcos, cared for me just the same.

When our American Airlines flight left for Florida in 1979, Dora Alicia came with us because she was part of our family. We needed her.

We drove to Chicago from there. I spent a memorable part of the drive hanging out of the car window, shirtless and yelling out at the top of my lungs, like Tarzan. Being a fearless boy of all of 5 years, I would not succumb to putting on a shirt—even as the winds grew colder and colder—even as we moved further and further north. My parents, they must've been too nervous to notice. Their eyes fixed on the road ahead. Dora Alicia was nervous too. When the truck driver pulled alongside our car, urgently gesturing to her, she looked straight ahead—dutifully heeding my Mom's advice to not speak to any stranger in this new country.

Later, we would discover that he was simply signaling that we'd dropped some luggage from the roof rack a few miles back.

I can't quite remember when we arrived in Chicago, but I recall there being a crisp in the air that I now recognize as that familiar signal that fall is arriving. I also don't remember exactly when Dora Alicia vanished. I may have been too young, or I may just not want to remember. She had her own dreams to pursue.

My cousins in El Salvador shared a home with a small tortoise that grew to become famous among our family. It was known for disappearing for days, weeks, even months on end, and then suddenly we would spot it treading along across the living room floor without a worry in the world, as if nothing had happened. It had no name. We just knew it as *la Tortuga*. We didn't even know if it was male or female. It moved from place to place, suffered through dry spells and torrential downpours alike, and always persevered. When found, we'd watch it for long moments at a time. The thing about tortoises is that they are completely incapable of moving backwards. They are anatomically built to only move forward, however slowly. To this day, I think it still roams the house.

I do not know if there's a method to what remains in one's memory and what doesn't. I remember this about those first few months in Chicago: that a single radio station transmitted Spanish programming for just a few hours a week, that cardboard boxes temporarily doubled as tables, that my brother was born in November, that we lived in a two-flat style house on north Mozart street with drywall so thin that one night the leg of a tenant upstairs crashed through our ceiling right above my brother's crib. That first winter got me frostbite when snow got into my woefully inadequate gym shoes after we went to play in the park with my class that winter. My first birthday/Christmas gift was an orange defectively-oblong Nerf football—a gift which, to date, I cannot fathom the sacrifice it meant for my parents to buy. I kept it for years to come, even as the sponge deteriorated. I remember my first fight. Some Polish kid called me spic, and although I didn't really know what it meant, I was told it was bad so I grabbed him by his jacket and threw him. I remember starting the first grade, speaking no English. I remember my parents' convincing argument to the school principal that I need not repeat kindergarten because my dad had already taught me to read, albeit in Spanish; and I remember my parents' drive instilled in me to keep moving forward.

I do not know what became of Marcos or Dora Alicia, but I like to think that they kept moving forward too.

CYNTHIA GUARDADO

# Eight Women in the Kitchen *y una Poeta*

San Salvador, El Salvador

The thump of palms on *masa*
resonates in the kitchen as two rabbits
cuddle in a corner close to the *plancha's*
heat. I am a guest here and sit at the table
with my notebook, pencil in hand—
draw rhythm with words: the curl
of the letter 'c' like a bass clef hooking.
The women prepare *pupusas*, next to me

oil dissolves into air. They tell me
I write too much; I listen to the music
of their fingers flatten *queso* into *masa*,
make perfect circles. We are in our late

twenties, still trying to figure out where
we will go. They laugh loudly
like a choir when I say I will write
about them. I watch their expert hands,

and they ask if I can make *pupusas*;
I let them instruct me on what I haven't
done since childhood. How much masa
is too much? When I clap I must rotate

my palms, they say, move my fingers
away from each other like wings.
They wonder if I am really
a *Chalateca* like them. I lift the *pupusa*

I've made like a symbol—a grand
finale—place it on *la plancha,* hear it
sizzle. Together we watch the *masa* smoke
as if it too will evaporate, ascend with time.

ROBERTO LOVATO

# Rich Eyes and Poor Hands

WHAT REMAINED of the blood stains and candle wax on the sidewalk streamed away, propelled by the curtain of water from the worker's hose. A small crowd—tourists, well-wishers, and the curious—gathered at the corner of Rues Alibert and Bichat. They leapt out of the way of the splashing water as young, cigarette-smoking Maghrebis in jeans and tennis shoes looked on from the doorway of their apartment, some with amusement, others with fear or disdain. Red and white rose petals, green leaves, plastic packaging, remnants of candles, handwritten tributes, and deflated mylar balloons floated in the puddles left behind, alongside the flecks of blood coursing—like so much other blood over the centuries—toward oblivion, down into the ancient sewers of Paris.

I'd come to the city to report on the crisis facing climate refugees, a topic world leaders decided, at the last possible minute, not to discuss. Left without a subject, I planned to go to Place de la Republique square to report on the students who were violating President Francois Hollande's ban on protesting after the attacks of November 13. Two weeks had passed since the attacks, but what really made my innards twist and tighten on that overcast Friday was the smell. Like someone cooking raw, rotting meat. There might have been a butcher shop nearby. My panic might have concocted the smell. *Or maybe it was the smell of death.*

This experience contained trace elements of my visit to El Salvador three months before. My parents' homeland had become the most violent place on earth, and I'd traveled there to witness and write about it. I was also researching the thousands of individual and mass graves, holes in the volcanic ground that had been left uninvestigated and underreported but remained sites of terror and trauma throughout the tiny country, since the war of the 1980's. I breathed formaldehyde, rotting flesh. Visits to forensics labs, morgues, and mass graves exposed me to chemical mixtures that made my stomach swell then, too.

But standing in front of Le Petit Cambodge, the Cambodian restaurant that was one of several sites of the November attacks that left 129 people dead, the facts on the wet sidewalk were undeniable. Paris, the city that helped me to love the lightness of life inherent in the word *légèreté*, had come under the grip of gravity. I'd first come to the city as a ten-year-old boy who wanted to rise up into the sky, like the boy in the magnificent French movie *The Red Balloon*, which I'd seen in Mr. Mathis' fourth-grade class. The story of a child who encounters a balloon with its own personality, befriending it as they walk, skip, and run through the rough, working-class neighborhood of Belleville-Ménilmontant, spoke to me. I was a lonely kid who grew up around the 26th Street projects in San Francisco's Mission District, and the balloon made me long for one of my own—so much so that I pestered my parents to let me fly to Paris on a kid's pilgrimage to see the land of balloons and levitating children.

*     *     *

The age of levity began in earnest on Sunday, November 21, 1783. At 1:54 in the afternoon, two Parisians—Jean-François Pilâtre de Rozier, a physicist, and François Laurent, Marquis d'Arlandes, a military officer—rose above the grounds of the Château de la Muette in the Montgolfier, the first aircraft ever to be untethered from the earth.

Named for Jacques-Étienne and Joseph-Michel Montgolfier, the two heirs of a growing global empire of luxury wallpaper, the royal-blue hot air balloon rising into the air that day bore the symbols of the king's earthly power: golden flourishes, *fleurs-de-lis*, zodiac suns. It had been designed by Jean-Baptiste Réveillon, a manufacturer of fine wallpaper hired by the Montgolfiers after they brought their invention from the countryside to his beautiful home and factory in the gritty Paris suburb of Saint-Antoine.

D'Arlandes said he felt like he was "being lifted by the armpits" as the balloon floated heavenward. The crowd of thousands beneath the two men grew smaller even as the earth and skies grew larger and more awesome. "This time we are rising!" d'Arlandes exclaimed to Rozier, who was himself astonished and quite frightened.

At over 5,000 feet above bustling Paris, the two men could see all that no one else had seen previously: the division of the city into a mostly wealthy right bank and a mostly poor left bank; the three cathedrals, forty monasteries, and over 100 convents of the city's largest landowner; and the hulking towers of Bastille Saint-Antoine, the prison symbolizing royal authority, which was a short walk from the Réveillon factory. But what most struck d'Arlandes was the uncanny silence.

As their chariot glided toward the southwestern part of the city, Rozier and d'Arlandes looked down. There at their feet was the city's highest and most hallowed structure, Notre Dame. Clergy, Crown, and commoner crowded on the roof looking up, looking like tiny black dots.

\*      \*      \*

"Guess where we're going?" my mother asked, collapsing onto the beat-up red and yellow sofa bed in our living room. Resting there for a few minutes was all there was between another long day of cleaning rich people's rooms at the hotel and starting to cook dinner for me, my siblings, and cousins, all of us living in the apartment on Folsom Street in San Francisco's Mission district. "We're going to Paris!"

It was 1973, and I was ten years old; my mother knew her announcement would make me, her youngest, fly. I jumped around our apartment's long hallways and danced around the living room. I looked out the rickety window facing the projects on 26th Street like I was Captain Nemo preparing the *Nautilus* to search for Atlantis. My mother's news filled me with visions of submarine voyages, exotic train rides, and wondrous balloon rides during which I disappeared into the air like the boy did at the end of his film, or like Phileas Fogg in *Around the World in 80 Days*.

By the time I was ten, I had already traveled far beyond the Mission. Thanks to my Salvadoran immigrant parents—my mother, Maria Elena, a maid at a five-star hotel, and my father, Ramón, whose job as a janitor at United Airlines got us free or discounted airline tickets—I got to see the world at an early age, with what Shakespeare called "rich eyes and poor hands." I'd return to the Mission with stories of the Colosseum in Rome, the bullfights of Madrid, and the pyramids of Mexico. In a neighborhood where the pull of our poverty had limited many of my friends' lives to a sixty-mile radius, my own red balloon turned out to be a United Boeing 747.

Most often, we flew to El Salvador. My parents' homeland was where most of our extended family lived, the only country we, my three siblings and both parents, visited all together. We spent most of our time in San Salvador, with my father's poor relatives, and in San Vicente, the more picturesque, semi-rural town where my mom's impoverished family lived beneath the green grandeur of the Chinchontepec volcano.

In the 1970s, El Salvador was a high-octane rocket. I had unlimited access to crates of firecrackers and the biggest, baddest barrel bombs in my explosive, expanding universe. On the radio, men in dark green military uniforms loaded with medals uttered the words *terrorismo* and *terrorista*. We kids cracked up watching my Tía Esperanza pop out her eyes, purse her lips, and march around her crowded living room as she mocked El Salvador's president, General Armando Molina. On streets paved with poverty, politics, and poetry, filled with graffiti calling for *revolución* and indicting the *fascista* government, I played soccer and *escondelero*, hide and seek, with my friends, some of whom didn't have shoes.

Just before we left for Paris, I was crossing the street near our apartment in San Francisco to buy a popsicle at Henry's liquor store, when I saw a lady in a yellow dress walking very quickly. A man came running behind her. When he caught up to her, they started yelling. *Fuck you bitch*, the guy screamed, and he pulled something out of his waistband. The woman screamed *No!* just before he started hacking at her stomach. To my ten-year-old ears, it sounded like he was slicing her skin with a potato peeler: *scht-scht-scht.* The woman cried out, each jab evoking *Noooooo! Help me!* as blood poured onto her hands and spilled onto the sidewalk. It looked to me like running red water. The man ran off. The woman stood there bleeding, staggering off to lean against a garage door before falling to the ground, where she lay twitching. I rushed home to tell my mom.

My mother sat me on the sofa and rubbed my stomach as if I was the one who had been stabbed. I felt unnerved every time I walked by Henry's store, long after the blood spilled on 25th Street that day had dried. It was a baptism in terror. Wherever I've traveled over the years, I've thought about how streets, and the cities they form, have all seen blood.

In the wake of the stabbing, going to Paris was all the more uplifting. The delight of visiting historic sights—the Eiffel Tower, the Pantheon, Napoleon's Tomb, Notre Dame—balanced the tedium of time spent looking for cheap souvenir scarves to give to every maid, domestic worker, and working woman from San Francisco to San Vicente. We didn't even try to find the Belleville-Ménilmontant area where *The Red Balloon* took place. But that didn't matter. The stairways around Montmarte allowed my imagination to take flight as if I was, in fact, strolling on sidewalks along the hills where the boy and his balloon played.

Coming back to San Francisco felt like coming back to earth.

\*     \*     \*

After the Montgolfier took flight, newspapers reported weeping crowds, people raising their hands skyward in a kind of religious ecstasy. Some who saw the balloons flying in rural areas thought they were moons signaling that the Apocalypse was imminent.

Balloons became the symbol of the *air du temps*, one of many objects of increasingly heated discussions and debates raging throughout Paris. Men and women, many sporting powdered wigs, engaged in spirited but tense conversations about science and society in salons, academies, coffeehouses, and masonic lodges that were the fashionable centers of polite conversation. Factory owners and merchants, some of whom financed balloon launches, started quietly questioning their allegiance to the Crown, while workers in factories cursed their wages and working conditions. Words like "*liberté*," "*nation*," "*souveraineté*," and "*citoyen*," were lifting up what it meant to be human in a world where one's place was typically predetermined by social position.

Not everyone shared the French faith in *légèreté* and the thrill of the balloon launches. English philosopher and statesman Sir Edmund Burke saw French levity as a negative force. Reading newspapers and looking across the English Channel from his seat in Parliament, the arch-conservative Burke grew impatient with the "frivolity and effeminacy" of the French "national character." He preferred to remain "standing on the firm ground of the British constitution," he said, "rather than attempt to follow in their desperate flights the aeronauts of France." (Unknown: Whether Burke's feeling about the French experiments in flying were influenced by his having had his watch stolen by someone in the crowd at a balloon launch.)

As an Anglican with a Catholic mother, Burke subscribed to ideas about the sublime that were steeped in gravity, declaring, in his classic *A Philosophical Inquiry Into the Origin of Our Ideas of the Sublime and Beautiful,* that "terror is in all cases whatsoever, either more openly or latently the ruling principle of the sublime." Burke considered feelings of terror crucial to keeping order in the body politic. His ideas about terror distinguished between less desirable fear and the more positive "salutary fear" that kept peasants and other commoners in "proud submission" or "dignified obedience." He was profoundly disturbed by the "strange chaos of levity and ferocity" among the Parisians he would later describe in his reflections on the revolution in France.

But the students of the sublime in Paris brought particular passion to their work. Born into a peasant home and best known for his prodigious writings—essays, pamphlets, and, especially, futuristic and salacious novels—Restif de la Bretonne developed early on the fever to name the new. He introduced the term *pornographe* (pornography) in his book about the need to legalize and reform prostitution. Searching for a way to describe his sexual pleasure and desire for women's feet, he invented the word *fétiche* (fetish). And in his novel *Le pied de Fanchette*, in a chapter about a character with a foot fetish, is found the first documented public use of a term inspiring radical revolutionaries like Gracchus Babeuf and others in Paris: communism.

Nicknamed *Rousseau du ruisseau* (Rousseau of the gutter) for his saucier writing, Restif was also one of the few writers to take nighttime strolls through the many Paris neighborhoods that were actually filled with gutters, and to write about the people living there. The dirty, smelly, narrow streets of Saint-Antoine were lined with the crowded homes of workers. The Réveillon factory, which was also located in Saint-Antoine, along with its owner's luxurious home, is where the first manned Montgolfier hot air balloons were manufactured. The factory's garden served as the launch site for the Montgolfier brothers' first tethered hot air balloon tests in Paris, prior to the November launch of Rozier and d'Arlandes's historic balloon.

The sublime invention literally rose out of the gutter.

\*　　\*　　\*

After my mother and I got back from Paris, things heated up in our apartment. My father, who we called *Papa Mon*, came home one day talking about *"esa compañía de mierda"* doing something or other to him and the other workers: janitors, baggage handlers, ramp workers, cargo and cabin service crews. Shortly after, workers and guys in windbreakers bearing the logo of a black hand shaking a white hand—the words "AFL" and "CIO" written on the wrists—would come to our house to drink and talk about work problems.

My dad became a shop steward. The workers, who loved my dad, were talking about "going on strike," and that phrase I came to associate with fun. I learned it from going into the street in front of the hotel where my mother worked, yelling slogans I didn't understand and marching while banging pots and pans with wooden spoons. After *Papa Mon* and the workers and union guys in the windbreakers had their talks, I learned that "strike" also meant stopping the flight of United 747's. Later on, I learned that French workers also stopped hot air balloons from flying.

The 300 workers at Folie Titon, the Réveillon wallpaper factory—the rag sorters, those wielding the mallets, the vat men, the couchers, the seamstresses, the loftsmen—were paid competitively, but still received little for their efforts. Toiling six days a week in a toxic factory for long hours at the rate of thirty-five to fifty *sous* per day, barely making enough to buy bread and subsist.

On April 29, 1789, the noxious air in the Folie Titon factory in Saint-Antoine caught fire. Shortly before, rumors began circulating in Paris that Jean-Baptiste Réveillon had written an essay calling for lowering wages. Though Réveillon was considered a fair and decent-paying employer, upon hearing (and misinterpreting) his statements, some 3,000 workers from across the city organized peaceful protests at his factory, and at the house where he was hiding. Sent to protect the factory, the Garde Française fired several rounds, killing 100, as other workers burned down the Réveillon factory in what became the dress rehearsal for the French Revolution.

*　　*　　*

I was eager to hear what my friend, Cherif, who lives in the Canal Saint-Martin area of Paris, had to say about the November attacks. He and I first met two years before, at the Tunisian and Maghrebi immigrant rights organization he volunteers at in nearby Belleville—the immigrant neighborhood that is my favorite part of one of my favorite cities.

A bookish-looking retired management consultant with a calm, fatherly demeanour gazed at me from behind large glasses. At the start of our friendship, Cherif made a point of telling me, "I was born in Tunisia, but my family and I are French. We are French." As we stood in front of Le Petit Cambodge, he spoke, in a soft voice cracking with anger, about the charged state that had followed the attacks, the "raids, arrests, and shooting of innocent people." Cherif was unhappy about what he deemed "repressive" measures that silenced criticism of acts he and others in his community found disturbing. He and his neighbors were, he said, unable to protest arrests that were happening without cause, police shootings in areas where bullets almost hit sleeping children, incidents where government security forces broke down the doors on the apartments of innocent families—all reported and documented at the community center.

Walking back across the wet sidewalk of Rue Alibert, we stopped to look at the small mountain of well-wishing in front of Le Petit Cambodge: the red and tricolor aluminum balloons, the plants and flowers, the handmade posters. The messages were in French, English, Arabic, and many other languages. The sliding metal doors of the restaurant were locked.

We walked on, across the Rue Alibert, to look at the gray wall of l'Hopital Saint-Louis. "Look," Cherif said. On a large black poster, oversized letters spelled out *VIVE LA REPUBLIQUE VIVE MA FRANCE* (Long Live the Republic, Long Live My France). The word *MA* stood out in even bigger yellow letters, for emphasis. Small letters below indicated that an organization called SOS-RACISME had produced the poster as part of a campaign to fight racism in France. When I looked at their website later, slick videos showed the faces of several light-skinned French people saying, *Je suis de la couleur de ceux qu'on persecute* (I am the color of those being persecuted).

"Whose France do you think they're talking about?" Cherif asked, his eyes wide, his question rhetorical. "Not mine." We walked back to Le Petit Cambodge. Chatib Akrouh, Abdelhamid Abaaoud, and Brahim Abdeslam—the three young men who attacked Le Petit Cambodge and Le Carillon—were French and Belgian citizens who worked for or ran businesses, liked hip-hop, and were described by some of their neighbors as "very nice." As such, they didn't fit the stereotypical image of the bearded terrorist. But it had also been poor, brown young men who were liked by some of their neighbors who told me, during my most recent trip to El Salvador, that they'd killed their fellow citizens. Most but not all of their victims had been affiliated with gangs. Both the young Maghrebis and the young Salvadorans bore the weight of a dehumanizing, destructive anger rooted in marginality, nihilistic rage that found a friend in the instruments of death. Though separated by thousands of miles, these men used AK-47's left over from wars in the Balkans and Central America. Those same guns, which can fire up to thirty bullets in three seconds, were the preferred weapon of the Salvadoran guerrillas who fought the U.S.-backed government in the 1980's.

Looking at the bullet holes in the windows of Le Carillon, the hotel and bar where twelve people were killed, I thought about the anger, disaffection, poverty, and absurd ideas that led El Salvador's gangs to kill 900 people in one month—August of the same year the Charlie Hebdo and November attacks left a total of 147 people dead in Paris. Some of the young gang members I had interviewed (many of whom were not ruthless murderers, unlike some of their peers) were labeled *terroristas* by the former guerrilla leaders now heading the government. I'd spoken to some of these same guerrilla leaders when they were themselves called *terroristas* by U.S.-backed military and civilian leaders of the wartime governments—which were also labeled "state terrorists" by opposition and international human rights groups in the 1980's.

The red and blue mylar balloons left by well-wishers brought me no relief.

\*     \*     \*

During my visit to Paris, my father called me several times a day to make sure I was okay. I didn't mind. In 1932, my father had witnessed the slaughter known as La Matanza, the massacre of tens of thousands of Indians and poor peasants in El Salvador killed on the orders of a dictator, one of the worst in Latin American history. I was the one in the family who discovered what he had remained quiet about for some seventy-five years, since he was a ten-year-old boy in his hometown of Ahuachapán, poor and often hungry. While teaching and doing research at Cal State Northridge, I came across reports that *Papa Mon's* hometown had been one of the epicenters of the massacre. I did the math and realized that my father had likely been living there when La Matanza began in January 1932.

When I asked him about it, he hesitated before nervously acknowledging for the first time what he had borne in silence for most of his life. He cried, and so did I.

"Things are fine here, Papa," I reassured him. "It's nothing like El Salvador, or even the U.S." I reminded him of both my safe visits to the dangerous parts of the motherland just a few months before, and of the spate of mass killings in the U.S. in 2015, only one of which was called a "terrorist attack."

I was telling the truth, but the whole time I was in Paris, there were memories I couldn't shake, memories of things I didn't tell *Papa Mon* about until long after they'd occurred.

In 1990, when I was working with refugee and displaced communities in El Salvador, Salvadoran death squads tried to capture and shove me into an un-marked van. In Los Angeles in 1992, members of the Salvadoran independence front and the Maximiliano Hernandez Martinez anti-communist brigade death squad—named for the dictator who perpetrated La Matanza witnessed by my father—threatened and harassed many of us who were denouncing human rights violations.

I left Le Petit Cambodge and Le Carillon and started heading toward the center of the city. As I crossed one of the small metal bridges over Canal Saint-Martin, I stopped to breathe in the poetic atmosphere: trees, gardens, bistros, and people walking and reading along a calm green river. My beatific moment was interrupted when I noticed that the *VIVE LA REPUBLIQUE VIVE MA FRANCE* posters were covering the walls on the side of the small bridge.

When I arrived at my apartment on a hill in Belleville, I was tired from a long afternoon of walking. I poured myself a glass of wine and drank it standing by the window, facing one of the concrete staircases that the boy in *The Red Balloon* rises up from, floating higher and higher before disappearing into the sky.

Looking out on the sublime gifts of Paris, I thought about my own inclination toward levity. Like my father, some in Paris after the attacks will live silently with terror, looking up and away for fear that the recent past will destroy them. Others, like my mother, will rise again and again, refusing to recognize the limits of terror's design, lifting those around them from imposed borders, never getting weighed down.

MELINDA PALACIO

# This Is How the World Ends

Blue wing feathers, soft rust bellies
no longer chirp in a bottlebrush hedge;
the high-pitched cry from the patient
nest sitter grows more frantic the moment

his cold bird body hits the dirt. The sound
eclipses any avian malice, no macho fight,
not pecked to death, jabbed by a rival's bill,
or snatched by the neighborhood cat.

His fallen feathers mean she's gone too,
flown the coop, in search of a live mate,
a warm body to settle her nest.

Ants, thirsty from drought, surround,
begin their slow feast. The army tackles
eyes no longer shiny. Yet dull orbs offer
answers, proverbial pearls of wisdom.

The garden is strangely quiet.
Imagine no buzz, no war of wings.
This is how the world ends

one bee
one monarch
one barren field
one hungry child
one state without water
one western bluebird

one
and then

MELINDA PALACIO

# All Things Precious

In death, some things never change.
Except for silence, where masked mimicry once filled
trees with car horns, ring tones, your child's laughter.

The starling's shiny eye turned dull reminds you
of glass. The moment black tail feathers turn purple.

Once a purple vase slipped through your fingers.
Broken, it left one smooth piece of ocean pretty.
Your fingers never held anything with the smallest chance to break.
Except for champagne flutes. You know how to hold a long glass stem.

Crystal clatters to a splat, sounds ugly on parquet,
unlike the palm-sized body's thump, soft as rain.

When you bury your grandmother in her favorite purple dress,
you wish you had kept the amethyst dragonfly pin for yourself.
An even exchange. Purple tail feathers for purple stones.
All things precious, except for this bird, end up buried in a box.

## ACKNOWLEDGMENTS

### Part 1: El Camino Largo

"War" by María Isabel Alvarez was originally published in print in the Spring 2016 issue of Arts & Letters, the literary journal out of Georgia College, and online at *artsandletters.gcsu.edu*.

The short story "Night Memory: The Mansion in the Middle of a Gully" by Carolina Rivera Escamilla is part of *...after...*, a book of short stories published in April 2015 in Los Angeles, CA, by World Stage Press.

"*La Masacuata*" by Alexandra Lytton Regalado appeared in Phoebe Journal. Runner-up, Phoebe Annual Fiction Contest, judged by Ramona Ausubel in 2015.

"*A la altura de la vida*" and "*Era tiempo de guerra*" by Dora Olivia Magaña was published in the book *Con los mismos ojos* in March 2014, Caza de Poesía Editorial, Los Ángeles, California. Also published in the book *Al calor del fuego*, in April 2015, POESIA Editorial, Los Ángeles, California, printed in México.

"*Guayaberas*" and "Bury This Pig" by William Archila were published in *The Art of Exile*, Bilingual Press, 2009. "Dig" was published in *The Gravedigger's Archaeology*, Red Hen Press, 2015.

"Guatemala" by Sara Campos was first published in Cipactli, Spring 2015, No. 19.

"Anthem" by Javier Zamora appeared in Narrative online magazine: *http://www.narrativemagazine.com/issues/fall-2014/poetry/put-book-down-javier-zamora*. "Pump Water from the Well" was first published in Ninth Letter, Online Vol. 2, January 2014, *http://www.ninthletter.com/web-edition/winter-2014/winter-2014-poetry#zamora2*.

"*Labriego en Libertad*" by Alexis Aguilar was published in 18 *Conejo, boletín literario de la editorial universitaria* UNAH (*Universidad Nacional Autónoma de Honduras*), No. 85, August 1996, Tegucigalpa, Honduras. *"Este Lugar"* and *"Me Enteré Que Era Hispano"* have been published in the literary blog *www.sopadefrijoles.com*.

### Part 2: En Voz Alta

"El Salvador at a Glance" and "Latinhood" by Quique Aviles were first published in the poetry book, *The Immigrant Museum*, an art book designed in collaboration with *Raices de Papel* and printed in Mexico City in 2004.

"Solidarity Baby" and "What It's Like to Be a Central American Unicorn for Those Who Aren't" by Maya Chinchilla both appear in *The Cha Cha Files: A Chapina Poética* (Korima Press, 2014) San Francisco, CA.

"Poor Westlake" by William A. González was originally published in the book *Blue Bubblegum*, January 16, 2015.

"Where is Guatemala?" by Patrick Mullen-Coyoy has been posted in a previous form in the personal blog at *aguacatemalteco.tumblr.com*.

*"Pupusas* or *Lucha"* by Willy Palomo published in: *vinylpoetryandprose.com/2016/05/willy-palomo/*. *"El Hombre Machete"* published in: *drunkinamidnightchoir.com/2016/10/20/three-poems-willy-palomo/#more-7872*.

"You Roque, Only You" and "In Case You Forget" by harold terezón published in the book *Hunting for Izotes*, and in The Acentos Review, May 2014: *www.acentosreview.com*.

"An Inchoate Symphony" by Susana Nohemi Aguilar-Marcelo appeared in In-flight Literary Magazine on July 2016.

### Part 3: La Poesía de Todos

"Midwestern Skulls for the Broken Latino" by Roy G. Guzmán originally appeared in Issue 16 of The Adroit Journal, May 2016. *"Amor Eterno"* originally appeared in Issue 23 of Assaracus, published by Sibling Rivalry Press, July 2016.

"Spoken Portrait" by Uriel Quesada appeared in The Iowa Review, 36 (Fall 2006).

"*Suelo* Tide Cement" by Christina Vega-Westhoff was published in Word For/Word 25 (2015), New American Writing, and in her book, *Suelo Tide Cement,* published by Nightboat Books in 2018.

"*Santiago Atitlán, Diciembre 1990*" by Claudia D. Hernández published in La Tolteca, *año cuatro, volumen tres*, Fall 2014. "*Kim ayu* (Come Over Here)" published in Poetry of Resistance: A Multicultural Anthology in Response to Arizona SB 1070, Xenophobia and Injustice, Fall 2015.

"Blister" by Francisco Aragón appeared in Mariposas: A Modern Anthology of Queer Latino Poetry, Ed. Emanuel Xavier (Floricanto Press, 2008), and is also part of the Poetry Foundation's web archive. "Dogs" (in an earlier version) appeared in Diálogo, Number 8, Spring 2004, Center for Latino Research, DePaul University. "January 21, 2013" (in earlier versions) appeared in Forward to Velma, Number 1, 2013; MiPoesías, Summer, 2014; Beltway Poetry Quarterly, Volume 17, Number 2, Spring 2016.

"The Stars Remain" by Claudia Castro Luna is forthcoming in *Whenever I'm with you* from Seal Press.

"Early Morning Chat with God" by Adela Najarro appears in the poetry collection, *Twice Told Over* (2015) and in Nimrod International Journal of Poetry & Prose 49:1 (2005). "After the 1979 *Revolución Nicaragüense*" appears in the poetry collection, *Split Geography* (2015) and in BorderSenses 19 (2014). "Star Variation in Blue" was published as "Incantation 2.1" in phren-Z 6 Spring (2013).

"Rich Eyes and Poor Hands" by Roberto Lovato appeared previously in the June 15, 2016 issue of Guernica magazine.

An earlier version of "All Things Precious" by Melinda Palacio appears in Off the Coast, Maine's International Poetry Journal, Summer Issue 2016.

## CONTRIBUTORS

*Part 1: El Camino Largo*

**María Isabel Alvarez** was born in Guatemala City, Guatemala. Her work has appeared in Black Warrior Review, Gulf Coast, and Arts & Letters, among others.

**Carolina Rivera Escamilla,** writer and documentarian, was born in El Salvador, went into exile in the 1980's, and became PEN Center USA Emerging Voices Fellowship.

**León Salvatierra** is the author of *Al Norte* (2012, National Autonomous University of Nicaragua Press). He is currently a Lecturer of Spanish Language & Literature at UC Berkeley.

**Alexandra Lytton Regalado** was born in San Salvador and raised in Miami. *Matria*, her poetry collection, winner of the St. Lawrence Book Prize, is forthcoming in 2017. *www.alexandralyttonregalado.com.*

**Jorge Tetl Argueta**, a native Salvadoran and Pipil Nahua Indian, is an award-winning author of picture books and poetry for young children. He has won the International Latino Book Award, the Américas Book Award, the NAPPA Gold Award and the Independent Publisher Book Award for Multicultural Fiction for Juveniles.

**Dora Olivia Magaña**, born in El Salvador and raised in Guatemala, has lived in Los Angeles for 27 years. Dora works as a Nurse Practitioner and has been writing for ten years.

**José B. González** was born in El Salvador. He is the author of *Toys Made of Rock* and the forthcoming, *When Love Was Reels* (Arte Publico, 2018).

**Rosanna Perez** was born in San Salvador, El Salvador. She also helped the founding of the first Central American Studies Program in the nation at Cal State University, Northridge in 1999.

**Darrel Alejandro Holnes,** a poet from Panama City, has been published in *Poetry Magazine, American Poetry Review, Best American Experimental Writing, Callaloo*, and elsewhere.

**William Archila**, born in Santa Ana, El Salvador, is the author of *The Art of Exile* (Bilingual Press, 2009) and *The Gravedigger's Archaeology* (Red Hen Press, 2015).

**Sheila Maldonado** is a Brooklyn-born Honduran and the author of *that's what you get* (Brooklyn Arts Press, 2017), her second publication.

**Sara Campos,** a native San Franciscan with Guatemalan-Salvadoran parents, is a multi-genre writer and a recipient of fellowships from Hedgebrook, VONA, Macondo and Las Letras.

**Adolfo Hernández** is a poet and comedian of Guatemalan descent. He maintains the Los Brainiacs Poetry website. Previously published in *Coiled Serpent: Poets Arising from the Cultural Quakes & Shifts of Los Angeles* (Tia Chucha Press, 2016).

**Felix Aguilar,** a Honduran L.A.-based poet and physician, has published and performed his poetry in Honduras, Guatemala, and the U.S. He works in community medicine.

**Gina Maria Balibrera** is a Salvadoran-American writer from San Francisco and a graduate of the Helen Zell Writers' MFA Program at the University of Michigan.

**Kelly Duarte** was born and raised in West Covina to Guatemalan parents. She is currently studying Creative Writing at the University of California, Riverside.

**Yolany Martínez** was born and raised in Honduras and came to the United States for the University of Oklahoma literature graduate program.

**Henry Mills** was born in Washington DC to a Salvadoran mother and a Jewish-American father. In 2016 he received an MFA in poetry from New York University.

**Andrés Reconco** was born in Acajutla, in El Salvador. He came to the U.S. in 1991. He teaches at a public school in Koreatown, Los Angeles.

**Lorena Duarte** was born in El Salvador, raised in Minnesota, and educated at Harvard University. She is a published poet and emerging playwright and has competed at iWPS and the National Poetry Slam.

**David Unger** was awarded Guatemala's 2014 Miguel Angel Asturias National Literature Prize for lifetime achievement though he writes exclusively in English and lives in the U.S. He has published several novels such as *The Mastermind* and *The Price of Escape*.

**Plinio Hernández** was born in El Salvador in 1979 and moved with his family to Oakland in 1985. He currently resides in Guadalajara, Mexico. Plinio's art practice and writing examines narratives of migration, history, and memory.

**Javier Zamora** was born in El Salvador and is a 2016–2018 Wallace Stegner Fellow. His first book *Unaccompanied* is forthcoming from Copper Canyon Press, Fall 2017. "Anthem" was first published in *Narrative Magazine* as "Put This Book Down," September 2014.

**Iris De Anda** is a Guanaca/Tapatia poet. Author of *CODESWITCH: Fires From Mi Corazon*. *www.irisdeanda.com*.

**Alexis Aguilar** arrived in the U.S. from Honduras as an unauthorized immigrant in 1979. He teaches college geography and lives in Santa Cruz, California. He maintains a literary blog: *www.sopadefrijoles.com*.

**Gabriela Ramirez-Chavez** is a Guatemalan-American poet. She is currently a Ph.D. Candidate in Literature at UC Santa Cruz, where she studies experimental poetics.

*Part 2: En Voz Alta*

**Quique Aviles** is a Salvadoran poet and actor based in Washington, DC. Writing and performing in the U.S. since 1980, his work has been featured on National Public Radio.

**Gabriela Poma** is a doctoral candidate in the Spanish section of the Romance Languages and Literatures department at Harvard University. Of Salvadoran and Nicaraguan parentage, she divides her time between the U.S. and Central America.

**Karina Oliva Alvarado** grew up in West Lake and Pico Union in Los Angeles. Salvadoran born, for the last four years she has taught in the Chicana/o studies department at UCLA.

**Ignacio Carvajal** is Costa Rican. He has lived in Lawrence, Kansas and Austin, Texas. He's a member of the Latino Writers Collective of Kansas City.

**Steve Castro** was born in San José, Costa Rica. Forthcoming work: *Latin@ Rising: An Anthology of Latin@ Science Fiction and Fantasy* from Green Mountains Review.

**Mario A. Escobar** is a U.S.-Salvadoran writer and poet. Escobar is a faculty member in the Department of Foreign Languages at L.A. Mission College.

**Maya Chinchilla** is an Oakland-based Guatemalan femme writer, educator, and author of *The Cha Cha Files: A Chapina Poética* (Kórima Press) and co-editor of *Desde El Epicentro: An Anthology of Central American Poetry and Art. www.mayachapina.com.*

**Mauricio Espinoza**, originally from Costa Rica, has lived in Ohio for almost 20 years. He teaches Latin American literature at the University of Cincinnati.

**Ariel Estrella** is a queer femme from Queens, New York City, Guatemáticx & Dominicanx descended scholar focused on fostering beloved communities through their advocacy and writing.

**William G. Flores** is a Salvadoran from South Central L.A. who graduated from Jordan High School in Watts. He's a Social Justice lover, fighter, and organizer.

**Camila Godoy Delgado,** originally from El Salvador, was raised in Puerto Rico and Miami. She holds a doctorate in psychology and works with immigrant families in Boston. Writing is a creative exploration of her everyday enigmas.

**William A. González** was born in Los Angeles California. He is of Salvadoran descent. He is the author of two books, *Black Bubblegum* and *Blue Bubblegum*.

**GusTavo Adolfo Guerra Vásquez** is a multi-disciplinary "GuatemaLAngelino" artist and educator born in Guatemala and raised (t)here and in "Los(T) Ángeles." His work has been featured in publications like *Revista Mujeres.*

**Robert Farid Karimi,** a Guatemalan Irani, was born outside Union City, California. An award-winning journalist/performer, and Pushcart nominee, his work appears in Asian American Literary Review, Mizna, and U.S. Latino Literature Today.

**Patrick Mullen-Coyoy** is a queer mixed-race Guatemalan based in Lansing, Michigan. As both a student and poet, he aims to center queer (Midwestern!) Central American voices.

**Willy Palomo** is the anchor baby of two undocumented immigrants from El Salvador. He writes book reviews for Muzzle and runs the Bloomington Poetry Slam.

**harold terezón** is a Bay Area poet and educator. His award winning poetry collection, *Hunting for Izotes*, explores his family's immigrant experience living in Pacoima, CA.

**Janel Pineda** is a Latina poet born to Salvadoran immigrants in Los Angeles. She is currently studying English literature at the University of Oxford.

**Mauricio Novoa** works in education with Latino high school students in Adams County, Pennsylvania. He was born in1992 to Salvadoran immigrant parents in Glenmont, MD.

**Susana Nohemi Aguilar-Marcelo** is a Salvadoran-born, Los Angeles-raised writer. Her work largely focuses on liminality, displacement, and intergenerational trauma.

*Part 3: La Poesía de Todos*

**Roy G. Guzmán** was born in Honduras and raised in Miami since he was nine. He is the recipient of a Minnesota State Arts Board grant.

**Silvio Sirias** is a native of Los Angeles and the son of Nicaraguan immigrants. He spent his adolescence in Nicaragua and currently lives in Panamá.

**Oriel María Siu** is a Chinese/Pipil mixed Central American born in Honduras. She left San Pedro Sula in 1997 and currently serves as professor and director of Latino Studies at the University of Puget Sound.

**Uriel Quesada** was born in Costa Rica in 1962. He has nine published books, including novels, short-story collections, and personal narratives. He works at Loyola University New Orleans.

**Christina Vega-Westhoff** is a Panamanian-American poet and translator. Her book, *Suelo Tide Cement,* was published by Nightboat Books in 2018. She currently teaches writing and movement in Buffalo, NY.

**Koyote The Blind** has been exiled from El Salvador since 1985. He is a published philosopher, writer, poet, and performer. He teaches writing and about Toltec art and philosophy in California.

**Suyapa Portillo** migrated with her mother from Copán, Honduras to Los Angeles, California in 1982. Suyapa is a historian and writes about gender, labor, and social movements.

**Krys Méndez-Ramírez** is a crip queer Ph.D. student of Ethnic Studies at UC San Diego. His research centers on border militarization and urban militarism.

**Claudia D. Hernández** was born and raised in Guatemala. She holds an MFA in Creative Writing from Antioch University and is the founder of the ongoing project, Today's Revolutionary Women of Color.

**Mixel Natalie Muñoz Bernardino** is the daughter of Honduran mother and Mexican father who arrived in the U.S. in the 1980's. She is a queer *mujer* who has been writing creatively for five years.

**Francisco Aragón** is the son of Nicaraguan immigrants. His books are: *Puerta del Sol, Glow of Our Sweat*, and *The Wind Shifts: New Latino Poetry*.

**Claudia Castro Luna**, born in El Salvador, is Seattle's Civic Poet (2015–2017), author of the chapbook, *This City*, and a non-fiction writer. She publishes widely.

**Jesús Figueroa Russell** was born in Chalatenango, El Salvador. He arrived in the U.S. at age six and is currently studying bio-anthropology at UCLA.

**Andrew Bentley** was born in Guatemala City, Guatemala in 1990. He is currently a PhD Candidate of Hispanic Cultural Studies at Michigan State University.

**Adela Najarro**, whose extended family emigrated from Nicaragua, is the author of two poetry collections. She teaches creative writing, literature, and composition at Cabrillo College.

**Ana Pérez** is a mother, a justice warrior, and a decolonizing Latina. She fled the Salvadoran civil war, grew up in Los Angeles, and now lives in Oakland.

**Raquel Gutiérrez** was born to a Salvadoran mother and raised in Los Angeles. Her work has appeared in *Izote Vos: A Collection of Salvadoran American Writing and Visual Art*, Huizache, and forthcoming in Fence. She is currently pursuing an MFA in Poetry at the University of Arizona in Tucson.

**Érida Mariela** is a Bay Area-raised queer latinegra educator, writer, and future lawyer with a larger-than-life Nicaraguan *mamá* and an Argentinean *papá*.

**Luis Oviedo** is an attorney who teaches legal writing at IIT Chicago-Kent College of Law and still thinks he's Tarzan. He is of Salvadoran and Guatemalan descent.

**Cynthia Guardado** is a Salvadoran-American professor of English at Fullerton College. She received her Master of Fine Arts from California State University, Fresno. And her book, *Endeavor*, is forthcoming from World Stage Press in 2017.

**Roberto Lovato** is a San Francisco native and the son of Salvadoran immigrants, Maria Elena and Ramon Lovato. He's also a writer/journalist whose work appears in numerous national and international media outlets.

**Melinda Palacio** is from California. Her estranged father was born in Panama. Her books include *How Fire Is a Story, Waiting* (Tia Chucha Press) and *Ocotillo Dreams* (Bilingual Press).